THE

Champion

REAL ESTATE AGENT™

THE *Champion* REAL ESTATE AGENT™

*Get to the Top of Your
Game and Knock Sales
Out of the Park*

Dirk Zeller

McGraw-Hill
New York   Chicago   San Francisco   Lisbon
London   Madrid   Mexico City   Milan   New Delhi
San Juan   Seoul   Singapore   Sydney   Toronto

1 2 3 4 5 6 7 8 9 0   DOC/DOC   0 9 8 7 6

ISBN 13: 978-0-07-148433-6
ISBN 10:   0-07-148433-7

This publication is designed to provide accurate and authoritative information in regard to the subject matter covered. It is sold with the understanding that the publisher is not engaged in rendering legal, accounting, or other professional service. If legal advice or other expert assistance is required, the services of a competent professional person should be sought.
—*From a Declaration of Principles Jointly Adopted by a Committee of the American Bar Association and a Committee of Publishers and Associations*

McGraw-Hill books are available at special discounts to use as premiums and sales promotions, or for use in corporate training programs. For more information, please write to the Director of Special Sales, Professional Publishing, McGraw-Hill, Two Penn Plaza, New York, NY 10121-2298. Or contact your local bookstore.

This book is printed on acid-free paper.

Library of Congress Cataloging-in-Publication Data
Zeller, Dirk.
    The champion real estate agent : get to the top of your game and knock sales out of the park / by Dirk Zeller.
        p. cm.
    ISBN 0-07-148433-7 (pbk. : alk. paper)   1. Real estate agents—United States.   2. Real estate business—United States.   I. Title.
HD278.Z45 2007
333.33023'73—dc22
                                          2006028077

Dedication

This book is dedicated to the two groups of people who helped with creating, forging, testing, and perfecting the process of becoming a Champion Real Estate Agent.

The first group comprises the coaches at Real Estate Champions, starting with Don Cunningham, the first coach I hired. We have come a long way since then. Thanks, Don! To Ann Arthur, your skill and loyalty are much appreciated. To Ed Schmidt, Jan Tomlinson, Tim Tully, Kent Jones, and Caryn Yates, your commitment to help people reach for their dreams is unparalleled in the industry. To Al Mayer, your experience and wisdom still astound me every time we talk. To Dave Doeleman, whose brilliance is still felt daily at Real Estate Champions, even a year after your retirement, I can say I learned from you every day we worked together. Thanks to all of you!

Finally, I need to thank a second group of people—the original group of Real Estate Champions' Mastermind Coaching members: Sheri Nasca, Shari Boyd, Julie Boyd-Elrod, John Gualtieri, Sheila Gunderson, Ann and Gordy Marks, Carol Park, Nick Peters, Dave Perry, and Evelyn Taibi. I will never forget the meeting in Orlando in the winter of 2002 when the perfection of the Champion Real Estate Agent system was our focus together. You each contributed significantly in listening and testing my systems, tools, and theories—and each of you became Champions yourselves.

Contents

PART III: CHAMPION SALES PRESENTATIONS

PART IV: BUILDING A CHAMPION AGENT'S BUSINESS

Preface

Success is a journey, not a destination. We have all heard that statement or something similar to it. It reminds us of a couple of truths. The first and most obvious one is that success is a process, that there is a pathway that we must follow over a period of time, possibly even years, to achieve success. Some of us will travel more quickly along that path, while others move more slowly and more steadily. Very few of us will arrive at success overnight. In some cases, it takes time even for the lightbulb to come on before we get it. We have all had those moments in life when we have been faced with a challenge, problem, change, or even crisis, and when the smoke clears, we see the whole picture. (It's as though we had been staring at one of those magic pictures—a picture inside a picture, the ones that were popular in the mid-1990s. You almost had to cross your eyes, blur your vision, and look *through* the picture to see the hidden picture.) I hope this book will help you achieve your "Got it" moment.

I recently had an additional coaching call with a client because he had an emergency that could not wait until the following week. I had been working with this client for a number of months. He is a good agent in New Hampshire who has the desire to be a Champion. When you are working with clients in a coaching relationship, they usually have a "Got it" moment. As a coach, you are hoping for that moment to come early in the relationship. Then, after a few months, you are just hoping it comes soon. After another few months, you are desperately praying that you will see it sometime in their and your lifetimes.

In this session, we were discussing a buyer client who was not following Mark's rules of engagement. His buyer client, because he was not following the rules we had set up together in a previous coaching session, was making the odds long that Mark would earn a fee . . . ever. Mark was calling to talk about what he should do. After a few minutes, it became clear to me that he *knew* what to do—he just wanted me to confirm it. My mind was thinking, "Did he just get it? After all these months of working together, did he just put the puzzle together?"

Before we hung up the phone, he said to me, "Dirk, I want you to know, I get it." That is the moment every coach, mentor, or parent would invest their whole life for—when you realize that all the sweat, worry, effort, and frustration have been worth it. I am hoping that moment comes to you before you put this book down, because that is the reason I wrote it. "Getting it" is the first step to "having it." I did say the *first step.* There is also a second step that most people miss.

The most important question isn't, "Do you know it or get it?" The most important question is, "Do you do it?" At the end of each day, we all know we need to spend less than we make. We all know that we need to take in fewer calories daily than we burn daily. We all know that citizens of the United States are more overweight and obese than ever before in the history of our country. We have more credit card debt and second-mortgage debt and a lower savings rate than ever before in our history. The question clearly isn't "Do you know it?" It's "Do you do it?"

My hope and desire is that this book will not merely offer you the knowledge to achieve Champion Agent status, but to motivate you, guide you, teach you to implement, and cheer you on to do it. The extravagant rewards in life are reserved for the doers. Because rewards are unequal in life and weighted to people who achieve Champion Performance, I hope that you will take on this challenge to become a Champion.

Your success will always begin with a single step. You have taken that one step by investing in this book. I will take the rest of the steps with you, as your guide, mentor, and coach, through the written word. Now that you are one of my coaching clients, I wish for you what I have always wished for and strived for with each of my coaching clients—to play all out, to play to the best of your ability, to play as close to your potential as possible, to leave it all on the field before the game is done, and to walk a way a Champion!

Acknowledgments

Behind any successful person or business or venture are numerous behind-the-scenes people who truly make the project a success. These people don't receive the accolades that the public face receives, but they are no less instrumental in the success. I want to thank these Champions for their contribution.

To my parents, Norm and Becky Zeller, the original Champions in my life, I offer my thanks. While their involvement in this book was limited, their involvement and guidance in my life has been unlimited. To Dianne Wheeler, my editor at McGraw-Hill, the commitment you had to me and this book was astounding. You went above and beyond to hit the shortened deadlines. You are truly a Champion! To the team at Real Estate Champions, you are Champion Performers. From the sales team to the coaches to the administrative staff, you all had a hand in this book. Many of you assumed more than "your job" to enable this book to become a reality.

A special thanks must go to Rachelle Cotton who labored over every unreadable handwritten word that I produced. Your commitment matched mine in maintaining the many tight deadlines that caused this book to happen. To Caryn Yates-Clowers, one of our excellent coaches at Real Estate Champions, who read and edited the manuscript, thanks for going beyond the call of duty.

Also, thank you to Dan Matejsek, vice president of marketing at Real Estate Champions, for your insight and thoughts in a few key areas of the book. Your wisdom is greatly appreciated.

Finally, to my wife Joan who labors to create a home of love and harmony and to nurture two small children and one big kid . . . *thanks!* I know the pressure and strain always increases for you when I am writing a book. You are my Champion!

Introduction

This book is not a theoretical view of Champion Performance or a theoretical view of how to be successful as a real estate agent—there are enough of those books. I will reveal the pathway up the mountain that I discovered well over a decade and a half ago and that I personally used. Through coaching people up that same pathway for almost 10 years, I have fine-tuned that pathway to speed up the journey for you and others. I want to be clear that this book is not written from the standpoint of, "I am already a Champion Agent. What do I do now to grow, expand, and increase." That type of book is really for less than 1 percent of the real estate population. This book is written for the agent who wants to get to the Champion Agent level. When I look at some of the recent bestsellers in real estate sales, they are books that are theoretical in nature; they describe the journey of wildly successful agents who have established large practices with lots of assistants. The question is, what did they do, say, think, market, prospect, monitor, and perfect *before* they reached the top of the mountain? That's what you will find contained within *The Champion Real Estate Agent.* This book will become your blueprint to success.

There are four distinctive parts to this book. In **Part I, "Portrait of a Champion,"** I want you to understand what a Champion mindset looks like, so you can recognize it in others and begin to raise yourself to that level in your attitude and activities. **Chapter 1** discusses real estate as an agent's business and how to expand it as a business. I delve into the four rules of business expansion, so you can minimize the risk of expansion while maximizing the return. I start the journey here because you need to know the truth in order to develop a clear pathway to the top of the mountain of success. **Chapter 2** identifies the attributes and characteristics of a Champion Agent and how to attain them. **Chapter 3** lays the groundwork for action, with the four probabilities of success and the four ways to increase production. These bedrock principles have guided Sales Champions for generations. **Chapter 4** focuses on the power source of your success . . . goals. I want you to move beyond success, so I include tools that will help you uncover the Champion's secret edge. Once you can do that, your rocket ship to the Champion level will be fully fueled. **Chapter 5** takes dead aim at one of the problems we have in sales (especially real estate sales)—getting people to believe that we are more knowledgeable, more believable, and more trustworthy than others they could select.

Part II, "**Champion Lead-Generation Methods**," not only identifies the common means of lead generation, but also explains how to perfect those methods—plus more. For any sales organization, the generation of leads is the first step to sales success. However, a lead alone is not a sale—it must be converted. **Chapter 6** looks at the prospecting side of the business. **Chapter 7** discusses leads from a unique perspective: how to enhance your ability to categorize, control, convert, and commit your leads. **Chapter 8** evaluates the steps to generating referrals. This segment helps you move beyond the cold referrals, or just getting a name and phone number from one of your past clients. I teach you how to upgrade the referrals to a meeting or a phone call from the referrer. **Chapter 9** explores the myths about the Internet. I explain my view of the danger for agents and the industry posed by the third-party lead-generation companies. I share strategies and tactics that are proven winners in lead generation and also have reasonable conversion numbers. **Chapter 10** looks at the implementation of IVR systems. These systems have transformed many agents' businesses, and I address the benefits and the land mines of using the IVR technology.

Part III, "**Champion Sales Presentations**," focuses your sales presentations. As a salesperson, you are constantly making presentations to prospects, customers, and clients. You have to be at your best when the sale is on the line. **Chapter 11** delves into the key moment with the seller . . . the listing presentation. I examine the structure, questions, delivery, objections, and characteristics of a Champion-level presentation. In **Chapter 12,** I coach you through ways to demonstrate your value, competitive advantages, and benefits to leave no doubt in the mind of your prospect that you are the right agent for the job. **Chapter 13** coaches you through the steps to acquire strong belief and conviction in your value. This chapter shows you the three core marketing messages, why commission shouldn't be an issue, and how to approach commission with the right attitude and expectations. **Chapter 14** deals with what most real estate salespeople hate and Champion Agents love . . . objections. I coach you through a six-step process that will guarantee your becoming a Champion Objection Handler. **Chapter 15** takes you deep into the world of the buyer. Being able to ask the right qualifying questions, quickly determine your prospect's motivation, and deal with all the buyer's misconceptions enables you to spend less time with each client. **Chapter 16** teaches you to demonstrate your value in quantifiable terms to the buyer. **Chapter 17** walks you through one of the most difficult discussions that agents have with a prospect—getting the buyer to sign an exclusive right-to-represent contract with you.

In **Part IV, "Building a Champion Agent's Business,"** I coach you through the initial stages of establishing a true business. This is an area in which agents fail miserably, even if they earn a six-figure income! **Chapter 18** explains how Champion Agents run high-net-profit businesses as Champion time managers. I teach you how to produce the greatest value from the minimum amount of time invested. In addition, I explain a new method of approaching time blocking and describe the four quadrants of your time. **Chapter 19** came about as a result of my work coaching thousands of agents to maximize their real estate success based on their behavioral style. It discusses the ideal method, systems, challenges, and solutions you can use to create the ideal Champion Agent practice. **Chapter 20** explores the three segments of your business and the seven key numbers to watch and monitor in a Champion Agent's practice. This chapter reveals the final truths about using your efforts to create your own business and personal wealth. Finally, **Chapter 21** contains my final thoughts on what it takes to become a Champion. I explain the importance of surrounding yourself with people who can help your business rather than those who hinder it. I also talk about how to attract the people who can help you and avoid those who can't. Finally, the **Epilogue** reflects my parting words to you—as your coach.

I have no doubt that this book will become a resource for you now and for years to come. It was not designed to be read merely once—but again and again. There is too much material to implement it all in the next week, month, or even year. The pathway to the Champion level begins with the first step. That first step is what stops most people. Let's take that first step together—to your new future as a Champion in your business *and* your life!

THE *Champion* REAL ESTATE AGENT™

PART I

PORTRAIT OF A CHAMPION

1

The Champion Agent's Business

Some would describe me as almost fanatical about my belief in the real estate business. I truly believe that the real estate sales business is one of the best business opportunities in the world. Beyond any other business, it creates tremendous opportunity for earnings, investment, freedom, and quality of life.

Real Estate Sales Business: The Best Business in the World

Incredible income and wealth are reserved for the few agents who decide to elevate their game to the Champion level. Anyone can earn a wonderful living in real estate sales. When I entered real estate sales in 1990, a mentor of mine said to me, "It's easy to make a six-figure income in real estate." The truth is, he was right. I made $100,000 the first year I was in the business.

The reason the business of real estate sales is such a great opportunity is contained in the *risk and reward* of the business. When we examine the business of most agents, they have very little capital invested in their real estate practice, which sways the equation of risk versus reward heavily in the agent's favor. Most real estate agents have less than $10,000 invested in a business that has the opportunity to create hundreds of thousands of dollars of net profit. When you compare the capital, risk, and access to prospects against the net profit, the real estate business has the makings of the best business model in the business world. When you couple that with the ground-floor opportunity one has to acquire other investments to build personal net worth along the way, you have an enormous upside without overexposure to risk.

My wife, Joan, has had an eclectic career. When we met, she was a flight attendant for United Airlines. She decided, after a few years, to take a year off from that career to pursue a new business in 1993: She became a general contractor for spec and custom homes and built a successful business over a five-year period. She has the ability to invest minimal personal capital by borrowing hundreds of thousands of dollars of other people's money to construct homes and earn a profit. This is another high-leverage business with potentially high rewards.

There are very few businesses for which your risk and personal cash outlay is limited and at the same time your earnings are high. Real estate sales is one; building and development is another. The reason I share this is to illustrate how most people who own businesses, like neighborhood dry cleaners, take-and-bake pizza parlors, restaurants, even retail stores, have to operate. Joan, after building her business, decided to open a retail store in Bend, Oregon, where we now live. She wanted to sell home design and decor items to this growing, tourist-based town. She began to research what it would take in capital, lease commitment, labor, inventory, accounting, and tracking to ensure success. A few months later, we were out to dinner when she gave me the news.

I must say, she was excited about the new venture. She began her discussion with the fact that we would need to invest nearly $300,000 for capital, equipment, and inventory to sell. We would need to sign a five-year lease, triple net, and personally guarantee the payment. When she said the words "personally guarantee," she made me nervous. Her final analysis was that she would probably need to work 12- to 14-hour days, six days a week, for the next couple of years to get the business up and running. The net profit would be in the neighborhood of $75,000 to $100,000 per year. It struck me at that moment . . . I was spoiled. I was in the greatest business in the world—the business of real estate.

As real estate agents, we don't have $300,000 in our business; we don't have long-term leases that we personally guarantee; we don't work 12 to 14 hours a day (if we are smart) for only $75,000 net. We have the greatest business opportunity in the world: limited risk and high return.

The truth is, in real estate, the biggest risk is in the broker or owner position. They have the space leases with the personal guarantees, the phone, furniture, staff, equipment, liability, and all the money invested. The agent has the least risk and can usually make the most money.

Don't Be Fooled by the Big Show

To be a Champion Agent, you have to be focused on the facts and reality. Champions are willing to search for the truth of their skills, the marketplace, their results, and to evaluate this with a keen eye.

The real estate business can be a big show. It is often the big show of egos and gross income. As agents trying to achieve Champion-level performance, we can be easily swayed by other agents who have already made it. I want to share a word of caution so that you avoid the mistakes of others.

Rule 1. If It Seems Too Good to Be True, It Usually Is!

Easy-money marketing strategies, easy lead generation, building a large team and heading to the beach to sip mai tais—these are some of the promises made by many trainers and agents who profess philosophies contrary to the laws of success in life. Tread carefully! You might achieve what they have in life and then find you do not really want it.

It's easy to project a larger-than-life image by overspending, not paying your taxes, and borrowing money. It's easy to always talk about gross commission income and sales volume and winning awards based on those factors. The awards and recognition in real estate sales are given based on sales volume and income, not on quality of the business, service to clients, and net profit after expenses. I know of an agent team that is among the top five in the country for a large national firm, but they discount their commission heavily. Would all the agents who respect them for their sales volume feel the same way if they knew how they acquired the business? Check the claims, look under the hood, and evaluate your options carefully. Anyone who makes claims to have found or developed the "secret to success," whereby success can be achieved easily and without work, will eventually lead you to destruction. You will fall far short of the Champion level of success in your business.

Rule 2. Objects in the Mirror May Appear Closer than They Are

Because of egos, recognition, and the rewards of real estate sales, it is easy to assume someone is doing well when often it is not true. Agents who dress well, drive fancy cars, and live in large houses may give the appearance of wealth and success, but it doesn't mean they are Champion Agents. The simple fact that they have a large team of assistants and high sales numbers doesn't mean they are Champion Agents.

Just because someone is on the superstar agent panel doesn't mean he or she has a profitable business model. Nor does it mean those agents understand how leads are generated; where their transactions, appointments, and commission income come from; what is spent in marketing; which marketing really works; and the return on investment for that marketing.

I recently began working with an agent who bought a moving truck to supply to his clients. I asked him why he did it. He said proudly that it would bring in business and referrals. I asked him how he was going to track the cost versus return. How many transactions did he need annually to make the payments and to pay for the gas, maintenance, cleaning, and equipment for the moving van? How much of his time or his staff's time would it take to manage, organize, and oversee the use of the moving van?

He finally admitted that he heard about it from a "very successful" agent and thought it was a great idea. What a great way to get his name out there and promote himself. He was swayed by the big show *that drew him into thinking that, with limited work and some expense, he could generate tons of leads. Instead, what he got was extra expenses, an administrative nightmare, and increased liability with a low return on investment. He also got his name and face plastered on the side panel of a moving van to feed his ego.*

Income versus Ego . . . You Choose

Studies have shown that most people will do almost anything for recognition; for most people, being recognized or getting their ego stroked is more important than producing income.

I have told hundreds of thousands of agents this truth, "You can build your business for income or build it for your ego, but you can't do both at the same time." You must choose which is most important to you. You must choose which is going to be the driving factor for you if you want to reach the Champion level in your business.

Does your ego drive you and your business, or is it your desire for a certain income level or net profit level? Which one controls your thinking, actions, and decision making for a greater percentage of the time? This question will really determine your net profit, personal time invested in the business, and quality of life for you and your family. Most agents never come to grips with this challenge. As a result, they can't move beyond it to become a Champion.

Big Hat . . . No Cattle

A number of years ago, I was speaking to a group of high-powered agents in Houston. I was sharing with them the six key numbers in a real estate agent's practice—the six key numbers an agent must monitor, watch, evaluate, and, for most, change. These six numbers, because I controlled them well, enabled me to sell more than 150 homes annually while working only Monday through Thursday and taking Friday, Saturday, and Sunday off. I didn't answer the phone, use the fax, or send e-mail on those days. I was off with my family. In fact, for most of those days, I was a three-hour drive away, at my vacation home. It allowed me to build a business of high net profit where I netted well over 60 percent of the gross revenue I created each year. You don't need to gross $2.4 million in revenue to net over $1 million in profit, as some experts will try to convince you. A Champion will cast an analytical eye on that model. (Chapter 20 explains these key numbers, how to monitor them, and how to improve them.)

I shared with the agents that most of their colleagues had no idea about these numbers. In addition, not being aware of the numbers allowed them to get out of alignment. The reality is, the numbers are so out of alignment that their net profit is poor. This is especially true for many agents who have superstar status. Achieving large gross incomes but low net profit numbers, they often live, spend, and have a lifestyle more reflective of their *gross* income than their *net* income.

I also shared a true story of being on a superstar panel in the 1990s with a prominent agent (one of the first to break the million-dollar-a-year gross commission income barrier) who admitted (after getting off the stage and getting real) that he was broke. He had nothing to show for his million-dollar gross income he earned that year. I can assure you, he wasn't projecting the image of being broke while he was on the stage.

═══════════════

As I shared these concepts and stories in Houston that day, an attractive lady in the back stood up. She was the "perfect" Realtor. You can easily picture her clean, professional suit, with diamonds just dripping off her fingers, wrist, and neck. She had the brooch as well as the hat. She graciously raised her hand to make a statement that I will never forget. She said, "Excuse me, Dirk. We have a saying for that type of person here in Texas. We call them 'Big Hat . . . No Cattle.' " She described the truth perfectly for many "superstar" agents. They are often big hat . . . no cattle.

═══════════════

Champion Agents recognize that the truth of their income, earnings, and quality of business is contained on line 32 of Form 1040. The Champion's scorecard isn't the gross income, the production awards, sales volume, number of assistants, or name recognition. The Champion's scorecard (when we are talking about money) is focused on line 32 of your 1040 tax return form. To be blunt, line 32 is your adjusted gross income (AGI). This is the amount that you get to live on, save, invest, and spend. It's the number that any bank will look at to determine whether to lend you money on the investment property you want to buy to build your net worth.

Reality is contained on line 32. Jack Welch, the former CEO of GE, has six famous rules for business success. The first is to face reality as it is, not as you wish it to be. Too often, we hedge, adjust, evade, and concoct a new reality that is too optimistic. Champions don't concoct a false reality to make themselves feel better. Champions deal with the truth and change the outcome. There is nothing based more in reality, with regard to earned income, than line 32 of a tax return. Nothing is more black and white with regard to earnings than line 32.

A Champion Agent's scorecard encompasses far more than just the money. I started with the money because that is what we generally recognize in real estate sales circles. It is also easy to count money to see how we are doing. When evaluating other areas of life, the counting is more difficult to observe and gauge.

A more challenging and certainly more meaningful area of development and growth in life is your relationships: investing the time to have vibrant relationships with your spouse or significant other, your children, parents, and friends. One advantage that your Champion business and income provides is the opportunity to earn more in less time, so you have additional time to invest in life's more meaningful pursuits. In order to become a Champion Performer, balancing career, money, family, health, and spiritual areas of life must be your aim. You don't have to be a Champion to earn a large income and bankrupt the other areas of your life while doing it. It doesn't take any particular skill to work too many hours, earn a large income, and blow up your family in the process. That would result in an A for income and an F for family, meaning your GPA is a C or less.

My goal throughout this book is to enable you to score As across the scoreboard of life; to in effect hit it out of the park; to play to your potential as a business owner, spouse, father, or mother (whatever role you have been blessed with in life); and to play that particular role—all out—at the Champion level!

Ensure Your Success

There are as many models of, trainers for, and philosophies about how to be successful in real estate as there are people. Each one of these people, including myself, has strong beliefs about the path one must take to be successful. The truth is, there isn't just one pathway to achieving success in real estate sales. There are a number of ways to prosper in the business. That is one of the exciting aspects of real estate sales. If anyone (agent, trainer, manager, or sales guru) tells you their way is the only way, run the other direction.

The real question is, what will be *your* way? There is a right model or pathway for you based on your experience, database size, market, commitment level, behavioral style, sales skills, and competitive nature. The way to ensure your success is to evaluate your own unique factors and build your business in a complementary way.

For example, for the past eight years, we at Real Estate Champions have been the leader in behavior assessments in the real estate industry. Through working with thousands of agents and benchmarking their behavioral styles, we have discovered patterns in how the different behavior styles can build a business that is effective and comfortable. Not everyone should call on for-sale-by-owner listings (FSBOs) and expireds, as some trainers profess. In fact, for a few behavioral styles, the success rate in prospecting to those sources is so dismal that it would be counterproductive.

Other behavioral styles are so competitive and focused that they struggle to create referral-based relationships even when they attend numerous seminars to learn referral techniques. Some agents sell more effectively by using facts and figures, while others use emotional connection and emotional techniques. Building your business around your natural gifts and skills, those given to you at birth and that you have spent years perfecting, is the mark of a Champion.

I once had a client who was frustrated because he didn't generate as many referral leads as his friend, whom I also had coached. Both were Champion Agents in their market. It really gnawed at my client, Eddie, that he couldn't generate as many referrals as Fred. When he finally shared that with me, I told him he needed to get over it, because he would never get as many referrals as Fred. After he calmed down, I explained that his intensity and focus, based on his behavioral style, was not as relational and people-oriented as Fred's. The outcome would be fewer referrals, no matter what he did.

Because of his high desire for competition and intensity, I convinced him to try working with expireds. Within weeks, he was taking at least six listings a month by working on expireds. He loved his business and was less frustrated. We then put a new assistant on his team to work with his past clients and sphere in order to maintain frequent personal contact and ask for referrals. The assistant had the same behavioral style as Fred, and the number of referrals increased by 25 percent in less than 60 days.

The way to ensure your success is to find your own system, strategy, tactics, lead generation, and conversion sources. Too many agents are looking for an off-the-rack solution in a tailor-fit world. We need to be willing to pause, to evaluate, research, and design the right long-term solution. People can do things that are incongruent with their behavioral style for a short period of time, especially if they are broke. The problem is that it's not sustainable. When we have made enough money or feel comfortable, we stop doing activities we don't want to do. (Chapter 19 reveals the secrets of building a business with your behavioral style.)

The search for your personal system and the perfection of that system will ensure your success. You still need to attend seminars and training sessions, listen to CDs, read books, and participate in coaching. However, if you work with a coaching company that is focused on helping you uncover your system rather than forcing you into its own, you have a higher probability of long-term success once the coaching is completed.

The second step to ensure your success occurs when you make the best decision on how you are going to generate leads—for example, past clients, sphere of influence, strategic alliances with other professionals (accountants, financial planners, family law attorneys, etc.), community involvement, FSBOs, expireds, REO properties. There are unlimited sources to choose from. However, once you have made your decision, stick with it. A Champion Agent tests new strategies long enough to modify the strategy a few times, retest, and then monitor all of the results. A huge error I see a lot of agents making is the *error of impatience.* They change strategies and tactics so quickly that they never get past the steepest part of the learning curve. They are moving from one ice mountain to the next, trying to find the secret path to the top. It isn't there; you have to climb to the top.

Most agents try a farm for three or four months; if they don't get any business, they scrap the farm. They try a newsletter to their past clients and sphere for three or four months, and then they decide that doesn't work. They call FSBOs or expireds for a few weeks without achieving the result level they want, and they stop that practice. In order for you to know whether something new works, you have to try it for at least six months. It takes that long to gauge the return on investment. It takes that long to tweak and perfect it. You won't get all the facts to make an informed decision about whether the strategy works for you before a six-month period of time.

Four Rules of Business Expansion

To be a Champion Agent, you must understand the four rules of business expansion. These rules are universal to all businesses, but especially to service businesses, where the competition is high and the opportunity for repeat customers and referrals is even higher.

1. Protect what you currently have.
2. Improve your market penetration with your target market or the people you already work with.
3. Expand horizontally in your core business areas.
4. Change, and create vertical expansion.

Coach's Tip: *Attack the rules of business expansion in this exact order. Always!*

These four rules control the level of risk you need to take in order to achieve a Champion Agent's business. The further down the list you venture, the more risk you incur, and the probability of achieving a return becomes even lower.

Champion Rule: *Protect what you currently have.*

Sometimes, you can get so excited about the new venture or opportunity expansion that you fail in your core business area. Your core business begins to slide and becomes stale, stagnant, and lifeless. Don't ever take your eye off the ball. Each of you has one or two pillars of your business that generates a sizable business without much extra attention, but it does need *some* attention. Don't throttle all the way back.

The vast majority of agents do a poor job of this. We are so excited about new techniques, new systems, and new lead generation sources that we neglect to protect the business, past clients, and sphere of influence that we have now. As I said to a new client when explaining the four rules of business expansion, "It's as though you're running a ranch. You spend all of your time buying new cattle that you find through a little prospecting or through marketing. The problem is that the back of your corral is open. Your freshly acquired cattle that haven't been branded yet are getting out into the neighbor's pasture. You have some fence mending to do."

The National Association of Realtors has done many studies over the years about our clients—their satisfaction and the retention levels of both buyers and sellers. The numbers are really quite shocking. In a recent survey conducted over a series of years, 69 percent of people were satisfied with their agent's service. When they checked back with this test group, they found out that only 24 percent of the people who conducted another real estate transaction did so with their previous agent. Only 69 percent, on average, of clients were satisfied, which is about a C– grade. Then only 24 percent of the total would even do business with us again—another 45 percentage point drop!

It gets worse. In the last year on record for sales, we closed 7.2 million transactions in the United States, with over 40 percent of those being investment purchases or second homes. That means almost 2.9 million transactions were done with people who had a previous relationship with a real estate agent. When all types of buyers and sellers were surveyed, it was found that only 13 percent, or only 936,000 transactions, were done with an agent they had used before.

What this says, boldly, is that we don't protect what we currently have, that too many of us are sending out trash and trinkets hoping that it will lead to referrals and long-term relationships with our past clients and sphere. The studies show this is obviously not working! However, Champions work first to protect what they currently have before moving down the ladder to improving market penetration with their target market or with those they already do business with.

But most agents go to number 3 on the list first. The reason is because it's new; it's fun; it's an adventure; someone recommended it; or they're bored. Figure 1.1 is a reminder that risk and probability are further down the list of rules you work. The risk is higher and the probability lower as you go to rules 3 and 4.

We must protect the farm we have (if we have one), our past clients, and our sphere of influence. You have to protect your position first. The way in which you currently generate business needs protection!

> **Champion Rule:** *Improve market penetration with your target market or people you already work with.*

Once you protect your current business, you need to expand your reach into your target market. Basically, the rule says that wherever you have strength or control, exploit that strength to get more. Identify ways to acquire a larger piece of the business in an area you have already penetrated. If you have a farm to work, increase your market share in that farm.

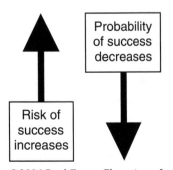

1. Protect what you have currently.

2. Improve your market penetration with your target market or the people you already work with.

3. Expand horizontally in your core business areas.

4. Change and create vertical expansion.

©2006 Real Estate Champions, Inc.

Figure 1.1 Four Rules of Business Expansion

I have a client who owns over 30 percent of the sales in her farm. Our first step was to create a strategy to increase her market share to over 45 percent. We did that by promoting her dominance compared to other individual agents, and even other companies. We also promoted the concept of a second opinion to the people who lived in the farm. She wanted to raise awareness of the changing marketplace and the fact that a second opinion costs nothing, but gives peace of mind that the client is making the right decision. That strategy worked beautifully. In the first few months, she increased her number of appointments in the farm by 23 percent. She is on track to easily exceed the 45 percent threshold of market share. She is getting a far better return in a short period of time with lower risk by working rule 2 rather than rule 3.

A *target market* is any market that you focus on to generate business. It could be geographical, as in my example. It could be FSBOs or expireds, provided you already do those. It is anything you are *doing currently and deliberately* to generate business.

Coach's Tip: *Convince your clients to invest in real estate. Do more deals with the people you currently do business with by getting their friends and relatives to work with you. (Ramping up your referrals is a rule 2 activity.)*

For the majority of the readers of this book, your core business area is residential real estate. It could even be resales, rather than new construction, in residential real estate. Your core business could be single-family homes rather than condos, multiplexes, or investment property. Whatever area generates 80 percent of your commission dollars is your *core business*.

Champion Rule: *Expand horizontally in your core business area.*

When you expand horizontally, you open up another section of your business or a new lead source while still remaining in residential real estate. You could begin to work with builders; market condos, multiplexes, investment property, FSBOs, or expireds; or establish a new farm area. You could move into conducting open houses, attending service clubs, or conducting seminars for home buyers, home sellers, or investors. You have endless options about what you can do in this category.

The key is to expand into this area *only* after you have hit the point of diminishing returns for rules 1 and 2. The law of diminishing returns indicates that you are getting close to the maximum returns in a particular area. The closer you get to the ceiling, the less growth you can achieve, regardless of your tremendous efforts and boundless resources. There's just not enough growth potential!

Champion Rule:	*Change, and create vertical expansion.*

To expand vertically would be to move to a similar, complementary business that is structured similarly to the real estate business or has ties to the real estate business. This rule allows you to take what you learned in real estate or use the contacts you have in real estate and build another business and an additional revenue stream.

The most common practice for agents working with this rule is to open a real estate brokerage office and recruit agents to work for them. You can also create a mortgage company, title company, or escrow company, or you can branch off into developing land, building homes, or dealing with investment real estate. I have even heard of agents forming a business partnership with a property and casualty insurance provider. If you have a good database and have communicated with your past clients and sphere frequently, you certainly have the option of serving their other financial needs.

Champions work to follow the four rules of business expansion. They focus on the risk and the probability of working to keep those both in their favor. I know of many agents who became Champion Agents merely by focusing on rule 1 (protecting what they have currently) and rule 2 (improving their market production with their target market or those they already work with). Because of their skill, database size, and frequency of communication, they can achieve exponential growth with limited risk.

Why Rise to the Championship Level in Life?

The Championship level affords you all the advantages of influence, recognition, and money. The people who climb to highest esteem live full, rich, and fulfilling lives. They have the resources to enjoy the finer experiences of life. I have found that while most Champions live well, the vast majority live below their means, and many even adopt the philosophy described in Thomas Stanley's book, *The Millionaire Next Door.* Stanley describes typical millionaires as those who can't be detected as such because their wealth has very few outward signs. They live in nice homes, but not in opulent palaces or in the latest "McMansions." They drive nice, well-kept cars, but not necessarily new vehicles.

They focus on protecting and growing their wealth and security. A Champion could certainly be in that fairly undetectable category.

There are a number of responses to the question, "Why rise to the Championship level?" "Why not?" comes to mind first. Since you are on the ride of life, you might as well make it an E-ticket ride. Before Disneyland made park admission all-inclusive, you paid admission and bought packages for rides based on a scale from A to E. The best rides were the E-ticket rides! As kids, we ran out of E-tickets long before the other tickets. A Champion wants an unlimited supply of E-tickets.

The greatest rewards in life are at the Champion level. The largest income, earnings, compensation, and wealth are at the Championship level. If you aren't there in your level of skill and ability as a business owner and real estate agent, the money you earn will be poor. If you are good, you will earn fair money. If you are great, you will earn good money. If you are a Champion, you will generate Champion-level earnings and Champion-level net profit; you actually skip over great money and go to the highest level.

The Power of Personal Satisfaction

There is nothing greater than the personal satisfaction and confidence you gain from being the best. To climb the success ladder and know that you are well on your way to the top is a feeling like no other. Your confidence grows, which increases your success. There is a connection between your competence and your confidence. When competence rises, so does your confidence.

Play to Your Potential

Champion Performers come in all shapes and sizes. The ones I respect the most are the ones who play the game of success closest to their potential. To me, that is the mark of a true Champion. A person who achieves a high level of production but still falls far short of what he or she *could* do, given that person's resources and skill, is not a Champion Agent.

Those who sell less but who are close to their capacity in terms of sales, are Champions. I could share numerous stories of agents who lacked extensive education and skills but who nonetheless managed, through their consistency, adherence to improvement, and determination, to increase their income in excess of $100,000 annually. They now make more money than most doctors, but they will never be million-dollar-a-year commission earners. In some cases, they won't even crack the $500,000 mark, but they are Champions nonetheless. They are playing all out at the highest level, based on the talent that God gave them.

Combat the Public Perception of Real Estate Agents

As Champion Agents, we must be constantly waging a battle to educate the public on our value and expertise. People often think we are overpaid and that we offer limited value, since they can find homes on their own through the Internet. We have to combat the opinion that we don't add value and that what we do is easy, that they don't need an agent unless the marketplace becomes tough or challenging, that when the marketplace has low inventory and high demand we are expendable in our service.

Through thorough and consistent communication with our sphere, past clients, and prospects, we can better educate them on our benefits and value. I believe it is a challenge to educate the masses. As an agent, I doubt that you can even do that via the mail or media. The objective is for each agent to handle the clients, prospects, and past clients in front of him or her, to focus on those people and to help them, through education, see value in the services of an agent.

You can choose to be a Champion Performer. It is within the reach for us all. However, you must make the commitment—right now—to achieve it.

2

What Is a Champion Agent?

For more than 20 years, I have been an entrepreneur in sales-based businesses. Throughout that period, I have diligently studied success by reading, attending seminars, listening to cassettes and CDs, as well as observing and analyzing the personal journeys to success (through trial and error) of myself and many others.

Link that learning (with numerous road abrasions and challenges) with a passion for excellence, and my life pursuit of first becoming a Champion and then coaching and teaching others to become champions comes into clear view. My passion for excellence was first forged by my mother and father. They endeavored to show me early on that a life lived through growth, personal development with excellence in clear focus, and not settling for less was one's true objective.

I aligned this ingrained wisdom with my competitive nature, forged through athletics (especially my years climbing the ranks in the sport of racquetball), to the professional level. Becoming a Champion has been a passion for more than 35 years of my life. The pursuit and perfection of a Champion mindset, actions to create the Champion's edge in the marketplace, whether in business or athletics, then distilling that Champion's edge to make it available have caused countless hours of work and sleepless nights. My belief is absolute that *everyone deserves to be a Champion,* that this level of high performance is available to anyone, that we at Real Estate Champions and Sales Champions (my two companies) can take anyone to that level, provided they have a high level of desire to become a Champion. The sad part is very few people really experience the exhilaration, satisfaction, quality of life, and wealth associated with playing all out, in life and business, at the Champion level.

Real Estate Agents Are Workaholics

Very few agents have achieved the Champion level; most agents are stuck trying to access it through the wrong trail. When we evaluate most real estate agents' paths to success, we find the preferred method to wealth and success in real estate sales is the workaholic path. The vast majority of people in the upper echelon of companies have given up free time, family, friends, and peace of mind to earn a large income. Realtors who work six to seven days a week and remain on call 24/7 can earn large incomes, but the cost to their health, family, and spiritual life becomes overwhelming. They eventually hit burnout or are forced to correct their behavior due to a catastrophic event (divorce, massive health issues, challenges with children, etc.). Catastrophes usually hit fast and hard, like someone swinging a ball-peen hammer at your forehead.

Real Estate Agents Are Excessive Marketers

The second most preferred method to success is to buy the business. Too many agents who are trying to grow their business to the highest level get sucked into the marketing game. They think that spending a larger and larger amount of money on advertising and marketing to get their name out there will drastically increase their business. There is no question that sending out thousands of postcards, newsletters, and promotional pieces can increase their business. The question is, by how much, and how much will it cost them. What will the return on investment (ROI) be? What will they net for all this effort? There are viable marketing strategies agents need to implement, but most lack the monitoring and control systems to manage and track their ROI.

I know many agents who have built large practices through this marketing method. It does work for some people to increase their gross commission income. The downside is that most of the money is used up in marketing, with little profit left. Many agents have the philosophy of "I will invest it all for a few years to get my name out there and then cut back." The truth is that few cut back when they achieve a high income level. They fail to realign the marketing.

When coaching these people early in my coaching career, I did not realize what a security blanket and stranglehold this marketing (buying the business) had on people. I also didn't realize that most people will panic if there is even a slight drop in leads or income. I would try to get them to quit cold turkey. The results were less favorable than I had hoped. I found the best approach is to transition away from buying the business over time. Create a one-year plan to continue the marketing while you open up other lead and income streams. This gives the other lead and income streams time to gain momentum, results, and earnings and enables you to feel confident about these new revenue creators. You can then slowly turn off the expensive and less profitable megamarketing-driven sales techniques.

Real Estate Agents Discount Their Fees

Another way I see agents buy business is through discounting their fees. Discounting and commission cutting has become more of a factor than ever before. With the massive influx of new agents and consumers' perceived ease of home selling, the fee structure for agents has become a major issue.

Agents who use discount strategies to buy the business can make it when the market is hot. However, when the market cools, days on the market increase; that in turn causes advertising and marketing dollars to increase because of the holding costs of listings; as a result, the small margins between their commission and the sales costs force these agents to change tactics or die.

I know of an agent team that is among the top five in terms of units sold, nationally, for a large franchise company. They heavily market their discount structure in their town. If we peek behind the velvet curtain of their business, it's not so glamorous. They sell about 350 homes a year. They have about seven buyer's agents plus the two of them. That's nine people to do about 350 units, or about 36 units per person. That would be solid production on a per-agent basis if they were getting a full fee. Since they are discounting, it's much easier to get listings and sales. However, 350 units is really not that impressive if you are willing to do it for free. There are an unlimited amount of prospects you can work for if you are willing to work for nothing!

A Champion Agent: Balance Business and Quality of Life

Very few agents achieve success in real estate by establishing a well-balanced business. A Champion Agent's business is to know how to produce the leads; where they are coming from; the conversion ratios of the contacts to leads, leads to appointments, appointments to clients created, clients created to contracts, and contracts to closings and income. A Champion Agent who has a balanced business knows the cost in each major category of the business, including advertising, promotion, car expenses, phone expenses, client care, office supplies, and brokerage fees. He or she knows the net profit of the business model, can project it in advance, and can track and monitor the cash flow of the business.

Champion Agents' well-balanced business model enables them to have quality of life. They receive ample days off weekly, a number of vacation weeks each year, and very few missed T-ball games or school activities of their children. Finally, the high net profit allows them to create a lifestyle of comfort while making investments for the future.

Less than 5 percent of the Realtor population has achieved the well-balanced business model or the Champion agent's model. Most have defaulted to the workaholic or buying-the-business model because they couldn't see another way. To become a Champion agent, you first have to make a commitment to yourself.

Decide to Be a Champion Agent

To achieve anything great in life, you must first decide to achieve it. You must decide that you are going to play at the Championship level. You can't decide you will *try* to do it. You have to decide that you *will* do it. I regularly have the pleasure of meeting agents all over the country through speaking engagements. After every speech, I have the honor of people coming up to share with me how I inspired or helped them. Many times, I get to talk with excited agents who want to share their goals. I often ask agents in those moments what their income or unit goal is for the year. Better than 60 percent of the time they start their next sentence with, "I would like to make." When I hear that, I stop them in their tracks. The truth is they have not decided yet. Something we "would like" is not something we have decided to do or made an absolute commitment to get. We haven't made the decision to lay it on the line to get it; to play all out and practice to improve the odds to acquire it.

Another 20 to 30 percent say that their income goal is a range, such as "between $200,000 to $250,000 for the year." These people are hedging their goal, which isn't a firm goal because it isn't defined and committed to. If you have income-range goals, you might as well consciously accept the lower number. Don't fool yourself by thinking you will achieve $250,000 in income when $200,000 is acceptable. You won't push yourself to the extra effort needed to earn another $50,000. The first step to becoming a Champion is to decide to be a Champion. This is true for every facet of your life.

When I established Real Estate Champions, I set a bold goal for the company to focus on creating Champion Performers. It wasn't to help people become proficient enough to earn an income in real estate sales. It wasn't to help people become top producers, but Champion Producers. My personal and company mission is "to teach and inspire people to use their God-given talents to create excellence in life," to rise to the Champion level in business and in life. When I first started working toward writing this book, I asked myself these three questions. I hope to answer them for you, as well.

1. What is a Champion?
2. What does it take for someone to become a Champion?
3. Why are some people Champions and others not?

By asking myself these questions, I came up with the following seven key characteristics or beliefs of Champion Agents.

Seven Characteristics of Champion Agents

Champion Agents exhibit seven traits that distinguish them from run-of-the-mill agents.

1. Champion Agents realize there is a price to be paid.   Once you are a Champion Agent, the opportunities come more frequently and easily; because you have arrived at the Champion level, everyone (buyers and sellers) wants to work for and with a Champion Performer. Generally, in the real estate market, it costs the same to work with a marginal agent as it does to work with a Champion Agent.

We all want to be successful. The question is, what are we willing to do to acquire it? Success does not care who acquires it. Success is available to all who are willing to pay the price that it requires. I admit my good fortune: being the son of Norm and Becky Zeller lowered the price for me to achieve success because of the environment they provided, their philosophy, the work ethic they demonstrated, and the education they afforded me. All of those factors, and others, helped me to advance up the success ladder faster than others who didn't have such incredible model parents. Nevertheless, I still had to pay a price for success.

Invest your time and resources.   The price of being a Champion is in both time and resources. You must be willing to invest time in larger amounts than other agents in direct income-producing activities (DIPA): prospecting, lead follow-up, buyer interview appointments and listing appointments, showing property, writing and negotiating contracts, and personal development time.

Invest in your personal development.   The edge for a Champion is created through the investment of personal development time. A Champion has the passion and invests the time in improving his or her mindset, skills, and business systems. A Champion invests time in reading, seminars, training CDs, coaching, and any other form of personal development.

━━━━━━━━━━━━━━━━━━━━━━━

In 1996, when Joan and I completed our vacation home in Bend, my personal development time kicked into another gear. I had always read and studied success from my first day in real estate sales. I attended countless seminars and listened to countless tape series in the pursuit of success. I hit a new level of investment in personal development because I had a new-

found freedom and location away from the distractions of life and business to immerse myself in personal development time. Joan and I spent many evenings in the library in that home in front of the fireplace, each sitting in a leather wingback chair devouring a good book . . . mine usually on business, sales, leadership, management, or finance.

I must admit, with four-year-old son Wesley and one-year-old daughter Annabelle the challenge to carve out enough personal development time to continue to grow and stay ahead of our clients and competition is more challenging than ever. A Champion is willing to stay up late or get up early when the house is quiet to stay at the top of his or her game.

───────────

Because of the competitive nature of this business, whatever brought you to your current level of success will not be enough to keep you there. To maintain your level of success, you must learn, advance, and grow. The competition will always get better. The marketplace will always be adjusting. If you don't have a passion to learn and improve, you'd better develop one, fast! If you have to study and learn just to keep pace, imagine what you must do to grow, expand, and get ahead. To grow, you must spend at least an hour a day on your personal development.

Most agents invest too little in their personal development. Think of the books, CD series, teleseminars, online seminars, and coaching as buying or investing in new equipment for your company. That new equipment will help you make sales in large quantities, faster and more efficiently than ever before. The investment in personal development will pay the largest dividend in your business—larger than a new computer, a new marketing strategy, a new Web site, or anything else.

Invest in your selling skills.   Another investment I have identified as a limiting step for most agents in the real estate business is a barrier to massive success. Until this step is removed, all the other changes, adjustments, and gyrations will bring about limited results. This limiting step is lack of sales skills!

Too many agents have invested too little time in their individual sales skills. The new agents coming out of sales careers where they have received exceptional fundamental sales training earn a large income early in their careers. There is a direct correlation between sales skills and high gross commission for most agents. A true Champion Agent has impeccable sales skills.

How are you at your scripts and dialogues that generate the lead and drive the lead to an appointment? What are your conversion ratios? How strong is your listing presentation, especially when you are competing against a good agent? How long is that presentation? Are you there more than an hour? Can you get buyers to come into your office for a consultation? Do they sign the buyer's agency contract every time after your consultation? How are you at responding to objections in sales? Do you really close on clients at the end of every presentation, or do you wait for them to close themselves? One of the key investments of your time resource needs to be in the sales skills development area. This is clearly part of the price one must pay to be a Champion.

Invest in your prospecting.   Another price is to prospect, consistently. It doesn't take a Champion to prospect and look for business when he or she is broke. Everyone (even poor performers) does a little prospecting when they are broke and have no listings or sales or good leads that will convert to dollars. True Champions prospect consistently and pay the price even when they are busy. They *find the time* and *structure it,* rather than *make the time* each day to generate new leads. You must invest your resource of time to create more revenue and success.

The real question is, *"Are you willing to pay the price?"* Deep down inside, you know what you need to do. The question is, "Are you willing to do it?" Are you willing to invest the time, energy, emotion, and money to become a Champion?

2. Champion Agents are ready and willing to make the sacrifice that is necessary. The challenge for most people climbing the ladder of success to becoming a Champion is knowing when and how much sacrifice is necessary. The key is making the right sacrifice needed for the situation. Too often, agents expect to give up too much. I was speaking with an agent the other day who wanted to be one of the top agents in his marketplace. Based on his comments, I knew he thought the only path to real estate sales success was being a workaholic. As we spoke further, he began to understand there were better avenues to success than a 70-hour workweek, that he could achieve a large, successful sales practice by putting forth the effort of sacrifice, plus a little bit more.

I don't believe people need to work 70 hours a week to achieve success. This only demonstrates how inefficient one is with the use of time in activities. It also speaks to a lack of skills that create revenue. Conversely, I do not believe people achieve wealth and success by working a typical 40-hour week, as most workers do. I know that to achieve success, wealth, and quality of life, you have to sacrifice by putting in a little more effort than the next person. Once you have increased your skills to the level of Champion, you can go well below a 40-hour workweek and still earn a large income. It's in the climb up the success mountain that too many people either don't give enough or give too much. In terms of work hours, if you are in a growth stage of your business, I believe around 50 hours a week is required.

Too many of us stop short of what is needed and required. Because we have allocated fewer resources than required, the results are guaranteed to fall short of expectations. Others sacrifice more than is needed, which is a waste of resources. You can kill a fly with a bomb, but it takes more sacrifice, resources, and power than is necessary.

The question is, *"Are you currently making the right amount of sacrifice to be a Champion Agent?"*

3. Champion Agents have the skill to focus in the moment.   The power of focus enables some people to accomplish greater production in a shorter period of time. Whenever we achieve a new level of success in life, it is preceded by a focused period of exertion. Focus always comes in front of any success. The most successful people have an enhanced power of focus.

The most significant challenges to a real estate agent's career are the distractions of the business. The structure and distractions make it difficult for an agent to have the time and mental energy necessary to focus on building one's business. The tightrope balance between being available to clients, especially prospects for new business, and the need for time spent in planning, strategizing, and implementing tactics causes most agents to fall.

Allocate time to planning.   My counsel is for a Champion Agent to allocate at least 90 minutes weekly to planning and strategy time. That time is really golden and must be protected. It is the focus time to improve your business. It enables a Champion Agent the opportunity to focus without distractions. The distractions will only intensify as business expands. It is better to establish this Champion habit before your business expands exponentially. When you set aside this time, be sure to turn off all access points to you: telephone and cell phone, pager, even your e-mail. Even the split-second ding that signifies "you've got mail" can take you out of focus, and you won't get the focus back for 5 or 10 minutes.

To focus better, I have clients who leave their office and go to a conference room or who leave the real estate office entirely. I have one client who goes to the library down the street. He can't go home because of the distraction of small children, and he doesn't do his planning time consistently enough when he stays at his office. Find your place to get in the zone and focus.

When you decide where this 90 minutes of planning time will be in order to increase your focus, treat it as an appointment. Do not let anything invade the time. It's an appointment with your business and yourself. I often tell clients it will be their most important appointment of the week and the easiest to cancel.

Goal diffusion is a problem.   Too many business owners have goal diffusion. Goal diffusion is when you are working on too many goals at once. You don't have clear objectives.

You can't focus with depth and intensity on your accomplishment. If you don't prioritize your goals with clarity, then you will struggle to complete them. The higher your position or ownership in a company (this includes entrepreneurial companies like real estate), the more potential growth you can experience. Along with this growth are increased responsibilities and additional staff, plus the higher probability of goal diffusion.

Divide your time into small segments. To increase your focus in the moment, divide your time into smaller segments. Insert specific activities inside the smaller segments. By single-mindedly focusing on one task rather than multitasking, you can increase your focus and results. Multitasking is a buzzword we have all adopted for doing a lot of things at once. By definition, it runs contrary to focus. How can you really focus on 20 things at once? Multitasking is a recipe for failure in business. It opens the door to distractions and lost productivity.

Take an honest look at your ability to focus, to immerse yourself in a mental state that takes what you are working on to completion before you move onto the next project or activity.

The question is, *"Do you have the mental discipline to become a Champion?"*

4. Champion Agents accept nothing less than excellence.   When you look at successful individuals and successful companies, good is not good enough. They are clearly striving for excellence. In Jim Collins's bestselling book, *Good to Great,* one of his premises is that good is really the enemy of great—that if we are willing to settle for good, we will never achieve greatness. I agree that to hit the Champion level as an agent, you can't be satisfied with midlevel skills, abilities, and mindset. You must resolve to raise your level of expectation and performance—first for yourself and then for your staff—to the predetermined Champion level.

Delegate and others will excel.   While a successful company must excel in all facets of business (sales, marketing, accounting, client care), it would be impossible for one individual to be that competent. Knowing the real estate business and knowing the areas in which you are personally most skilled can raise your performance. It is paramount that you delegate the areas in which you will never achieve excellence to others who have the capacity to excel in those areas.

Perfection is not excellence.   It is easy to confuse perfection with the pursuit of excellence. To many, they look the same. On further analysis, one can see the distinction between obsessions with the most minor details, which is *perfection,* and wanting to hit the upper echelon of the zone of success, which is *excellence.* One means trying to achieve a 100 percent standard (perfectionism), while the other says that 95 percent is clearly in the excellent range. We must ask ourselves if 90 percent is still an A in our business. Can I live with 90 to 95 percent, or must I reach 100 percent? If your response is 100 percent, you have a perfectionist problem that is holding you back from becoming a Champion.

The truth is that to close that last 5 percent gap from 95 percent to 100 percent requires a considerable amount of resources. You can produce a lot more sales and income by looking for other opportunities rather than by pushing that 95 percent to 100 percent. A Champion knows the fine line between excellence and perfection. He or she works to stay on the right side of that line.

I frequently see agents working to perfect their systems. They spend hours and weeks designing flyer templates, follow-up procedures, letters, marketing pieces, closing checklists, buyer checklists, seller checklists, seller activity reports—the list is endless. However, before you assume I am against systems, let me say that you must have these systems to provide quality customer service, good follow-up, and the ability to make sales. If the systems are 90 to 95 percent effective, you don't need to invest hours of time to make them perfect. You need to invest your time generating more leads to run through your systems. A system for service is valuable, but revenue growth comes from running more people through your service system, not from perfecting the system.

Execute the fundamentals, exceptionally.   You can become a Champion, easily, through exceptional execution of the fundamentals. Most people fall short in the fundamentals of their core business. The reason is that the fundamentals are harder to master. They aren't really exciting, sexy, or full of public accolades when you do them. They just work to produce significant results.

_____

As a professional racquetball player in my twenties, I was not the flashiest player with the most diverse shot arsenal. I had a couple of shots from a handful of positions on the court. When I positioned myself in those areas, it was point over. If I got into those zones more often than my opponent, it was game over. In racquetball, the objective is to control the center of the court a few feet behind the service line. If you are in that zone for more of the time than your opponent, you have a 90 percent probability of winning the match. My objective was to control that center court area. When my opponent had it, I wanted to hit a shot that moved him out of the area and me into it. That is fundamental racquetball. That approach, while not as flashy as some of the spectacular shots my opponents would sometimes execute, allowed me to win a number of prestigious titles during my career.

_____

As a Champion real estate agent, the fundamentals are prospecting, lead follow-up, presentation, objection handling, and closing skills in the sales process. In client care, it's the communication frequency and systems. In marketing, it's copywriting, strategy, tactics, and implementation. Throw in two more fundamentals, time management and money management (in both business and personal life), and you will be a Champion. When you evaluate that list, it's not very exciting to look at . . . especially the sales processes. What I find is that most agents are better at marketing and client care than at sales processes, time management, and money management. However, I rank those three (sales processes, time management, and money management) as the top three in a Champion Agent's business. If you don't have impeccable skills in those three core areas, you won't be a Champion!

The question is, "*Are you ready to do what it takes to develop impeccable skills in sales processes, time management, and business management?*"

5. Champion Agents realize it's not *what* happens but *how they react* to what happens that counts.   When I speak, I often ask groups if they think that an agent who sells 100 homes a year has more slumps, challenges, struggles, problems, and distractions than one who sells fewer. Most agents say that the high-production agent has fewer challenges, not more. The truth is, these agents have *more,* not fewer. They usually have more staff, which automatically means more problems. They have more exposure to problems because they are doing more transactions. It increases the number of times they have to work with challenging co-op agents, difficult sellers, and problem transactions. The real secret to their success is that they let difficulties affect their performance or mindset for a shorter span of time than do other agents.

Champion Example

What happens when you think you have a listing in the bag and you lose it? How long does it affect your personal performance? Does it affect your desire and motivation to prospect and do lead follow-up? Does it make you hesitant, cautious, a meeker closer with the next prospect? Does it wipe you out emotionally for a few days? I frequently see low-performing agents become wiped out for the rest of the day or even the rest of the week when hit by a negative occurrence like this. A Champion will not let that happen. He or she will be disappointed, for sure; however, that disappointment will not be allowed to control the rest of the day. In fact, a Champion will not even let it control the rest of the hour.

Reaction is key.   A Champion doesn't let feelings and reactions determine whether he or she will be successful. A Champion executes the fundamentals, even when he or she doesn't feel like doing them. That is the mark of a Champion. The reaction is more important than the situation.

Coach's Tip: *Control your reaction, and you have a chance. Don't control it, and you have no chance.*

6. Champion Agents know that selling is the name of the game.   When I think of a Champion Agent, I think of a Champion Salesperson—someone who understands, accepts, and embraces the fact that sales and sales skills are the name of the game. The essence of selling in real estate is to create leads that you convert to clients, then clients you convert to commission checks.

I often ask agents, "If you had to choose to be exceptional in *one* of two areas of your business, *creating clients* or *keeping clients,* which one would you choose?" More than 75 percent say "keeping clients." Before I go any further, I want to state clearly that I think you have to do both well to be a Champion Agent. You have to be able to create and serve with success. But the question was specifically worded that way for a reason. One is a sales function: creating clients. One is a customer service function: keeping clients.

Create clients.   Most salespeople select the wrong one when given the choice between the two. The correct answer is "creating clients." Again, I am not advocating such a narrow-minded approach, but you do need to establish priorities when running a business. You need to work on the strategic skills that create the greatest return. The truth is, you won't have anyone to serve if you aren't able to create clients with regularity and consistency. Client service excellence is the direct result of a client's service experience. Client creation is the necessary prerequisite to outstanding client service.

Client creation is harder than client servicing. It requires sales skills, consistency, and persistent prospecting for clients. You must acquire a level of sales skill and confidence to pick up the phone and call people you know and people you don't know to ask them for the opportunity to do business with them.

The question is, *"Are you ready to both create clients and service them successfully?"* Will you ask all of your clients to refer you to others who might benefit from your service?

7. Champion Agents understand their focus is always being a listing agent.   Many agents feel the market should dictate how they generate their revenue. When the market is more neutral or even swinging to a buyer's market, they swear off listings. When the market is robust, they work to acquire more listings. Their theory is that the business model or business mix should reflect the overall marketplace.

Listings = revenue.   I personally don't subscribe to that thinking. I believe that, no matter the marketplace, your objective is to be a Champion Listing Agent. The current and emerging market trends play a very small role. The market trends can influence the type, location, price range, and even motivation level of the clients you represent in selling their homes. The market conditions might cause you to require a larger inventory of homes because the listings-sold-versus-listings-taken percentage is askew or the days on the market are lengthening.

The question is, *"Can you continue to focus on being a listing agent, no matter the condition of the market?"*

> **Champion Rule:**   *The area in which you invest most of your time and resources will be where your revenue comes from.*

Shift your time mix to accommodate listing revenue.   I meet too many agents who want to become listing agents, but when we evaluate their investment of time, it becomes obvious why they have a limited revenue stream from listings. If you spend 35 hours of a 50-hour workweek working the buyer side of your business, your revenue will be heavily slanted to the buyer's side. The only way to change the revenue mix is to change the time mix. It is as though you are planting corn and hoping for green beans. If you plant corn, you will be harvesting corn. This seems like an obvious truth, but most agents miss it.

The question is, *"Can change your time mix, right now, or will you have to do it over time?"* You can cut out buyers—cold turkey. You can shift a large amount of time to prospecting and lead follow-up—specifically for listings. The challenge for most agents is that the corresponding revenue drop is not pleasant. Can you weather the financial challenge for 90 days in order to select this option?

Balance your business with family time.   The next step is to ask permission from your family to cover both areas for 60 days. In effect, to add a few hours to your regular schedule daily for the next 60 days until you get your listing levels and listing inventory up. You have a valid reason for needing to invest the little bit extra to advance your earnings, stability, and quality of life. Your family will support you, provided you don't abuse this favor they are granting. You also need to be able to explain to them that it's for their benefit. You might design a reward for the family to share when the 60 days are completed. You must figure out a way to reallocate your time to focused listing and listing lead generation.

The question is, *"Can you reallocate time to focus on listing lead generation?"*

Create Leverage in Your Business

There is a growing belief that creating a large team of producing agents under you creates the best leverage in the business. There are more agents today trying to create leverage through people than ever before. While I agree that the approach is valid, you must ask yourself whether now is the right time for you make that play. Are you personally ready to build and use that time? More important, have you used the easiest and greatest form of leverage in real estate before you start exploring the people leverage?

Be a Champion Listing Agent

The easiest and most profitable leverage in real estate sales is being a listing agent. Too many of us do not using this leverage to establish the foundation of our success. We are getting drawn into the more-people-bigger-team mentality before we dominate as listing agents. Once you have the skills and production of a Champion Listing Agent, you can then more easily build a team of producing agents.

Being a Champion Listing Agent spawns opportunity that carries new risk and high rewards. As a Champion Listing Agent, you can enjoy the following benefits.

1. Gain leverage by employing numerous people to work for you at no cost. How many licensed agents are on your board of Realtors? That will be the number of people you will employ to sell your inventory each day. The best part is that all of these people are working for you at no cost! There are no wages, withholdings, taxes, insurance, workmen's comp, or equipment charges (telephone, desks, and office supplies). There are no expenses of any kind. I know that many of you are saying, "My company covers all that because of the commission split." That may be true, but you still have to manage these people and deal with personal problems, mistakes, low motivation, and interpersonal office politics.

If you focus on being a great listing agent first, you don't have to manage and lead any of these co-op agents who are out selling your property until they actually write a contract. You employ all of these co-op agents for little time investment, no cost, and no risk. With buyer's agents on your team, you take a risk in terms of your leads and how they convert them. You invest large amounts of your time to train, coach, and direct them to success. Champion Listing Agents eliminate the risk and receive the reward.

I want to stress, again, I am not against teams or buyer's agents. I do, however, believe that in our excitement to achieve a Champion level real estate practice, we may take higher risks and lower net rewards because we heard an "expert," or because we really didn't evaluate the return on investment or the risk/reward equation.

2. Generate multiple streams of income. The residual value of a listing, in terms of additional business creation, brand recognition growth, market share, and market presence, develops leverage. By taking a listing, you are in effect creating a storefront from which to sell your services. A listing creates sign calls and ad calls that convert to both buyers and sellers. It allows you to raise your personal profile in a neighborhood to generate future business.

What is a listing worth to you beyond just making a commission from the sale? One of the numbers I tracked was additional revenue and additional transactions created through securing a listing. For me, I tracked an average of 1.68 transactions for every listing I took. By pounding a sign in someone's yard instead of working with a buyer, I enjoyed the leverage of another 0.68 of a transaction. Track the buyers generated and converted from your listings, the sellers who buy through you, and listings you generate additionally because you sold the house down the street. You will find leverage from every listing you take. I am sure your ratios will be as good as, if not better than, mine.

3. Maintain a client, even if the transaction fails. When representing a seller, if a pending transaction fails to close, you still have a client. You can put the home back on the market, salvage the relationship, and sell the home. Buyers have the option to not do business with you in the future. They can decide to use someone else to represent them on their purchase. The seller provides more security to your income should something fail to close or go smoothly.

4. Gain control of your life. As a listing agent, you will be able to create a business devoid of the working weekends and evening hours that most agents must put up with. You can build a business that is more family-friendly for your children and spouse. While you are away, you will still be generating activity on offers if you are a listing agent. I remember very few Monday mornings (after a nice long weekend with Joan at our vacation home) when there wasn't a contract waiting on one of my seller's homes. I didn't know about it until I walked in the door on Monday morning.

5. Invest less time per transaction. It takes less time to represent a seller than a buyer. There will be a transaction every so often that will be the exception to that rule, but over time, the seller clearly requires a lower investment of time. Because the seller uses small amounts of your time, you are able to invest that time elsewhere to create more income.

═══════════════

A few years ago, I went to a dentist other than my father for the first time in my life. This dentist was going to install a gold crown on a tooth that needed an upgrade from the amalgam filling my father had put in years before. I was really astonished at how long my new dentist took to install one gold crown on my second appointment. He took well over an hour to install that crown.

Later that evening, I called my father and asked him how long it typically took him to install a crown and how many he could usually install in an hour's time. He told me that one crown was usually about a 30-minute appointment, that waiting for the Novocain to take effect took longer than the installation, and that he could usually install around four crowns in an hour of work. He was saying that he could make at least twice and possibly even four times the amount of money my new dentist made for the same hour of work. Could you make two to four times the amount of money per hour by becoming a Champion Listing Agent? Absolutely!

━━━━━━━━━

I believe that our focus as Champion Listing Agents isn't to achieve a 50/50 mix of buyers and sellers. The objective is to be weighted to the seller side—for example, 70/30 seller to buyer, or even 80/20. The only way your mix should be 50/50 is if you have two or more buyer's agents working for you. Listing agents ultimately dictate the marketplace. They set the terms, conditions, and the control level of the marketplace. Tap into the tremendous leverage of being a Champion Agent before you hire your first producing agent assistant (e.g., a buyer's agent).

The Champion Listing Agent's Unstoppable Edge

There are so many advantages that a Champion Listing Agent has, it would take the whole book to list them all. I have shared a few with you, but let me share some more that might not come to mind instantly.

1. *Discipline.* Becoming a Champion Agent takes discipline. To many of you, the word *discipline* has a negative connotation, either physiologically or psychologically. It's because you have a negative view of the word. The truth is, discipline is a primary tool that must be acquired to achieve success in life.

━━━━━━━━━

A number of years ago, I started to plan what I wanted to teach my son, Wesley. What were the tools, skills, characteristics, knowledge, and atti-

tudes I wanted to instill in him? Once I had completed my plan, I asked my question. If I could ensure he got only one of these because my life was cut short, which one would I select? It took me a few minutes to decide which one. My decision was discipline. *You might select something else for your child. I selected discipline because, if he had that, he could acquire the others in my plan when he needed them. If he really needed something later in life, his discipline would give him the basic building block to achieve it. I also recognized at that moment that, if he learned and acted in a disciplined way, his success would be guaranteed. It doesn't mean he won't have hardships and challenges; it does mean he'll have the primary skill necessary to work through them. A Champion Listing Agent is no different. To really be at that Champion level, you have to acquire discipline.*

2. *Sales skills.* When you are a Champion Listing Agent, you have acquired the skills to put you in the highest category of sales performers. You have mastery of your scripts, dialogues, presentations, qualifying, appointment setting, personal value, objection handling, and closing. The marketplace, other agents, your company, and your broker-manager don't determine your success; you do. It's great to have confidence in and control over what will happen in your business and life.

3. *Quality of life.* A Champion Listing Agent has a better quality of life. You have greater control of your schedule and thus have more and better-quality time off with family. You have more stability of income because you can project and control cash flow and regular closings. It would be impossible to close 8 to 10 buyer transactions monthly for an extended period of time. However, it is relatively easy to create and close double-digit listing transactions monthly.

As with anything in life worth accomplishing, becoming a Champion Listing Agent isn't the easy road. It isn't the superhighway that all can or will travel on. It is the road less traveled. The path to a Champion Listing Agent will be much harder. There are more skills and disciplines required to achieve success. It is also harder to find and secure a seller than it is a buyer. That's why Champion Listing Agents are the minority rather than the majority. You have to ask yourself, "Do I want to be in the minority? Am I willing to exert the effort necessary to reach the level of success to join the minority?" That's where all the fun is in life!

Attitude and Commitment Come First

For over 20 years I have studied successful people. I have studied how they think and react and what they do in many different situations. After years of study, thought, observation, and analysis, there are four core areas that Champion Performers monitor and improve. I call these "The Four Probabilities of Success." It doesn't matter if you are a real estate salesperson, a doctor, a dentist, an accountant, or a ditch digger. You will increase your income when you work to improve these four areas. Any one of these four will dramatically influence the probability of your success.

The Four Probabilities of Success

The four areas are *knowledge, skill, attitude,* and *activities.* When you work to improve any of these, you increase the odds of becoming more successful and generating greater wealth, improving your relationships, and improving your health. Everything in life is governed by these four areas.

Because everything in life is also governed by priorities, one of these four is always more important than the other three. There is an order of importance in which to attack and improve these four success factors: Knowledge, Skill, Attitude, and Activities. Before you read on, I want you to rank, or prioritize, the probabilities. Write a 1, 2, 3, or 4 next to each of these.

____Knowledge   ____Attitude
____Skill   ____Activities

Don't proceed until you complete the exercise. I have presented this exercise to hundreds of audiences over my speaking and training career. The breakdown never changes much. About 5 percent of people believe that either knowledge, skill, or activities is the first priority. About 85 percent of people say that attitude is the number one influencer of increased success.

I think one could make a valid case for attitude being the highest priority, that without a good attitude, your growth is stunted, as well as your earnings and quality of life. Like many others, I believe that is a logical argument.

Engage in Success-Producing Activities

My research in working with thousands of successful people has led me to another conclusion. Most successful people have a good enough attitude to be producing at a much higher level than they currently do. The barrier to reaching the Champion Agent level isn't attitude, but rather *activities.* It's engaging in success-producing activities with focus and consistency and allowing attitude, skills, and knowledge to produce the results desired.

Too many people want their attitude to get better before they start to engage in a challenging task. One of the fundamental questions people who are trying to rise to the Champion level in life must ask themselves is, "Does my attitude influence my activities more than my activities influence my attitude?" *Please read that question again!*

Simply stated, does how I feel control what I do? If you answered yes, then there is a barrier between you and your life's goals and dreams. This barrier will stop you from becoming a Champion Agent. If you are waiting for your attitude to improve before you begin doing some of the tougher things you know you need to do as a salesperson, you could be waiting a long time. You're like the person standing in front of the stove saying, "Give me some heat and then I will put wood in!" We have to put the wood in before we can experience the heat. There is a direct link between your activities and your income. There is also a direct link between your activities and an improved attitude. You can't let whether you feel like doing something that needs to be done control whether you will be successful.

━━━━━━━━━━━

A number of years ago, I met a future Champion Agent in John Gualtieri. John and I talked because he was considering working with a coach to help him improve. John had been stuck for a number of years at the same production level. He was, at that time, a 15-year-plus veteran of real estate *sales and was making around $300,000 a year. If you have to be stuck, $300,000 isn't such a bad place to land for a while. (I'm sure some of you who are reading this book would give your left arm for $300,000 a year in revenue.)*

The truth is, within 15 minutes of talking with John, I knew that $300,000 was far too low an income for him to earn. He was worth much more than that. His attitude, skill, and knowledge really demanded that he earn more. The problem was that he didn't do the necessary activities consistently enough to earn a greater income. The interesting part of our discussion was that he was the typical agent searching for the "secret" to growth in income. He wanted the magical piece of knowledge or skill that would transform his business, life, and bank account. After listening and taking notes for about 15 minutes, I shared a statement with John that he later told me smacked the truth straight into his head.

"You are mentally clogged. You don't need a bunch more information and techniques. What you need is implementation. You need to put into action what you know and what you know needs to be done. You don't need to learn more stuff that you can't or won't do."

My friends, it's all about *doing.*

A person with greater knowledge and skill, but without activities, has no advantage over someone who has no knowledge or skill. The activities create opportunities to use your knowledge and skill to your advantage. For many, it's more important to hear something they know and fail to do than to hear something new. Most agents are in the constant search for new ideas and new techniques, which is good. The problem is, if you do not engage in sound activities or invest your time wisely, the new ideas and new techniques will bring limited results.

My client and friend, John Gualtieri, shared this quote with me years later: "To know and not do is not to know." When John started putting activities first, his income increased by over $200,000 a year each year for three consecutive years. His knowledge and skill in running the real estate business became the best that I have seen in North America. When you define a Champion Agent, you will see a picture of John Gualtieri.

Build a Team for the Right Reason

The latest trend to grip real estate is the establishment of large teams. I want to state that I am not against teams. In fact, I was one of the first agents in my area to establish a team of people working and creating leverage for me. The reason most agents establish teams, however, is to avoid doing the key activities of the business. The key activity they are trying to avoid is prospecting. I see agents who are fairly new in the business or who don't have sufficient prospects establishing teams. My question is, "How can you teach and coach what you cannot do effectively yourself?"

If you are establishing a team so you don't have to focus on the activities or the prospecting specifically, you are establishing a team for the wrong reason. Agents who are considering joining a team should do so only when the lead agent engages in activities that generate leads—like prospecting. You don't necessarily have to prospect using methods like cold calling or FSBOs and expireds, but you do have to prospect your past clients and sphere through the telephone and face-to-face.

I want to tell you about another Champion Agent I work with, Kim Heddinger. Kim is an agent in Eugene, Oregon. She does a large volume of business with a small team. She has increased her income by over $200,000 each year over the past two consecutive years. Her secret is the consistency of her daily activities. She doesn't miss a day of prospecting. When I get her weekly report, she always works around 40 hours a week. She never works more than 42 or 43 hours. She always hits her goal of 50 contacts a week. Her consistency equates to stable, increasing income—year after year. Her net profit is outstanding because her value for an hour of her time is so high. She has a simple, growing, stable, high-net-profit, low-maintenance business. The truth is, I would stack up her net any day against most agents with teams four to five times her size.

Champion Rule: *Your personal productivity is the most valuable asset in your business.*

You lose productivity and profitability when you lose focus on the key activities. What you do with your time and how you invest it for the highest return determines not only your gross revenue, but your net profit. You will never be able to hire someone as skilled as you to bring business in the door. If you managed to secure that person, he or she wouldn't stay long. Why would such an agent stay and split the revenue with you if he or she were as skilled as you in producing it?

Increase Production and Revenue

Champion Agents focus more of their time on activities that create revenue for the business than do good agents or low-producing agents. Champions focus on connecting with people in a personal, direct, and focused way. When you break down a real estate agent's business, there are only four ways to increase production and thus revenue: (1) number of contacts, (2) method of contacts, (3) quality of the prospect, and (4) quality of the message.

When you begin working on any one of these, you have taken a step to becoming a Champion Agent. Once you have raised your level of performance in each of these areas, you can call yourself a Champion!

Number of Contacts

Whether we like it or not, real estate sales is a full-contact sport. Too many agents are trying to devise ways to avoid making personal contact with people. We use massive mailing programs to raise our image and build our brand. We develop elaborate Web sites and e-mail contact systems so we can hide behind the computer every waking hour of the day. Some of us do this because we don't interact well with people. Some of us do this because it is beneath us to prospect for business. Others of us do it because someone told us this is what we need to do.

Definition of contact.   In the end, the number of contacts matters. My definition of a contact is probably different from most people's. I define a *contact* as talking to someone over the age of 21 about real estate. This person must have the capacity to buy or sell or be able to refer you to someone who can. A contact can be face-to-face or over the phone. A contact, for the purpose of my definition, is not an Internet e-mail address or a mailing piece you send. It can only be face-to-face or phone-to-phone. You can make a contact at an open house, during floor time, at the grocery store, or at your child's soccer game, provided you really make it a contact by discussing real estate and discussing referrals.

Sales ratios.   Numbers matter in life and in business. One of the ways to know the health of your business is to know your sales ratios. By knowing your sales and conversion ratios, you can determine your income before the year, the quarter, or even the month begins.

Some of the most powerful pieces of information you possess are your sales ratios, but only a Champion Agent knows what those really are.

═══════════════

Within the first year of my real estate practice, I understood my sales ratios of contacts to leads, leads to appointments, appointments to representation contracts, and contracts to closings. Clearly knowing my ratios allowed me to create a plan that I could follow to earn what I wanted to earn. The reason that such a high percentage of our clients at Real Estate Champions earn what they want to earn is because we teach them that contacts matter and that sales ratios are king.

═══════════════

Coach's Tip: *Just because you tracked your sales ratios once doesn't mean you can stop tracking them. You must embrace tracking your sales ratios for the rest of your career. Your sales ratios will usually improve as your skills improve: your ability and skill to ask for referrals, to ask for appointments, to conduct Champion-level buyer and seller interviews.*

There is one exception to that rule. The sales ratios can change negatively or adversely if the market changes adversely. You might see, as some of our clients have, the number of contacts needed to create a lead go up and the number of leads needed to generate an appointment go up as well. In some markets, the number of appointments rises because the sellers are unwilling to do what is necessary in terms of price to be competitive. You might have to walk away, as some of our clients have, from a few more listings. When that happens, you have to have an attitude of acceptance and a commitment level to do what it takes. Jack Welch, the famous retired CEO of General Electric, has six rules for business success. One of the rules is, "Face reality as it is, not as you wish it to be."

Champion Agents have that attitude and commitment. When the marketplace dictates that sales ratios will change and things will get tougher, they deal with the reality of the marketplace influence on their business. They realize and accept the marketplace influence and increase their number of contacts to reflect the new sales ratios that will enable them to reach their goals.

Method of Contacts

How we choose to make contact with people determines our success level, or outcome. Having been in the real estate business for the better part of 16 years, I can say that in the past 8 years we have shifted away from the face-to-face, belly-to-belly, phone-to-phone business that I started in. I contend that we are less personal today in business than ever before.

The Internet is not the standard for making contacts.   We rely more on communication via e-mail and mail than ever before. We rely on the Internet to create leads, convert prospects, and sell homes. I believe the Internet and e-mail are wonderful tools. They create an ease of communication in marketing. They fall far short, however, of the standard for making sales.

In the late 1990s, we had a large volume of Internet prognosticators who forecast a future of real estate sales via the Internet. Through Web sites, pay-per-click ads, organic traffic, and virtual tours, we were all going to sell homes easily. They would come to these magical Web sites, watch virtual tours of the homes, and click the "buy it" button at the bottom of the page. We would have then sold a home! However, the Internet prognosticators missed the fact that people would never make such a large personal and financial decision for their family via a few digital pictures and a click. The public still wants the personal service, expert counsel, market knowledge, and market interpretation of trends that a Champion Agent provides.

Personal contact increases your odds.   When you look at the method coupled with the number of contacts, the pathway to success seems obvious. The number of contacts you need to make decreases as the method you select becomes warmer and more personal. You would need more than 1,000 mail pieces to create a few leads. In direct mail, companies expect only a couple of percentage points of return. When using the telephone for cold calling, you need only a few hundred calls for the same level of return. I am not an advocate of cold calling; the odds are still too long to achieve a satisfactory result. (I define *cold calling* as using a crisscross directory to call people randomly.) At best, you might work geographically.

Target groups produce more leads.   When the method changes to target groups, the ratios improve to around 50 contacts to produce a few leads. Calling absentee owners, a geographic area you mail to, a school directory list, orphaned past clients of other agents who have left your company—or any group created by combining mail and phone targets—can work. The results improve when you combine mail and phone and maintain contact over a period of time. This is not a once-and-done strategy. Select targets you can work with profitably over the long run.

Warm prospects increase your odds even more.   The last category is warm prospects. When you work to create revenue through this method of contact, you increase your odds to 25 contacts for a few leads. The contact points are your current clients, past clients, and sphere-of-influence people in your database. Most agents merely mail these people something periodically but never call them. When the method of contact is exclusively mail, the results move back up to the thousands when they should be in the teens. I also place expireds and FSBOs in this 25-or-less category. Because of their previously demonstrated motivation, you are at least making contact with more motivated individuals, so your odds of lead generation and lead conversion to appointments is markedly better.

Quality of the Prospect

The quality of the prospect is an area that really separates non-Champion performers from Champion Performers. Our ability to separate the wheat from the chaff will lead to a dramatic increase in our value per hour, gross income, low frustration level, better clients, and more and better referrals.

Lead follow-up versus lead creation.   The natural tendency for most salespeople is to work with current leads rather than to prospect for new ones. Most salespeople, in real estate especially, do primarily lead follow-up rather than prospecting or lead creation. The problem with that approach—what happens if your leads aren't any good?

Most agents have a group of bad leads they are trying to convince to be good leads so that they don't have to prospect. Let me give you a hint: you can be the greatest salesperson in the world and yet you will rarely convince a bad lead to convert to a good lead. You are far better off investing your time in finding better leads.

Identify high-quality leads.   It takes less effort, time, emotion, and frustration to convert and serve high-quality leads. The question is, how do you determine whether the prospect you just created is a high-quality lead. I frequently ask agents that question. I get a variety of answers, including "by asking prospects qualifying questions," "by evaluating the source of the lead," and many others.

Ask for a face-to-face appointment.   The Champion's technique is to ask prospects for a face-to-face appointment. By asking them for an appointment, you cut through the smoke to see whether they are real. The last place on earth a low-motivation prospect wants to be is in front of a salesperson.

The 80/20 Rule

There are many prospects whose sales resistance goes up in direct proportion to the length of your litany of prequalifying questions. Questions, even well-scripted and well-directed ones, can lead to sales resistance. I am not saying don't ask questions; you need to use them to keep the discussion flowing, so you can ask for an appointment again in a minute or two. The most efficient way to determine the viability of prospects is their willingness to meet with you.

There is a rule that governs success and people. This rule was formulated in 1895 by a man in Italy named Vilfredo Pareto. He observed, at that time, that most people had little influence, power, or money in the marketplace. He called this group of people the trivial many. *He decided that these people made up about 80 percent of the population. He then theorized that the remaining 20 percent had all of the influence, power, and capital of the society. He called them the* vital few. *He postulated the 80/20 rule that has governed success for more than 100 years. The 80/20 rule applies to your prospects, as well.*

According to Pareto's rule, 80 percent of the prospects you work with will create 20 percent of your income. The amount of time, effort, and energy is disproportionately not in your favor. The odds of becoming a Champion Agent when working with this group are long indeed. The devastating part of working with this group is that you spend 80 percent of your time, capital, effort, energy, and emotion to create a 20 percent return on investment. These numbers are not in line with a successful business.

A Champion works with the elite 20 percent of the population that creates an 80 percent return on investment because they gain an added return or unequal return on their investment. This elite 20 percent doesn't mean that you have to work only with those who would be defined as the upper crust of society. (Although, working with high-priced buyers and sellers certainly can have a positive effect on your income.) In evaluating the quality of prospects, you must determine their level of motivation, financial capacity, how easy they are to work with, realistic expectations of service, and what they can purchase. I have met high-priced buyers and sellers who were also high maintenance; to be fair, I placed them in the 80 percent category, not in the 20 percent category. The question you must quickly resolve: "Does this prospect fit into the 80 percent or the 20 percent category?"

Coach's Tip: *You have limited resources to invest in terms of your time, effort, energy, emotions, and dollars spent. Your objective must be to select clients who use low levels of resources with high levels of return. That is what a 20 percent prospect allows you to do.*

| *Champion Rule:* | *Sales is a margins game, not a volume game.* |

Increase sales margins by selecting better prospects.   We must focus on the sales margins, not just the sales volume. Our objective is to enhance or expand the margin between the resources we expend and the return we get. One way to influence the margins is by selecting better prospects to serve. You must reduce the resources of time, effort, energy, emotion, and dollars that you invest in relation to the return of money, job satisfaction, and future revenue (in the form of referrals and repeat business). Better prospects create better margins. Don't be fooled by the sales volume game. The margins in business and life are what really count.

I would not have been able to work only four days a week (having off Friday, Saturday, and Sunday), sell 150 homes a year, fund my wife's initial start-up for her construction company, develop subdivision land, buy investment property, and fully fund our retirement accounts (starting my first year in real estate sales) without strong margins in my business. However, there are lower risks in running a high-margin business. You are better able to weather the storms of life and business that will come. In addition, it's easier to adjust to market changes.

I had a client a number of years ago who was one of the best agents in the marketplace. She was one of the top five agents in gross income and sales volume in a major metropolitan city. I could see when I started to work with her that she was in trouble. This lady had zero margins in her business. Her expenses, staff, and marketing were too high to support her gross revenue. She sold, on average, about 10 homes a month, but she was in trouble. She had operated for years like this and had little to show for it in personal assets. I could tell by the marketplace change that she had about 180 days left before she would be gone. When I say gone, *I mean out of business. I couldn't get her to see what I saw.*

To this day (about seven years later) that still haunts me. She struggled on for another 120 days before she was forced to take a corporate training position with a large local company. She made more net money doing that than she had in her real estate practice (because of her poor margins). She was one of the nicest people I have ever worked with. I was really sorry she couldn't make the transition. That's what happens when the margins get out of whack.

The 20/50/30 Rule

There is one last rule I want to share with you to help with the quality of your prospects and your business margins. It's the 20/50/30 rule. The 20/50/30 rule separates prospects into three distinctive categories. This categorization will help you determine your approach and actions with the prospect.

The 20 percent. The 20 percent are people who are easy to work with. They convert quickly and trust you easily. They decide quickly because their motivation is high. They treat service providers with respect. They are really the golden group. Your marketing and prospecting should focus on generating more of these prospects. Most trainers will try to tell you that the only way to get people in this group is to work their referral system. That's a load of hogwash. You can secure prospects that fit into this group from any source. I have personally gotten prospects in this group from referrals, past clients, FSBOs, expireds, ad calls, sign calls, open houses, divorce attorneys, other agent referrals, and countless other sources.

My best advice in dealing with the 20 percent is to get out of their way. Let them trust you; lead them and sell them. Tell them when the home is right for them as the buyer. Ask them to make a decision and to make it now. Don't be afraid to guide them to the culmination of the sale. For example, if you have a buyer in this 20 percent, and you see that the home you are standing in is the right home for them (it has all the amenities, location, and features they want) and has an emotional connection for them, buying signals are flying. Don't show them another home; sell them this one . . . get out of their way. Far too often, I see agents missing the emotional buying moments and confusing a prospect (especially in this group) by showing more homes and giving them more options and driving their client to confusion.

The 50 percent. This is the group that Champion Agents convert at a higher rate than other agents. Anyone, even a new agent, can convert a 20 percent prospect eventually. It's with this 50 percent group that Champions excel.

The first observation is that this group is large, but the problem is that they need convincing. They need to clearly understand the benefits and service advantages of working with you over all the other agents they could choose. To convert these people who are on the fence, you must convince them that the grass is greener on your side. The only way to do this is through a compelling benefits-driven presentation that is first delivered over the phone to set up a face-to-face meeting. Then the face-to-face meeting must clearly answer the base question, "Why should I hire you?"

This is a competitive group to access, unlike the 20 percent group. These people will not roll over and sign an exclusive right-to-represent agreement without knowing the facts.

Once you begin to service members of this group, it is possible to move them up into the 20 percent, but you have to convince them to do this. With increasingly greater competition in the real estate market because of more agents, more company options, more service models, and greater media exposure, you need to be ready to compete.

My belief is that the real estate community doesn't dramatically influence the number of transactions that are done annually in the marketplace. In 2004, a record number of transactions were completed in the United States . . . about 6.8 million sales. In 2005, there were 7.2 million sales. The real estate community didn't cause the additional 400,000 increase in sales from 2004 to 2005. The market conditions, interest rates, and law of supply and demand influenced the upward movement of the sales.

The only way for us, as agents and companies, to increase sales is to take sales and market share from others—from other agents and other companies. Some people don't like it when I say that, but what I am telling you is the truth. Sometimes you have to play hardball to secure more prospects. To secure this 50 percent group as clients, you will have to compete with other agents. Don't make the fatal error of assuming you are the only agent who knows about this prospect's desire for real estate. Don't assume just because this person was referred to you there is not another agent that you are competing against for the business. When prospects are in this 50 percent group, you need to be prepared to compete for the business. In most cases, the agent who secures a face-to-face presentation will be the victor!

The 30 percent.   This is the group that can really gum up an agent's business. The quality of these prospects is so low that you need to quickly move on. I would affectionately call these people "toxic." These people will suck the marrow out of you. This group is death to your business. They will drain your battery fast! They will expend your energy and emotion in such large quantities that it will affect all other areas of your business and life. Are you working with toxic clients right now? The only solution is to run away fast. You must screen out these people quickly and move on to your next prospect.

The law of attraction.   There is an age-old law called the *law of attraction.* The law of attraction basically says that you will be attracted to what you are looking for. If you decide you will buy a new Jeep Grand Cherokee in black, whenever you drive down the road for the next few weeks, you will see such cars everywhere. Your mind will seek out things, situations, and people consistent with your focus.

The law of attraction applies to sales as well, in two areas. The first is that people are attracted to people who are like themselves. When you evaluate your friends, you will find that they have values and beliefs similar to your own. People tend to congregate based on their values and beliefs. In sales, we are all trying to establish a referral base for our business. If people know, hang out with, and influence people similar to themselves in values and beliefs, what types of referrals will you receive from the toxic 30 percent even if you decide to arduously serve them? You will get a whole new batch of 30 percent prospects. My contention is that one such group is bad enough. I don't want any more. By working 30 percent clients, you wear yourself out physically and emotionally for limited return and zero residual value to the relationship.

If you focus on attracting the 20 percent through deliberate prospecting and marketing to this group, the law of attraction will enhance your referral business. It will lead to higher margins in your business. In targeting the 20 percent, you will still receive a large quantity of 50 percent category prospects as well as a few of the toxic 30 percent variety. The quality of prospects in your sales business matters.

Quality of the Message

This is where the Champion Agent really excels over other agents. The message you present is essential to your success. What you say, how you deliver your message, your tone, and your body language influence the results you achieve. Homes are not bought, but sold. Professional representation services are not bought, but sold. We have to sell to be at the Champion level. Most agents have never taken formalized sales training of any kind. They have had a couple of weeks of introductory training as a real estate salesperson that their broker provided . . . that's it.

Correlation between sales skills and income.   When sales skills go up, income goes up. There is a direct correlation between sales skills and ability and income. I know there is a large group of skeptics reading this. Let me illustrate my point. To be successful in any profession, you have to achieve mastery of the primary tool of the profession. There are secondary tools that help, but the primary tool is the cornerstone to success. Without mastery of it, you will always be brushing up against a ceiling of production; you will never explode through it.

―――――――――――

My father was a dentist for over 30 years. As a successful dentist, he had one primary tool that he worked for years to master. As secondary tools, he had explorers, drills, polishers, Novocain, a dental chair, lights, scrapers, probes, amalgam fillings, sealants, gold crowns, different types of adhesives, X-ray machines . . . you get the idea. All of these were secondary tools.

What is the primary tool of a dentist? What is the one tool that must be controlled to let all these other tools work their magic? For dentists, it's their hands. *A dentist without skillful hands isn't a good dentist.*

━━━━━━━━━━━━━━━━━

As a real estate salesperson, you have laptops, BlackBerrys, Internet sites, lockboxes, lockbox keys, marketing pieces, mailings, flyers, customer relationship management (CRM) software, computers, tracking forms, your car, your clothes, MLS, and countless other secondary tools. What is the primary tool of a real estate salesperson? It's the *words* that you say and how you deliver them. The message you present and convey either causes prospects to work with you or sends them away. All the secondary tools will not make up for a lack of skill in the primary area—the words that you say and how you deliver them.

Most agents invest far more in their wardrobe than they do in themselves and their skills. I have listened to hundreds of very good agents' tapes—prospecting, lead follow-up, buyer consultation, and listing presentation. I have never listened to one that I thought, initially, was awesome. The tapes I have listened to have come from some of the best agents in the world. That's why I can say confidently that the vast majority of you reading this book, even if you are doing a lot of production, have a message or presentation that is not very good, either. I am not trying to cause you to toss this book aside, never to pick it up again, by making such a bold comment. I am merely trying to get you to face the facts of how important your message is and how you can change it to improve your business.

━━━━━━━━━━━━━━━━━

For a number of years, I worked with a client who was an excellent agent in Cleveland, Ohio. Sheri Nasca was one of the best salespeople I have ever worked with in terms of sales skills. When she was forced to move and restart her business in the Chicago area, she closed on 60 sales in her first year without knowing a soul. She was able to do it because of her superior sales skills. I think selling 60 units in your first year without market presence, a sphere of influence, or past clients is outstanding. Sheri did it because she is the consummate professional in her sales skills.

━━━━━━━━━━━━━━━━━

A professional football team will practice for 40 to 50 hours a week in preparation for a 60-minute game. How much time do you invest weekly to practice your craft of selling?

Most agents will spend at least $500 on a good outfit, another $75 on a quality shirt, perhaps $75 on a nice tie or other accessories, $12 on socks, and $200 on a pair of quality shoes. All told, we will invest nearly $850 to walk out the door dressed for success, yet we hesitate to spend a dime on what matters most—our mind and our sales skills to create, convert, and service our customers well.

Champion Rule: *Real estate sales is an odds-based business.*

Know Your Odds and Improve Them

As salespeople, we operate in a game of odds and probabilities. Being deliberate in knowing the odds and improving them is what a Champion does. You must be able to balance the odds of the marketplace, the odds of the prospect, the odds of creating a delighted client, the odds of expending your resources, the odds of a higher return, and the odds of your time. All of these odds have to be evaluated and factored into your decisions.

Casinos earn large returns for the owners because they play the odds in their favor . . . always. They don't do it sometimes; they do it always. There is not a game in any casino in the world where the odds are against the house . . . not one game! Some games are more favorable to the player than are others. You stand a higher probability of winning in blackjack than in roulette. The odds are still less than 50/50 for the player, though. The casinos know that if you sit there long enough and frequently enough, even if you win in the short run, you won't win in the long run. It is certainly better when you are the house. How do we become the house in the business of real estate? The first step is to understand the aforementioned odds by tracking and analyzing the odds of the marketplace, the odds of your skills, and the odds of the prospect.

Champion Rule: *Wants and needs don't change the odds.*

Wants and Needs Are Different

Too often, we believe that if we want or need something, that fact alone will swing the odds in our favor. I would have loved to have played professional basketball. I really wanted to be a power forward, like Maurice Lucas, Karl Malone, or Buck Williams. But at 5 feet 11 inches when I graduated from high school, the odds were heavily against me. Even after I grew another four inches before I started college, the odds were extremely long. How many 6-foot 3-inch power forwards have there been in the past 30 years in the NBA? *None!*

Perhaps a seller says, "You don't understand my problem. I really need to net $100,000 from the sale of my home, so we need to list the home for $350,000 in order to net that amount." If you know that the house needs to be at $299,000 to get a buyer for the property, does the seller's need to net $100,000 change the value and sales price of the home? What are the odds of finding a buyer who is willing to pay this seller a $50,000 premium for the home because the seller really needs it? *Zero!*

You, as a salesperson and an entrepreneurial business owner, must play the odds. The better the application of odds, the better the income, results, and time off with your families. When you are, in effect, playing against the odds, you can still make money, but it will cost you more time than is necessary. When I see agents working six or seven days a week, it tells me they are ineffective at evaluating and playing the odds. It tells me that there is a lot of wasted time and emotion in their business model. This correlates to lower-than-necessary hourly rates for what they do based on their skill, lead volume, market presence, and experience.

Hourly rate reflects the odds of your business.   One of my key objectives, when I work with people in a coaching and consulting capacity, is to double their hourly rate in the first few months of working with them. Your hourly rate directly connects to how well you are doing and will be doing in a sales business. It also demonstrates the odds of your business and how well you play those odds. Your value per hour is a critical computation of success. I describe it as one of the six key numbers in a real estate agent's practice. Your hourly rate is the pulse rate of your business . . . similarly indicating its health.

Champion Calculation

To calculate your hourly rate, write down your gross commission income for the past 12 months. Your *gross commission income* is what you make before expenses or company split. (You created the gross revenue, so use that number. Your split is really a cost of sale, not a cost of your time value.) Then write down the number of hours you work in a day, on average. Next, estimate the days you work per week and weeks you work per year. Multiply all of those work hours, days, and weeks together to get the total hours worked. Then divide your total hours worked by the gross commission income.

_____ × _____ × _____ = _____ ÷ _____ = _____
Hours/day   Days/week   Weeks/year   Total hours   Gross   Hourly rate
                                               worked   commission

You can work the same number of hours and make twice as much money as you normally would, or you can cut your hours in half and make the same as you were making before. Most agents choose neither of these options. They usually choose a combination of more income and better quality of life. The best news is, you

Coach's Tip: *Your goal should be to double the number you just wrote down—in the next six months. If you double your hourly rate, you have created dramatically more options in your life.*

can now choose, where before you had no choice. Champion Agents continually raise their hourly rate through improvement of their skills, knowledge, attitude, activities, and the odds of the business.

Champion Rule: *Consistent commitment of effort and consistent commitment of resources will change the odds.*

Champion Agents Are Consistent

True Champion Agents are agents of consistency. They consistently do the activities that generate high profit margins for the company. They consistently prospect, do lead follow-up, and book appointments. They operate in a world of consistency. They consistently engage in self-improvement, listening to CDs, attending seminars to learn, or coaching. They consistently evaluate the financial performance of their company and their personal assets. They consistently engage in health-related activities like working out and monitoring their eating habits. One of the characteristics of Champion Performers is consistency. Most people are too inconsistent to be of Champion caliber.

Let me illustrate the power of consistency. You decide to lose 10 pounds, and in order to lose those 10 pounds, you need to move your body 60 miles. You are now faced with a choice of odds. You could decide to go all out for three days and get it over with by going 20 grueling miles each day to reach your goal. You could also run one mile a day for 60 days. Which of these approaches would increase the odds of your success in losing the weight? The answer is obvious to us all. The binge approach, lacking consistency, would leave us far short of the 10-pound weight loss. If we eat reasonably and exercise over 60 days, we are more likely to achieve our goal.

The same is true in our sales business. To go out and make 50 contacts today, to binge and get it over with, rarely works. A Champion has developed the skill and discipline to invest in success-producing activities daily (e.g., prospecting and lead follow-up). A Champion Agent doesn't binge in this area . . . ever! He or she has learned to control the personal environment, schedule, access points, and emotion to engage in success-producing activities every day. The consistency of activity is the key.

Gain Financial Independence

Most agents begin their real estate careers with the hope of gaining financial independence. They are attracted by the possibility of earning large sums of money. Even when agents make more than a six-figure income, the vast majority have not dramatically improved their financial balance sheet. After looking at hundreds of agents' profit and loss statements and personal spending habits, I've determined that real estate agents are poorly prepared for financial independence. (Why should real estate agents be any different from the American population in general?)

According to the Social Security Administration, out of a randomly selected 1,000 people from age 25 to age 65, statistics indicate the following:

- 190 would have died (19 percent)
- 150 would have incomes over $30,000 (15 percent)
- 660 would have incomes less than $30,000 (66 percent)

Let's look at these numbers. Of the people still alive, 66 percent exist on less than $30,000 per year. Which group do you want to be in? Which group are you heading for based on your financial plan, investment choices, and savings plan?

These are the top three reasons people fail in their finances:

- They never create a financial plan.
- They make poor investment choices.
- They put off starting a savings plan.

Let me share with you a few simple rules that will ensure that you don't join the 66 percent with low incomes. I have used these rules with hundreds of agents to transform their financial picture in a short period of time.

Track Your Expenses, Both Business and Personal

You must know where your money is going. Separate your business expenses from your personal expenses. Establish a business checking account and pay all business bills through it. Too many agents commingle their business commission checks and business bills with personal and household expenses. It is more difficult to control your money when you can't track it. Enter all of your expenses and revenue in an accounting software program. (I think the easiest is Quicken. Quicken will allow you to accurately track your costs to run the business; then you can run a monthly profit and loss statement to see where you are spending your money. The money you earn in real estate can come in bunches. It can become very easy to spend that large commission check that's burning a hole in your pocket.)

Adjust Your Lifestyle

Spending less than you earn makes up 90 percent of financial planning. The premise involves saving money and making sacrifices. The ability to pay now, in the form of adjusting your lifestyle and saving the difference, will allow you to play later. To play later, you will need more than $30,000 per year. Thomas Stanley, who wrote the book *The Millionaire Next Door,* summed up how the vast majority of his subjects accumulated their millions: "They lived well below their means." Living beyond our means is a national epidemic. Consumer credit card debt in the United States is in excess of $528 billion. Roughly two-thirds of Americans who have credit cards do not pay off their monthly balance. We are clearly living beyond our means. Take a close look at your monthly obligations and evaluate where you are spending your money.

Aggressively Reduce Your Debt

There is an old proverb that speaks of the borrower being a servant to the lender. The weight and pressure of debt can be crippling. I have seen this happen to agents for years. I have even seen it manifested in my own life. I have not always made the wisest choices with my money. Fortunately, I have made more wise choices than foolish ones.

If you have credit card debts, make a decision to pay them off. Start with the card with the highest interest rate. Decide on a monthly amount that you can commit to to start reducing your debt. If you stretch, you will be able to find a few hundred dollars per month to pay toward your debt. Most credit card companies require you to pay 2 percent of the balance owed monthly.

Champion Calculation

Let's say you have a debt of $2,705 with an interest rate of 18.38 percent. Your 2 percent toward the outstanding balance would take you 27 years and two months to pay off. You would pay $11,047 of total interest. How do you feel about eating out more often now? If you increased your payment to 8 percent, or to $216.40 per month, it would take two years and one month to pay it off. You would pay $94.00 in interest. You need to accelerate your payments to reduce your debt. You must adopt a cash mentality. This cash mentality will allow you to charge only what you have funds to pay for.

Create a Savings Plan, Now

The biggest enemy in financial planning is procrastination. People wait too long to start saving. The truth is becoming a millionaire is not very difficult. The power of compounding interest will take care of your needs. According to *Investor's Business Daily,* a 20-year-old person needs to invest only $1,014 per year, or $2.78 per day, with an annual return of 11 percent to save $1 million by the age of 65. Look at the daily number of $2.78. Who couldn't save that amount per day, even at the age of 20? Even someone working for minimum wage could do that with ease. My mentor, Jim Rohn, used to say, "What is easy to do is also easy not to do." It's easy to save the $2.78, but it's also easy to buy a latte every day at Starbucks instead of saving. Choose financial independence planning rather than the latte.

Coach's Tip: *Transform yourself into a saver. Savers pay themselves first. Create a system to automatically remove a portion of money toward savings when you first receive it. It's amazing how little you miss money that never comes into your possession.*

The secret to saving is writing the check to savings first. Do it before paying other bills and obligations. Savings is a habit to be forged. Here is the formula I used on each of my commission checks for many years:

> 20 percent went to a tax account.
> 10 percent went to a retirement savings account.
> 10 percent went to a business savings account.

These percentages ensured that my taxes were always current and my retirement account was always fully funded. There were also reserves for an investment opportunity or a slow closing month. The more you make your money disappear into protected accounts, the more you will have later.

Time Invested versus Return on Investment

It's easy to trick ourselves into thinking we are doing what must be done consistently and well. Let's say that you set a goal of 50 contacts per day. Assume I have inspired you about the importance of regular contacts, at a minimum, with your past clients and sphere, and you resolve to start Monday, bright and early. Next week comes, and you do your 10 contacts on Monday. Tuesday comes around, and you have an office meeting and tour, which shoots down your morning, so you get only three done. On Wednesday, you are right back on it, with 10 that day. Thursday brought a few problems with clients and transactions, so you manage to make only eight contacts. Friday is a beautiful day, so you get in four contacts before you hit the golf course for the rest of the day. My question to you: Is that a great week, a good week, an okay week, or a disastrous week?

Since you have not prospected previously, most people would say that it was a good or even a great week. "I improved; I didn't hit my goal of 50, but I did get to 35." The truth is, it was an improvement, but it was still a disaster if repeated over time. The results of that type of week repeated for a year would be 15 weeks of no prospecting at all. Those 15 weeks are equivalent to almost four months of prospecting. How do you feel about that week now? It is very easy to get fooled into thinking something is good when it falls far short of the standard.

I will never tell anyone they have to make hundreds of dials a day and 50 to 60 or more contacts a day. I won't ever tell people to dial two phones at once and wear two head sets. If you have to make that many dials and contacts, you're playing a game of very low odds.

I had an initial consultation with an agent who was a cold call cowboy being coached by another company that promotes that type of prospecting. He made 75 contacts a day and spent five to six hours a day prospecting. More than 85 percent of his time was spent just cold calling a geographic list. He did that day in and day out for years. He secured eight transactions the previous year from his cold calling and invested 85 percent of his time prospecting them. I asked him why he did it. He said his trainer and coach told him to.

I quickly calculated that he spent close to 850 hours in the previous year to generate eight transactions. He made less than $50 an hour to make all of those calls to secure leads . . . poor odds. Why invest that amount of time for such a limited return? He was skillful in his consistency, but applied it in the wrong area for too little a return.

The 5-5-5 System of Success

All most Champions need to do is 5-5-5 a day to grow their business. The 5-5-5 system stands for 5 past-client calls a day, 5 lead follow-up calls a day, and 5 new contacts a day. That is 15 total contacts needed each day to reach your production goals. Very few of my clients do more prospecting a day than that. Some of them might have to make a few more lead follow-up calls than that due to their volume of leads. The number of their past clients and size of their sphere can also push the numbers up a little for some of them. The vast majority of our Champion Agent clients follow the 5-5-5 system. They use it to create consistency in order to establish and maintain momentum.

Real Estate Is a Momentum Business

One of the challenges for non-Champion agents is to establish and maintain momentum. A tremendous amount of energy is required to create momentum. It requires consistency of resources and effort for you to acquire a certain number of listings and a reasonable number of pending transactions. If you are in an airplane, it takes a large quantity of fuel and thrust to take off from the runway and achieve a cruising altitude of 36,000 feet. You can feel the captain throttle back once you reach cruising altitude. I did say throttle back, not cut the power. If he cut the power, the plane would instantly dive back to the ground.

Too often, when agents get to cruising altitude, they cut the power of their prospecting and lead follow-up. They could be tired because it takes energy to get a listing inventory. They could be focusing on servicing their clients. The danger with their strategy is that they lose momentum. Most agents' income goes through up-and-down cycles at least four times a year. The up-and-down cycles are caused by up-and-down momentum of prospecting and lead follow-up by the agent.

If you look at your income swings, you can trace them back to 90 days earlier when you switched away from prospecting and shifted to lead follow-up. You might even have shifted your time almost exclusively to serving listings, buyers, and pending transactions. Prospecting and lead follow-up create production-supporting activities. If you engage in prospecting and lead follow-up, you will create opportunities to serve people. Serving people will take more of your time, but you have to avoid letting it take all of your time.

> **Champion Rule:**   *A Champion does prospecting and lead follow-up even when faced with the need to service a lot of clients.*

Operating with an on/off approach to prospecting and lead follow-up leads to inconsistency of income, burnout, and frustration in your business. Lots of folks can prospect when they are broke, have no leads, and have plenty of time. It doesn't take a particular skill or set of disciplines to do that. That is prospecting out of desperation. A Champion, however, prospects even when he or she has business, prospects, clients, and transactions to close.

Use the Learning Curve to Your Advantage

We all deal with learning curves in our lives. The question is *where are you on that curve?* You have to use the learning curve to your advantage to create a greater return. You also need to be careful that you don't overexpose yourself by trying to engage in the steepest part of the curve too frequently.

There is a rule we all need to understand regarding the learning curve. Figure 3.1 is a common picture of the rule.

Everything is hard before it becomes easy.

The amount of effort we must put forth to climb the learning curve is substantial. My daughter, Annabelle, is 13 months old. She is trying to walk, and the effort she is putting out is large. Her return has been limited to bonks on the head, plops on her rear end, and a few shuffles with her feet by hanging onto anything she can get her hands on to maintain her balance. She is at the steepest part of the learning curve. I can see it in her face; she gets frustrated at times. The lack of success in walking like her four-year-old brother, Wesley, gets to her attitude once in a while. She is committed to overcoming this challenge of life. One day, in the next few

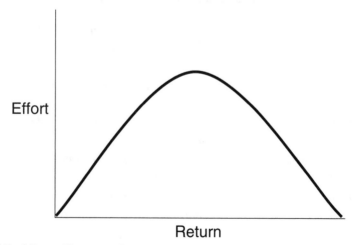

©2006 Real Estate Champions, Inc.

Figure 3.1 Learning Curve

months, she will be over the steepest part where the effort drops and the return stays constant or improves slightly. It will just take her time.

===

Be Persistent and Focus

There are two mistakes I frequently see as a coach and trainer of people. Both of these mistakes prove to be equally detrimental to an agent's success. The first is not "sticking it out" and being persistent enough to continue to climb to the top, where it becomes easier. We often become frustrated and quit. This often happens when we are close to the summit of the learning curve. The reason we quit is because we are not tracking our progress during the climb. We don't, for example, see the increase in lead generation, because we are looking only at the number of listings or the commission income. Since we are not tracking the baby steps, only the scoreboard of commission, we miss our progress. This makes it difficult to gauge where we actually are on the learning curve. We might be approaching the top, but we don't know it.

Keep your tools for success clearly focused and in front of you daily. When you don't have your objectives in clear focus, the trials that come along sometimes overwhelm. They can often cause you to stumble and quit before you obtain your objective. Don't allow yourself to be sidetracked by adversity.

===

Florence Chadwick wanted to be the first woman to swim the English Channel both ways. For years she trained and disciplined herself to keep going long after her body needed rest. When the big day arrived to challenge the channel, things went well until she neared the coast of England, where heavy fog, cold, and rough waters impeded her progress. Not realizing she was within a few hundred yards of the shore, she became completely exhausted and quit swimming. Think about it . . . she quit a few hundred yards from her goal after swimming miles and miles! She was quoted by reporters saying, "I'm not offering excuses, but I think I would have made it if I would have been able to see my goal." She tried again after she developed a mental image of England and the coastline. She memorized every feature of the distant landscape and held it firmly and clearly in her mind. Again she was hindered by fog, frigid water, and high, turbulent seas, but this time she accomplished her objective. The reason she was able to accomplish it was because she never lost sight of it. It was in her mind's eye the whole way across.

———————

When you lose sight of the learning curve, it can cause you to leap prematurely to another goal—one that you feel holds more promise. One of the failures of salespeople is that they don't do anything long enough to fully understand and test the progress and results of their initial efforts.

Coach's Tip: *Amazing things can and do happen when you keep your objective in sight. Don't lose sight of yours. Even losing sight for one day can cost you thousands of dollars in lost revenue for your business.*

We leap to what seems like the latest and greatest thing—the new gimmick for success, wealth, happiness, and prosperity.

The late-night infomercial industry was founded to take advantage of these feelings. A recent study determined that 80 percent of the infomercials on television could be categorized as get-rich-quick schemes or weight-loss methods. Both of these types of infomercials are designed and produced to lead us to believe that results are easy, requiring no effort, that the learning curve has been flattened to nothing, that success, results, income, wealth, and quality of life are guaranteed. This is certainly faulty thinking.

The second mistake I see agents make is that they have too many learning curves going at once. Attacking the steepest segments on 4, 5, 6, or even 10 learning curves at once is a clear and certain recipe for disaster.

Focus Precedes Success

Your ability to focus always precedes your success. Focusing, testing, practicing, and perfecting your systems, skills, attitude, knowledge, and activities will speed your climb to the top of the learning curve. I often meet agents who make the commitment to prospect, but they want to prospect their past clients, sphere of influence, FSBOs, and start a geographic farm. My response is always the same. If you want to fail and be frustrated, proceed forward with your plan. Why not spend the next 90 to 120 days perfecting your relationship, connection, and contact with your past clients and sphere of influence? They offer similarities in how you contact them, how you raise your connection and intimacy level with them, and how you add value and serve them. Don't do anything other than focus on these two. That's enough of a learning curve for anyone.

Once you hit the top of the learning curve and the effort needed starts to drop (and your results are consistent or growing), then you can implement another revenue stream. You can't do it all at once. (Generally, we overestimate what we can do in a day or a week or even a quarter, and we underestimate what we can accomplish in six months, a year, or even three or five years.)

The *X* Theory of Success

It always takes us *X* number of times to become proficient at anything. That *X* will be different for each one of us based on our internal, God-given gifts and previous experiences and skills that complement what we are trying to learn.

As an example, it might take some of you reading this book 100 practice sessions to really perfect your listing presentation, to be able to deliver it with power and conviction, to handle all of the objections that will naturally come up, and to convert the seller to sign the contract the night you are there. I might be less skilled than you and have a tougher time perfecting it. My effort segment on that learning curve is longer and steeper than yours. I may need to practice it 200 times before I perfect it. It doesn't matter that I take twice as many repetitions as you to achieve success; the important point is that I have an idea of what number *X* is and that I am working toward it regularly.

The *Y* Theory of Choice

I now have a *Y* theory of choice. Since I know I have to practice my presentation 200 times, I have a *choice* of how long I will take to reach *X*. That is the *Y* theory of choice. I can take 10 years, 5 years, 2 years, 1 year, or perhaps even just six months. If I conduct my listing presentation only in front of live sellers, and I am in front of sellers three or four times a month, it will probably take me more than five years to reach my goal of 200. That is, unfortunately, the mistake that most agents make. They have a poor attitude and lack of commitment to speed up the time frame to hit *X*. Their *Y* theory of choice is way too long to build a successful career. Your success is determined by crossing the finish line of *X* and using the shortest amount of time *Y* to get there.

The far better approach a Champion Agent would apply is to use a combination of presentations in front of sellers and a larger number of practice or role-play presentations to speed up the learning curve process to reach the *X* theory of success. My personal goal, years ago, once I postulated the *X* and *Y* theories, was to do a listing presentation every day. If that presentation was live in front of a seller, wonderful. If it was a role-play presentation, that was fine, too. For a little over six months, I did a listing presentation each day. My role-play partner (my wife Joan) got very tired of hearing my presentation. In fact, she could probably do it better than most agents because she listened to it hundreds of times in a six-month period.

As I got closer and closer to my *X,* I got much better at my presentation. As I got close to the peak of the learning curve (about four months into my six-month daily routine), a transition happened. The number of practice presentations started to diminish. The number of real presentations in front of motivated sellers increased. By combining the *X* theory of success and the *Y* theory of choice, I increased the speed at which I reached the Champion level of production, and so will you if you apply the same principles.

Accept the Results and Move On

A Champion Agent doesn't whine about the results. Don't complain about the changing market conditions, increased competition, changing consumer views, or anything else that can affect the results. A Champion applies what I call the *Four Rules of Real Estate Success:* (1) show up, (2) focus mentally, (3) tell the truth, and (4) don't be attached to the outcome.

1. Show Up

There are a few elements of showing up. The first is showing up on time. Be on time for your appointments. I know a large percentage of agents are in the habit of running late. For a segment of the public, that is the kiss of death. It reeks of "my time is more important than yours." I am one of those people who quickly crosses off doing business with people who are late. I know this seems rudimentary, but too many agents are guilty of tardiness.

Showing up also means being consistent in the things you know you need to be consistent in. Show up for your prospecting; show up for your lead follow-up; show up when you agree to be at work. I was always in the office by 7:00 a.m. That commitment to show up at 7:00 a.m. didn't mean 7:15, 7:10, or 7:05 a.m. It meant 7:00 a.m. or before. Because we are independent contractors, we often give ourselves a pass. You can't do that. If you change or relax the standard there, you will relax it other places as well.

You also can't expect that, on the climb up to the Champion level, you can work for 30 hours a week and grow your business. A Champion is willing to work for a greater amount of time than others to achieve success. When you are growing your business, anything less than the average workweek of 40 hours won't get you there. On the other hand, investing 70-plus hours will burn you out. You have to find a middle ground, beyond 40 but less than 60 hours a week. You will have to be the judge of what is necessary, based on your goals, time frame, database size, competitiveness of the marketplace, and market conditions.

Coach's Tip: *There are two great books I recommend if your focus is lacking:* **The Power of Focus** *by Jack Canfield and* **Focus** *by Al Ries. Both books are excellent resources for people who are challenged to focus mentally.*

2. Focus Mentally

No matter what you are engaged in, your focus needs to be at the highest level. Most people struggle with their ability to focus for extended periods of time in order to take what they are working for to completion.

3. Tell the Truth

In all situations, you need to tell the truth. This is especially the case when dealing with yourself. Too many of us live in dream worlds. We concoct stories in our heads. We use creative score keeping to make ourselves feel better. All we do is fake ourselves out. I am a believer in affirmations as long as you affirm your progress in truth. (To say that you are worth $1 million when you are bankrupt is the start of delusion.)

An agent must tell the truth to the client. If a client has an unrealistic view of the value of his or her home—say so. If the buyer is hoping for a better deal than is probable, based on market conditions—say so. You might as well tell your client now. A day of reckoning will appear sooner or later, but guaranteed, it will appear at the worst time—when you least expect it.

4. Don't Be Attached to the Outcome

Sometimes, your well-laid plans and well-conceived activities don't produce the wanted results. This is especially true if you are looking at a short time frame. Even a Champion goes through peaks and valleys. By the end of the year, the highs and lows have evened themselves out, and if you have been diligent and consistent in your activities, you will achieve your goals.

All agents lose listings we thought we had. We have buyers who turn up in the disloyal category and buy with someone else. We have transactions that suck large amounts of time and don't close. This happens to the Champion Agents as well.

Stay on track.   The secret of a Champion Agent is not to let the negatives wipe you out. How long does it take you to get back on track after a negative outcome? If your answer is more than an hour, it's too much. What do you need to do to change that? It isn't that Champion Agents have fewer negative outcomes. In fact, I could argue that they have more than other agents do. They have greater exposure to them because they do more transactions. Their edge is the span of time they are off track until they get back on track and focused again. That time span is much less for a Champion Agent!

C H A P T E R

Setting the Sail

We all have dreams, wishes, and desires for how our life and business will be in 1 year, 3 years, even 10 years down the road. However, you must be able to develop a clear picture to accomplish these goals or objectives.

I am amazed by how foggy agents are in terms of their goals in life—even agents who reach high levels of production. Numerous studies have been done on desired goals, written goals, and their results. The net result (short version) is people who have written, defined goals accomplish them. People who don't have written, defined goals don't. The studies also have indicated that less than 3 percent of people ever construct written goals. Wherever you are today, either in the 3 percent or not, this chapter will help you broaden your approach toward the use of goals. It will help you look at goals in more than a business sense. It will help you develop health goals, family goals, spiritual goals, and financial goals—to name only a few.

What Is Financial Independence?

I have yet to meet an agent who didn't have a goal for financial independence. We all got into real estate with the desire to have the choice to work or not to work. In talking with agents, we all banter about the phrase *financial independence* as if it were a tennis ball in a tennis match. We hit it back and forth in our conversations. It slams around in our brain at least weekly or even daily. The question is, what is financial independence? The more important question is, is financial independence for you?

To me, *financial independence* has two possible definitions. The first is a little broader: "the ability to live off of one's assets without working directly to create more assets." It's the ability to live off of your stocks, bonds, CDs, loans you have made to others, and real estate. There are unlimited assets one can own to produce income.

When you really look at financial independence, it is fundamentally a number. That's the second definition, which is more specific and of higher value than the first. I think one of the reasons we have trouble developing numbers-based goals is because you can't fake it or fool yourself. (You either hit the number or you don't. When it's a number, you know where you stand at any given time against the goal.)

Net Asset Amount or Net Worth Amount

The financial independence number can take two forms. It is either a *net asset amount* or a *net worth amount.* This is a gross number that you have calculated based on achieving a reasonable return of investment that will allow you to be financially independent—to live off of those assets without working. The other option is that it's an income level that is created monthly from the assets you possess. It's a certain number of rental properties that create a net cash flow of X per month. It's an annuity you purchased that pays you X per month until you die. In my case, it could be writing books, like this one, that give me a small income from each book that is sold. But too often, we don't have a clear understanding of the result we are looking for.

Create Your Goals

Stephen Covey, in his book *Seven Habits of Highly Effective People,* introduced to the masses the concept of the need to start with the end in mind. That is what you are fundamentally doing as you set goals in writing. You are establishing the end before you write the chapters or the forward of the book of your life. Many of the goal programs I have studied or evaluated have you writing your obituary. That is certainly starting with the end in mind. There is nothing on this earth that is further out than your death. Picking a time line somewhere in the future and working backward is an effective technique to establish the road map to your success.

What are the things that you want to accomplish before you leave this earth? What's on your life list? What do you want to do and accomplish before you are finished? I will share with you one of my life goals.

=====

I wanted to have two children—a boy and a girl. This goal was written before all the pregnancy problems, fertility treatments, a miscarriage, and the eventual realization that Joan and I would be unable to have children as most couples do. Without actively seeking an adoption, our son, Wesley, dropped into our laps like manna from heaven. Our daughter was not quite as abrupt, but was an equally miraculous blessing. Goals and divine intervention are a powerful combination.

═══════════════

Goals are not to be evaluated based on the odds of getting them. Many of us are too conservative in our approach to goals. It's not about what you think you can have or what is reasonable. It's about what you want. If you let your imagination go, what would you desire? If you could have anything you wanted, what would it be? What would create joy, enjoyment, and pleasure for you? What do you want to be able to buy and own? What do you want to be recognized for? Where do you want to live? Do you need multiple homes? Where would they be? How would they be furnished? Where do you want to travel? What experiences do you want to have in life? What skills or abilities do you want to acquire? What do you want your business to look like? These are the types of questions you need to ask and answer in order to craft your path in life.

Coach's Tip: *Stop reading this chapter right now!! Take out a clean sheet of paper and write out your goals, based on the questions I just asked. I want you to write at least 75 to 100 goals that you have for the rest of your life. Write out your business goals, financial goals, family goals, relationship goals, spiritual goals. Create a list of what you want to do, see, and accomplish before you die.*

The Champion's Power Source . . . *Why*

Many people get caught up in the *how* of reaching the goal. They spend little time focusing on the clarity of the *why*. Why you want something is clearly the power source. If the *why* is large enough, the *how* becomes easy. We often focus on the wrong end of the equation. Why do you want to be financially independent? Why do you want to build a real estate sales business to a large scale?

I don't think there are hundreds of whys in your life. I think you have a handful of whys that interconnect your goals and dreams. This small handful of whys creates the power source in your life to become a Champion Agent, Champion Parent, or Champion Spouse, and it creates a Champion Legacy for your life.

═══════════════

I have become known worldwide from my sales career—being able to sell 150-plus homes a year while working only Monday through Thursday and taking off Friday through Sunday. That outcome of success in sales and quality of life was born out of a big why in my life. It was the why of creating an environment for myself and my family that I grew up in. My father, as a dentist, worked only those days. He was always around on Fridays when I came home from school. The biggest benefit to this was in the summer, when we left Portland every Thursday afternoon to spend three days at a second home on a lake that was a quarter of a mile from the Oregon coast. Some of my fondest memories as a child and youth were swimming, sailing, water skiing, walking the beach, and playing at our family lake house. I wanted to replicate that life exactly. It was a huge why as I built my real estate business. It drove my production, business skills, and time management skills. It caused me to build a vacation home in Bend, Oregon, where Joan and I spent three days a week for over five years.

A why can come from a past positive or negative experience. There are thousands of stories of successful people who grew up in abject poverty, and that fueled their why. There are stories similar to my own, of growing up privileged, and that also can fuel the why. There is really no difference between the two pathways to the result. Each person taps into their unique why to power themselves to the Champion level in life. The why can come from a desire to achieve the highest level of personal performance.

Discover Your Why

No one can give you a why. You must discover it for yourself. As a coach, I can ask questions and guide a client to his or her unique set of whys. However, I can't give clients their whys. A big value to having a coach in the early stages of your career is that a coach has the ability to help you draw out the whys buried inside you. Your why can come from your envisioned future of your life and business. Your why can come from your love of another and the devotion and commitment you have for that person.

I knew that my father's why was born out of his love for my mother. The reason for his financial success was the challenge of multiple sclerosis, and my parents faced it together. My mother was diagnosed with MS when I was three years old. By the time I was in the second grade, she never took another step. The last years of her life were spent without the use of her arms, legs, hands, or feet. My father's big why for wealth was to provide her with the most extraordinary life possible during each stage of her dis-

ease: to be able to travel with three sons and a wheelchair-bound wife to Mexico, Asia, Hawaii (annually), and many other locations. But mostly, he wanted to be able to care for her in her aged years in their home, with the help of full-time caregivers, so she could live where she raised her children and so she could have the best quality of life imaginable for someone in her condition. That was his *why. What's yours?*

What Will You Become?

I learned from my friend, Jim Rohn, that life is not about what you acquire, but about what you become. We set goals to become the person we need to become to accomplish the goal. I had to become a different person to attract the success that I have had in real estate sales. I have had to become a more skilled and more knowledgeable person to become a coach and speaker.

However, the change in your thinking, your knowledge, your skills, your discipline that you must undergo is the real value. The achievement of crossing the finish line of the goal lasts a week, a day, or even just a moment. The improvements you make to cross the finish line of that goal last a life time. You get to invest that newfound knowledge, skill, thinking, and discipline for the rest of your life to create abundance and accomplishments.

I believe that's why most financially successful people create the largest portion of their wealth between the ages of 55 and 65. Numerous studies have profiled wealthy individuals and discovered that successful people make more money in those 10 years than in all the preceding 30-plus years combined. For most of us, it takes us that long to acquire the wisdom, skills, knowledge, and discipline to achieve fantastic returns for our efforts.

It's difficult to work on all of your goals at once. You must choose and prioritize your goals to be able to create and implement your plan for achievement. You need a plan of action and achievement to successfully check the goals off of your life list. You must look at the resources in life that need to be employed to ensure the achievement of your goals: the resources of money, skills, knowledge, time, and other people. These are the resources of life that you can invest in achieving the Champion level of life. For each goal, you need to determine the resources to invest as well as how much and when to invest them.

Select Your Top 10 Goals

Because none of us have the capacity to work on all of our goals at once, the more focused and specific you are, the more successful you can be. Figure 4.1 can be used to develop a chart of those "written" goals.

Goal Action Plan Tool

Money

- Is there an amount of money I need to invest to accomplish this goal?
- Where can I acquire the money to reach the goal?
- Do I need to take it out of my working capital or savings, or borrow it?

Skills

- What skills must I acquire and perfect to reach this goal?
- What is the best way to acquire those skills in terms of ease, time frame, and cost?

Goal to achieve and time frame	Resources needed
1.	**Money:** **Skills:** **Knowledge:** **Time:** **Other people:**
2.	**Money:** **Skills:** **Knowledge:** **Time:** **Other people:**
3.	**Money:** **Skills:** **Knowledge:** **Time:** **Other people:**
4.	**Money:** **Skills:** **Knowledge:** **Time:** **Other people:**
5.	**Money:** **Skills:** **Knowledge:** **Time:** **Other people:**

©2006 Real Estate Champions, Inc.

Figure 4.1 Goal Action Plan Top 10

Knowledge
- What knowledge must I secure to achieve this goal?
- Is this knowledge specific or general?
- What's the best pathway to obtain this knowledge in terms of ease, time frame, and cost?

Time
- What time investment must I make personally?
- What's the timing or order of steps to ensure the accomplishment of this goal?

Goal to achieve and time frame	Resources needed
6.	**Money:** **Skills:** **Knowledge:** **Time:** **Other people:**
7.	**Money:** **Skills:** **Knowledge:** **Time:** **Other people:**
8.	**Money:** **Skills:** **Knowledge:** **Time:** **Other people:**
9.	**Money:** **Skills:** **Knowledge:** **Time:** **Other people:**
10.	**Money:** **Skills:** **Knowledge:** **Time:** **Other people:**

Figure 4.1 Goal Action Plan Top 10 *(Continued)*

Other people
- Who can help me?
- Who can help me reduce the time or timing?
- Does who I know make a difference?
- If it does, who do I need to know and how do I get to know them?

The process of setting and achieving goals is a process of clarity and commitment. It's easier to have the commitment you need if you have the clarity of your goals. I am a firm believer that everyone has the opportunity to live a grand and glorious life. Everyone has the opportunity to accomplish anything he or she desires. The biggest barrier between you and your dreams is the time you take to clearly write down what you really want out of life.

5

Building Credibility
and Trust

Two basic sales models and sales customers have evolved over time. They are *transactional selling* and *relationship selling.* For too long, sales and, especially, the real estate sales arena were transaction based. We provided the conduit of access to the information and the properties. We secured and facilitated the closing of the property. The service usually ended at the conclusion of the transaction. That is not an effective model from which to create a long, successful business, but we controlled the information, access, and fee structure.

The pendulum started to swing rapidly as our control started to slip away. When we lost exclusive access, along with other factors, the speed increased. Agents needed to establish a more relational selling approach for survival and success, so we moved to a relationship model of sales. In fact, I would contend that we have overcorrected in many cases and that the use of relationships to an extreme is rampant in many agents' businesses. The *relationship* is the reason for doing business, not expert guidance and high credibility that leads to high levels of trust.

Evidence of this outcome is the intense competition for commission dollars and the fees we charge. According to a recent *Harris Interactive and Real Trends* report, 62 percent of sales professionals feel pressure to negotiate commission, and 81 percent of those said it was because of the competition. When all you have is a relationship with a prospective client, it's not enough to sustain your exclusive position as their Realtor. It's not enough to protect your commission and value. The fact that you are a nice person and send a calendar each Christmas is not enough to position yourself as the expert.

Move Beyond Bonding

The buzzword in real estate sales over the past few years has been "relationship selling." To bond, connect, find common ground, soft sell, let the customer lead are a few of the many phrases and acronyms that we speakers and trainers use to get our message across. The overcorrection into extreme levels of "relationship" sales or "consultative" sales is just beginning to be seen in our sales performance. This is because the marketplace made it so easy to make a sale in the past few years. This overcorrection has allowed some agents to feel better about themselves in a sales career. I am not trying to offend anyone here, but it has also created a new breed of wimpy salespeople for whom the relationship is everything and the skills of selling are inconsequential.

Rather than focusing on building the relationship exclusively, I would encourage you to focus on building credibility and trust. The process of building credibility and trust should make up about 40 percent of your sales process, followed by identifying wants and needs, which should represent 20 percent. Don't mistake this new focus of building credibility as a way to get around having to develop sales skills, as most did with relationship building. There is no substitute for Champion-level sales skills. You need to sell the prospect on your credibility and trust through knowledge and expertise.

Use Key Market Statistics

By using the resources that are already available, you can set yourself apart from other agents. You have a large pool of resources that you can easily access, but few agents do. You merely need to ask the right questions and contact the right people. The information is available.

Your Local Board of Realtors

1. *The number of agents in the marketplace.* This information will help you calculate per-agent productivity, average listing per agent on the board, and segment stats in your core geographic area based on agent production. You can also see the agent count and find out whether it's growing or shrinking. With this information, you can also show your prospects that their odds of selecting an ill-equipped agent are moving either against them or for them.

2. *The average production of agents in units and volume.* You will be able to compare your performance to the new agents and other agents in the marketplace. It will allow you to segment production into the top 10, 20, or 50 agents in the marketplace. It is essential for you to know how you compare with other agents in your marketplace.

3. *Experience (in years) of agents on the board.* Most boards keep exhaustive studies in this area. For some reason, the public is swayed by the experience number. The funny thing about that is an agent with 20 years in real estate could have one year of experience 20 times over.

4. *Percentage of licensees that would be considered part-time.* This number, coupled with the experience number, can be used to illustrate to prospects the transient nature of salespeople in the real estate industry. This statistic is extremely effective in building trust in a changing marketplace.

Your Local MLS

You can secure valuable statistics and information from your local Multiple Listing Service (MLS). The MLS can give you key market stats such as the following:

- Days on the market averages
- Inventory levels of active listings
- Geographically active markets inside your service area
- Active markets based on price point inside your market area
- Listing price versus sales price ratios
- Listings taken versus listing sold ratios

National Association of REALTORS™

Some of the most valuable and least used services that NAR provides are their reports, market studies, and analyses of the national and regional real estate markets. NAR issues reports and studies on every segment of real estate sales (second-home markets, investment property, an annual home buyers and sellers report, Internet popularity in real estate sales, and many others).

The association also conducts studies and surveys of home sellers and buyers, probing why people select a certain agent, consumer satisfaction levels with their agents, home amenities that buyers want most, what services consumers want from us, and a host of other factors. This knowledge, in the hands of a Champion Agent, can easily be used to build credibility and trust. It will clearly provide value that will be unmatched by your competitor.

Use Market Trends

You need to understand the current and emerging market trends. You need to understand the economic influences of your region and how that will influence the marketplace in the future. Having the skill to evaluate the present against the past in order to forecast the future can separate you from others in the marketplace.

Total Sales Volume and Number of Sales (Year-to-Year)

Evaluate the total sales volume and number of sales on a year-to-date basis and against the previous year. This will allow you to see where you have been and where the marketplace is trending.

- Is the number of homes sold going up or down?
- Is the total volume increasing or decreasing?

Number of Listings

Evaluate the number of listings taken. Remember that real estate is influenced by supply and demand. The amount of inventory is the supply segment of the equation.

- Is the number of homes for sale up or down?
- Do buyers have a greater selection than at this time last year?
- Is the number of homes for sale rising or falling compared to this time last year?
- Is the mix of inventory for sale the same in town homes, condos, and single-family residences? Is it the same percentage of the overall market as this time last year?
- Is there more inventory in certain geographic areas than this time last year?

Champion Rule: *When inventory of active listings increases, most people panic.*

The average agent will have a hissy fit when the inventory increases. The reason is that it signals a change in the marketplace. The media will pick up on the inventory increase and start broadcasting the change as gloom and doom or the "bubble bursting." This further increases the consumer's negativity toward the real estate marketplace.

———————

Recently I led a coaching call with a client in San Diego who is a Champion Agent in that marketplace. The marketplace in San Diego has seen rapid increase in inventory of homes for sale in the past year. That has caused the media, consumers, and even agents to portray gloom and doom across the marketplace. While the days of selling homes within 24 hours of listing, receiving multiple offers for more than the asking price and with escalator clauses, is gone, the marketplace is still a great one.

When my client and I compared the current numbers against the previous year's numbers, there were some startling facts that were contrary to the gloom-and-doom prognosticators. Inventory had increased by 68 percent in his service area. Certainly, the increase in inventory would influence the marketplace. At the current rate of growth of the inventory, the marketplace would eventually have price and value corrections.

The list-price-to-sales-price ratio in the marketplace, however, was still solid and respectable against historical standards, at 96 percent. Now, against a marketplace where everything was selling above asking price, it was a change, but against the long-term view, 96 percent is a good number. The average days on the market for homes that sold was 61 days. That told me that a home priced competitively would sell in a reasonable period of time.

The sold properties per month was what really clarified the picture. The sold properties were within a few homes either way each month for the previous last 18 months in his service area. When the marketplace was explosive, there were about the same amount of sold properties per month as there were at that moment. The sales had not dropped in my client's market area.

The net result was that homes were still selling. The sellers were still getting close to their asking price in a reasonable period of time. The key is that the sellers could achieve a sale only by being competitive on their price. With the high inventory levels compared to the previous year, there is now more competition, but that competition has not positioned itself competitively via price. The media and most consumers are wrong about the marketplace. My client is one of the few in the marketplace who has the correct view of the overall picture.

Average Sales Price (Year-to-Year)

Evaluate average sales price this year versus last year.

- Is it going up or down?
- Is the marketplace depreciating or appreciating in value? Calculate this statistic on a quarterly basis.
- Is the inventory aligned with the demands? You need to know if you are experiencing a net gain per month or net loss in the inventory levels.

Percentage of Appreciation for Average Sales price (Year-to-Year)

Evaluate the percentage of appreciation for average sales price last year versus this year.

- Is the appreciating percentage decreasing or increasing compared to the same time last year?
- Is the marketplace gaining or losing strength?

Coach's Tip: *To be a Champion Agent, you must have greater marketplace knowledge than your competitors. An agent can increase credibility and trust with a prospect or client through important, current marketplace knowledge.*

Compile a Marketplace Analysis

Before investing the couple of hours a month building your own marketplace analysis, check to see if your local board of Realtors or MLS compiles market trend reports. I have found that most do something on this order, but are not as comprehensive in price ranges. They do mainly geography-based reports for all price points. You need price segmentation. If the essential data isn't available, set a couple of hours aside and construct the analysis on your own. Use the following formula to gain accuracy of the trends in your marketplace.

Segment Your Marketplace Geographically

Your objective is to view the macro and micro of your marketplace. The macro would be the marketplace broken down geographically. The micro is the price segmentation you need to use. You could also break your areas out via school boundaries. The broader view works well to gain a flavor for the marketplace. The close-in view will be used heavily in showing properties to clients.

The easiest way to create segmented market areas is by using the existing MLS geographic regions. Most real estate statistics and data are already segmented in that format. Another option is using the areas as featured in your newspaper's real estate classified ads, as long as it works with what is considered standard marketplace knowledge.

Segment Your Marketplace into Five Price Segments

While most consumers, real estate agents, and the media view the marketplace as one entity (or even a couple, based on geography), that approach is too narrow. Price plays a significant factor as well. Once you decide on a geographical area or segment, you need to segment via price point. You need to divide your marketplace into five key price segments:

entry, low middle, middle, upper middle, and upper. Each segment can be vastly different from the others.

Your sellers and buyers *say* they want to know the overall health of the marketplace. What they really want to know is what's happening in the specific marketplace in which they are trying to buy or sell. The only way to convey that information is by price point comparison.

Know Your Available Inventory Levels

All markets are influenced by inventory levels. The inventory levels in turn affect the percentage of homes that sell every month. The higher the inventory, the lower the percentage of homes that sell monthly. Another term used for the percentage of homes sold is *listings-sold-versus-listings-taken ratio.* In a normal or neutral market, the listings-sold-versus-listings-taken percentage will run 65 to 70 percent. In an inventory-short, robust, high-level seller's market, the number will be well above 90 percent. You need to know the level of competition sellers and buyers will face based on the marketplace inventory levels.

Determine the Number of Sales in the Previous 30 Days

Notice I didn't say *sold* or *closed properties.* I said *sales* or *pending sales.* We want an accurate analysis for the previous 30 days. If we count closed transactions, we are really reflecting the marketplace inventory from 30 to 60 days ago, not from 1 to 30 days ago. You always want to reflect the activity from 1 to 30 days ago.

Calculate the Absorption Rate or the Number of Months of Inventory

This last calculation is the linchpin of the whole analysis. This is where most people fall short in terms of marketplace knowledge. You need to take current inventory levels at each price point and divide that by the pending sales for the month. This will give you the number of months of inventory left if sales remain constant. You are also making an assumption with this calculation that no new available homes will come on the market before the entire present inventory is sold. We all know that assumption is false.

Champion Calculation

As an example, you have 100 homes for sale at the entry-level price point. On average, 20 sell every month. You clearly have five months' worth of inventory left. A seller will need to be competitively priced to be one of those that sell next month. What you are doing with this calculation is providing a clear picture of the current supply and demand mix in the marketplace.

Champion Calculation

If there are 300 homes for sale in a given geographic area, and 30 of them are pending this past month, divide 300 by 30 and end up with 10 months. In contrast, one of my clients in Southern California submitted her market stats from a year ago. They showed 98 properties available, with 176 pending on a monthly basis. That's quite a bit different than the one with 300 actives and 30 pendings. One has 10 months' worth of inventory and the other has about two to three weeks. The strategy, tactics, and counseling of the clients will be very different for these two marketplaces. One is a "list at all costs" type of marketplace; the other is "you'd better secure the listing at the right price."

The seller has to be informed or you are wasting your time.

1. Which market allows the seller greater control?
2. Which market do you think is appreciating faster?
3. Which marketplace inspires the greatest seller greed?
4. In which market will homes spend fewer days for sale?
5. In which market do buyers have the least control and the greatest need to meet seller demands in order to make the purchase?
6. In which marketplace do the sellers put more pressure on agents to cut their commission rate?

The marketplace with only two to three weeks of inventory is the correct answer to all these questions. The other marketplace is behind on all counts.

The trends of the marketplace are predetermined by the inventory of listings, pending sales, and number of months of inventory. Your marketplace will not magically go against the grain of the law of supply and demand. The key is knowing what the law is saying about it. Don't leave your office without your monthly analysis!

Use Your Evaluation of the Market

Figure 5.1 is a market trend report form that you can replicate for your own use.

Figure 5.2 is an example a client's marketplace trends grid for one month. There is a significant difference once you cross the line from the middle segment of the marketplace to the middle-upper and upper segments. Agents, consumers, and media will report only the good news. In this case, they were expressing the robust nature of the marketplace—that no inventory existed and that homes were selling fast. The truth in the middle and the

Monthly Report

Month: _____

Price Range	Current # of Listings	Avg. # of Sales per Mo.	Selling Price % of List Price	Avg. Days on Market	Remaining # Months Inventory
$ Entry					
$ Low middle					
$ Middle					
$ Upper middle					
$ Upper					

Previous month's statistics

Month: _____

Price Range	Current # of Listings	Avg. # of Sales per Mo.	Selling Price % of List Price	Avg. Days on Market	Remaining # Months Inventory
$ Entry					
$ Low middle					
$ Middle					
$ Upper middle					
$ Upper					

Same month last year's statistics

Month: _____

Price Range	Current # of Listings	Avg. # of Sales per Mo.	Selling Price % of List Price	Avg. Days on Market	Remaining # Months Inventory
$ Entry					
$ Low middle					
$ Middle					
$ Upper middle					
$ Upper					

©2006 Real Estate Champions, Inc.

Figure 5.1 Real Estate Market Trends

upper-middle segments was quite different. The inventory levels were 6 to 12 times greater. While homes were still selling, sellers had to be competitive.

Develop Credibility in Your Marketplace

Until my client had this knowledge, she was unable to articulate, with credibility, to prospects and clients what she felt the marketplace was doing. She was right, but didn't have empirical evidence to back up her assertions. Prospects, agents, and sellers can't argue with the facts. Her sellers who were in the upper price point category were calling to ask why their homes hadn't sold yet. They were hearing from friends and the media that the marketplace was great and assumed their agent was doing a less-than-stellar job. The truth was that their prices were less competitive in a marketplace that had over a year's worth of inventory and only six sales. The question then became, did they have what it would take, based on *true* market conditions, to achieve the sale? What it takes means having one of the top properties, in terms of price and conditions, because only a few will sell every month.

Update Your Clients on Their Investments

When you have a strong market trends report, you will be able to do a number of strategic things that add value to your prospects and clients. This report should include at least the current numbers and should be sent out quarterly. You are giving your clients an update about how their investment is doing. You're giving them a clear picture in case they want to sell or buy another home or make an investment purchase.

When you send out this market trends report, beneath the numbers write a couple paragraphs of analysis about what is happening in the marketplace. Then write a call-to-action

Monthly Report

Month: _____

Price Range	Current # of Listings	Avg. # of Sales per Mo.	Selling Price % of List Price	Avg. Days on Market	Remaining # Months Inventory
$0–$300K	125	201	99%	6	.62
$300K–$500K	337	286	98%	14	1.20
$500K–$650K	247	179	96%	11	1.40
$650K–$800K	101	15	95%	37	6.70
$800K and up	75	6	95%	68	12.60

©2006 Real Estate Champions, Inc.

Figure 5.2 Example Real Estate Market Trends

paragraph at the bottom of the page. The call to action could point out the opportunities in the marketplace. You might highlight a new property you just listed and ask whether your client knows of a buyer for it. There are unlimited calls to action.

Secure Prospects

You can also use the newfound knowledge to secure prospects over the phone and in person. With this knowledge, you can position yourself as the expert in the marketplace. Use your knowledge to inject urgency, reveal motivation, and convey your market knowledge.

- Were you aware that we have only about three weeks of inventory in the price range you want to buy in?
- Did you know that we had 22 percent appreciation in the marketplace last year? This same home would have been almost $50,000 less a year ago. You could have bought it for $225,000 last year instead of the $275,000 now. I wouldn't want you to waste another $50,000 by waiting until next year! Would Wednesday or Thursday this week be better for us to meet?
- Have you been told that a well-priced home in great condition and at a solid location lasts only three days on the market right now?

Using key marketplace knowledge and statistics is really an easy way to build credibility and trust. It sets you apart from the other agents. It increases a prospect's desire to meet with you. Your clients will listen to your counsel more attentively, and more important, they will actually *do* what you counsel them to do.

PART II

CHAMPION LEAD-GENERATION METHODS

Dialing for Dollars

People who read the term "dialing for dollars" usually react negatively. Most of us equate the work of prospecting, or "dialing for dollars," with something negative.

―――――――――――――――――――――

I spent my whole career with one company. There was a time when my broker and I were going through a rough spot in our business relationship, and during that time, I contacted another successful broker with multiple offices who was rumored to be opening an office in my service area. We met for lunch to discuss the potential of my changing companies. After we dispensed with the initial warm-up, the first question he asked me was, "When are you going to stop all this prospecting and become a real real estate agent?" I was stunned by his comment . . . meeting over! We talked real estate for another 45 minutes, but my desire to go to work for him ended the instant he revealed his myopic viewpoint. I sold more houses than probably any other agent he had in his firm at that time. His view was that a "real" agent didn't prospect . . . especially expireds, which I did constantly and very successfully. He lost the chance to land a very successful agent because of his limited view point.

―――――――――――――――――――――

Champion Rule: *Prospecting is the first step in the sales process. You are in sales; you need to prospect.*

Prospect Options

You really have an unlimited supply of prospects. Webster defines *prospecting* as "seeking a potential customer; seeking with a vision of success." In the definition, it doesn't say waiting for the phone to ring, sending out postcards, hoping someone calls me. It clearly says that prospecting is a *seeking* activity.

The second segment of this definition is that we need to "seek with a vision of success." Webster must have worked in a real estate office at one time. He knows how other agents can try to pull you down or away from prospecting. You could even have brokers who, like the one I mentioned, try to belittle you because of your prospecting. Webster was saying, turn your mind to the positive, expect good results, focus on that, and you will succeed. Don't let others' negativity influence your vision of success.

The question isn't whether you should or shouldn't prospect; the answer is yes, you should. The options of *what* to prospect are wide open. There are unlimited sources to prospect for generating new leads and appointments. It's critical to be able to sort through the more competitive sources versus less competitive sources, reactive sources versus proactive sources, the possible sources and the probable sources to find your niche.

Figure 6.1 illustrates the many options you have with regard to prospecting sources, categories, competition level in those categories, and the controllable influence you have on your business success through prospecting.

Competitive Prospecting Sources

You have the option to select more competitive sources to generate your leads. These more competitive sources mean that you are not usually the only agent who knows about this prospect's desire to buy or sell. Those more competitive categories are open houses and/or sign calls, Internet contacts, even floor time. These are general sources for future business.

Other excellent competitive sources are FSBOs and expireds. There you will be competing with the top-level sales-skilled agents in the marketplace. You have to possess Champion-level sales skills to compete and win clients in these two categories with consistency.

Less Competitive Prospecting Sources

The less competitive options are referral leads from other agents, personal relationships, and referring businesses. A referring business could be your mortgage organization, insurance agent, or home inspector. All these sources are less competitive because these people aren't referring their business to 20, 10, or even (in most cases) 5 agents in your marketplace. Other less competitive sources would be geographic, demographic, or psycho-

**More   Less
Competitive**   **Competitive**

Reactive Sources

Possible sources of their current or future **direct** business

*   Open house contacts
*   Ad and sign calls
*   Internet contacts

Probable sources of others' current or future **direct** business

    Referral leads from other agents   *
    Referral leads from "referring businesses"   *
    Referral leads from "personal relationships"   *

Proactive Sources

Possible sources of their current or future **direct** business

    General/cold calling   *
    Specific activity/warm calling   *

Probable sources of their current **direct** business

*   FSBOs
*   Expireds

Specific groups that are sources of their **direct** future business

    Geographic/demographic farms   *
    Spheres of influence   *
    Past clients   *

Specific groups that are sources of others' current and future **referral** business

    Past clients   *
    Spheres of influence   *
    Geographic/demographic farms   *

©2006 Real Estate Champions, Inc.

Figure 6.1 Real Estate Business Sources: Categories, Competition, Controllability

graphic farms, spheres of influence, and past clients. Again, the number of agents working the same people that you are trying to serve and secure as clients status is very low. Geographic farms are the most likely of all these sources to have multiple agents working an area.

Cold calling and warm calling.   Some of you may be wondering why I put cold calling and warm calling in as less competitive. It's because very few agents actually do them. Even fewer agents do them since the advent of the no-call list. We all know what cold calling is, but warm calling is merely creating a more targeted list and possibly sending a door-opening marketing piece. An example of an effective strategy with little competition is to send a marketing piece to a non-owner-occupied property and then to make a warm call to the owner after a big run-up in real estate prices followed by a softening in the marketplace.

I am personally not a proponent of cold call prospecting—calling down a list in a criss-cross directory for business. That is really the definition of cold call prospecting. Agents, and even sales trainers (especially the "magic pill guys" and "referral gurus"), usually try to categorize anyone who is a prospecting proponent as a cold call proponent as well. I sometimes get painted with this broad brush, but it's not true. Even calling your past clients and sphere needs to be called what it is . . . *prospecting.* You can easily be in favor of prospecting and against cold calling, as I am. I am not against cold calling because it doesn't work . . . it does. I am against it because the return on investment is too low. The margin between your effort and your results is not large enough. There are much higher probability lead generation sources for your prospecting effort.

Proactive Prospecting Sources

When evaluating the sources, you must also evaluate the ability to create the business or react to the business. If you spend your time in the proactive sources, like past clients, sphere of influence, farms (if you call them as well), FSBOs, expireds, and cold or warm calling, you can track the numbers and return on investment from your effort.

Reactive Prospecting Sources

With the reactive sources, you have less control over creating your desired outcome. In reactive sources, you don't know the volume or time frame of the leads as completely. With an open house, for example, you don't really know whether 2 people will show up or 20. With the Internet, you have no idea of the number of leads or when they will come. These are clearly reactive sources for prospecting and leads. The same is true of referrals from agents, referral business, and personal relationships. With all of these, the factors of when and how frequently are uncertain.

Possible versus Probable Prospecting Sources

The last option is the evaluation of the possible versus probable sources. A *possibility* is something that happens 50 percent of the time or less. A *probability* is something that happens 51 percent of the time or more. The mark of a Champion is investing your time and effort in an area where the odds are better. Increasing your effort, time, energy, and expertise in past clients, sphere of influence, FSBOs, expireds, referrals from other agents and referral businesses, and personal relationships will increase the results that you will receive.

Establishing a Lead Triad

When you evaluate Champion Agents' prospecting and lead generation, you will find these people have more than one source. Your objective is to establish a lead triad. A *lead triad* is at least three sources of business that each generate leads accounting for at least 15 to 20 percent of your overall revenue or units.

When I evaluate most agents' businesses, either they have one source that they rely on too much (creating an imbalance of leads and a vulnerability to their business) or they have too many lead sources that generate low levels of leads and business. They may have 10 lead sources, and most of which represent less than 10 percent of their business. Both these bookend errors are equally disastrous. You need to have three to four lead sources that can account for a substantial amount of business. When you have a lead triad in position, if a prospecting and lead follow-up source dries up or diminishes because of intensifying competition, marketplace or industry changes, or just bad breaks, you have already established, tested, and proven methods of prospecting and lead generation that you can shift your resources to. You can ramp up those sources to a high level quicker, which saves you stress and a cash flow crisis.

If you don't have a lead triad, your probability of weathering the storm is lower. It will take a greater toll on you to navigate the storm. If you have too many sources, you have to pick one or two without knowing whether you selected the right ones or whether your strategy will work. With only one solid source, you are starting from scratch, attacking the steepest part of the learning curve and hoping for quick results. Either approach can be deadly.

> **Coach's Tip:** *If I am describing your business, I have a word of caution for you: don't try to add too much too soon. The natural tendency is to rush to add two, three, even four sources now. The better approach is to select one and commit to that one. Track the results and make the changes and requirements necessary to increase the results. Don't change your source or add another one for six months, until the strategy, tactics, and implementation have been fully tested.*

Prospecting: The Efficient Lead Generator

Prospecting is the most efficient lead generator ever created. All it takes is time and a little bit of skill. You don't need large amounts of money to prospect well. When I entered real estate sales, prospecting was my only option, since I was undercapitalized in starting my business (translation: *broke*). Developing and implementing a large marketing and direct mail campaign was out of the question. I was forced to prospect for business. Looking back now, I would not have traded my desperate situation in the beginning for anything. It freed me to learn, early in my career, a primary skill of every salesperson's success. There is no method of lead generation that deals as well with the law of cause and effect. The law states certain causes create certain effects. Making phone calls and talking to people creates leads in bunches . . . period.

Only Two Types of People

You really have only two types of people you can call: people you know and people you don't know. The question is, which of these categories is bigger? I'll give you a minute to think about it. The group of people you don't know is larger. There are more potential prospects in that group. The group of people you know is smaller, but the odds of you doing business with them are greater.

Four Pillars of Prospecting

The four pillars of prospecting are the four steps you need to focus on to ensure your success. In order to achieve the revenue goals for your business, you need to master the following four disciplines: (1) set a daily time and place for prospecting; (2) fight off distractions; (3) follow your plan; and (4) be faithful to yourself and finish what you start.

Set a Time and Place for Prospecting

You have to work your day around your prospecting. You can't work your prospecting around your day. You must establish the habit and discipline of prospecting on a daily basis. You have to create an environment that is conducive to prospecting, with limited distractions. This environment must have your prospecting tools, scripts, dialogues, and objection-handling scripts ready and available for use. Prospecting needs to be done at the same time each day to build consistency.

In my early career, I set up a prospecting station in my office that included a stand-up area, a computer, and telephone with a headset. I stood up because my energy and intensity is high when I stand. I know that body language comprises 55 percent of my communication power. I needed every advantage possible. You can increase your energy and intensity by standing up. You can intensify your focus as well. Having a headset enabled me to keep my hands free so I could engage my body in communication as if I were speaking directly to my prospect in person.

I tacked scripts on the wall of my prospecting station to use when contacting expired listings and FSBO prospects, past clients, and those in my sphere of influence. I also posted all of my objection-handling scripts, including a few options for each objection. Although I had them

> **Coach's Tip:** *A headset is one of the most important tools for a salesperson to have. It enables you to keep your hands free. I know that the people over the phone can't see you, but it doesn't matter. What matters is the manner in which you come across over the phone. With the headset, you can task or gesture with your hands, which informs your tone and your body language. Spend the money to get a good headset; the vocal quality matters. You'll spend at least $200 for a good wired one and $300 to $400 for a good wireless one.*

memorized and practiced, it was great to have a backup for the moment when I might be caught off guard.

Fight Off Distractions

For most people, any distraction is celebrated as an excuse to not prospect. Some obvious distractions are an incoming e-mail, an inbound phone call, a home inspection question, a problem transaction, an agent who wants to talk, a broken nail. For most agents, anything will do to help them feel like they have something more pressing to do than prospect. I call this creative avoidance, and real estate agents are masters at it.

It doesn't matter where you are in your career, the distractions never go away. My belief is that Champion Agents have even greater potential for distraction because of the volume of business, the size of the listing inventory or the number of active buyers and sellers, and the client base. The difference between engaging in creative avoidance and doing the prospecting comes down to the question: What do you do when the distractions hit? Do you postpone prospecting while you put out fires? Do you decide to make just a few calls to settle the issues now, or delay them until later? Your answers to these questions reveal whether you're an agent who tends to engage in creative avoidance.

To fight off distractions, you have to limit their access by doing the following:

- Ask the receptionist to take messages for inbound calls during your prospecting sessions.
- Turn off your cell phone and pager.

- Put a sign on the door that basically says, "Don't bother me. I'm prospecting."
- Turn off your e-mail so the "you've got mail" icon doesn't tempt you.
- Tell anyone who asks for a meeting during your prospecting period that you already have an appointment, because you do—you have an appointment to find a potential prospect.

Follow the Plan

To get your prospecting steps and order correct, you need to create and implement a prospecting plan. When you set up the plan, you need to know who you are going to call each day. You need to know the reason for the call. You need to understand the objective you are trying to attain before the close of the call. The primary objective of any sales call is to book an appointment. The best approach to creating a daily prospecting plan is to create it the day before—to create it in advance for the next day.

Coach's Tip: *Affirmations will help you get into "the zone" so that success can come more easily. Their repetition will help raise your intensity, confidence, and focus. This small action will help you to begin your prospecting with the expectation of achieving a successful result.*

If you wait to put your prospecting plan together on the day of your prospecting, the probability increases that you'll talk yourself out of more calls than you will actually make. If you walk in the door without your prospecting plan ready, you're too late. In your mind you begin to think, "This person will think I'm calling back too soon" or "This person won't buy or sell right now."

If you schedule your prospecting the night before, there will be no excuses to stop you from just doing it when you walk in the door. To be successful in your prospecting follow these steps:

1. Do your research, establish your plan, and set up for the next day's prospecting a day in advance.
2. In the morning, quickly review your calls and your daily goals.
3. Spend 20 minutes before each prospecting session practicing your scripts, dialogues, and objection-handling techniques.
4. Review affirmations:
   - "I will generate leads and appointments before I'm through today."
   - "I'm a great prospector."
   - "When I prospect, people love to talk with me and set appointments with me."

Be Faithful to Yourself and Finish What You Start

The hardest part is actually getting started. Once you start, the hardest part becomes finishing what you started. My best advice is stay faithful to your daily objectives. Make all your contacts for your daily goal, down to the very last one. Don't settle for less than your daily goal. If your goal is 10 contacts a day, make 10. Don't allow yourself to make eight and feel good. The goal was 10. Accept nothing less than the standard you set for yourself.

Set the Right Level of Prospecting Goals

Selecting the right level of prospecting daily is essential to your success. When you begin prospecting, the number of daily contacts is at best an educated guess. You haven't been prospecting, so you don't really know your sales ratios for contacts to leads, leads to appointments, appointments to committed clients (signed listing agreements or signed buyer representation contracts), or committed clients to closed transactions. These ratios are essential to understand the activity level necessary to reach your goals.

I find one of the most stressful things for agents, especially if they are coming off a banner year, is the start of a new year. The vast majority of them have no real idea how they achieved their banner year. The stress and tension arises because they come to the realization early in the year that they have no plan, and they don't know how to make more money, let alone the same amount of money they made the previous year.

I had a client who lived that vicious cycle of coming off a good year and then being worried about how to duplicate that achievement the next year. He went through this cycle for many years of his career before he became my client. After working together for a while and beginning a new calendar year together, he then knew his business sales ratios and had a solid numbers-based business plan. He told me a month into the new year that in the past he had always dreaded the new year. He had always felt like a fraud because he really didn't know how he was going to achieve more. The truth is, he had been sitting on the same production plateau for six years before we met. He increased his business income over $200,000 that first full year of coaching.

He said something profound that day that I will never forget. "Knowing my sales ratios, prospecting daily, having a numbers-based business plan, and showing up every day to work is an easier way to live!" He had spent *the previous handful of years trying to cover his tracks. My dad always told me when I didn't do well in school, "You had to work harder to get a poor grade than you would have to get a good one." Both of these men were right. When selecting your prospecting goals, start small. Prospecting is about building momentum and consistency. It's about establishing the habit of controlling your time, emotion, and the distractions of your business to do it daily.*

5-5-5 System

I would suggest that, if you want to take your business to the Champion level, you apply the 5-5-5 system each day. The 5-5-5 system is five past client calls, five lead follow-up calls, and five new prospect contacts each day. This is a minimum level for a Champion Agent. This will take you about 90 minutes a day to complete. The key adjustment is that if you have more than five lead follow-up calls that need to be made, based on the motivation and number of leads, be sure to make them all.

Prospecting will generate *some* new business for you right now, but it will mostly produce leads. These leads need your attention and effort as well. I am frequently asked, "How can I do more transactions next month?" or "How can I catch up to my goal for the month, quarter, or year when time is short?" The answer—focus on your leads. These are the people who are closest, in terms of time and connection, to doing something with you. Call them all, even the ones who seem a few months away. True motivation can change quickly.

Do Enough Prospecting to Drive Your Business

You don't need to make 50 cold calls a day to achieve prospecting success. In fact, if that is your primary method, I would question your decision-making ability. You need to do enough prospecting activity to drive the business. Picking a more effective medium than cold calling is the mark of a successful businessperson. When you prospect consistently, which is the key, it doesn't take much. I caution you: it is easy to think we are making progress when we are merely treading water at best.

Say you set a goal to make 10 contacts a day. On Monday you do 10, on Tuesday 3 (because of an office meeting), on Wednesday another 10, on Thursday 8, and on Friday you do four (because it was beautiful and you wanted to play golf). Was that a good week of prospecting? When most agents are asked that question, they say yes. The truth is that such a week repeated for a year would be the equivalent of 15 weeks of zero prospecting. Now how do you feel about that week?

If you have some name recognition or market presence, a little prospecting will generate explosive growth. Established agents and Champion Agents receive more benefit from prospecting than new or low-producing agents. The reason is because your sphere of influence, past clients, and other sources know that you are busy. Because of the volume of business you do, they are not expecting a call. When you do make prospecting calls to them, it carries more of a *wow* factor.

This is also true for the more competitive forms of prospecting. If you have good market share in an area and you decide to make calls to expireds or FSBOs, you will hear frequently from the prospects that they see your signs everywhere. You can parlay that into a huge advantage in securing a listing presentation. Don't make the mistake that most agents do when they achieve a little or even a lot of success. They stop doing what brought them their success. The time to increase is at hand; do not cut back.

Coach's Tip: *My friend John Gualtieri shared this statement with me a few years ago, which I quickly wrote down. "On the road to success, you have to chop wood and carry water. When you become successful, you have to chop wood and carry water." The need for your daily prospecting doesn't change when you become a Champion!*

How Do *They* Do It?

The truth is, most agents want to share with you how they achieved success; they passionately share their techniques and the mentors, coaches, or speakers who helped them. I caution you—more than 95 percent truly have no idea or can't quantify their success for you. They don't really know how they got there or what it cost to produce it. They heard about or thought of a great idea, put it into place, but haven't tracked it to really know the return on investment (ROI).

In the movie *The Wizard of Oz,* Dorothy, the Scarecrow, the Tin Man, and the Cowardly Lion were all terrified of the great and powerful Oz. They shook with fear at the shear intensity and volume of his voice. Toto was the one to reveal that Oz was only a little man behind a curtain who used a sound system to produce the illusion of greatness and power. Too often, the great Oz is parallel to the great Realtor. We need to pull back the curtain to make sure what we are seeing is real.

Too often, agents are mesmerized by the promotional gimmicks and marketing strategies that other agents say "work like magic." There is nothing wrong with marketing, provided you are doing the real work of pulling the prospecting levers behind the scenes. Prospecting makes it's own magic over the short and long run.

Ask the Right Questions

The big challenge is, how do you pull back the curtain? How do you find the truth? You have to ask the right questions so you can gain the answers that reveal the truth. If someone approaches you with great and powerful business-generating techniques, ask these types of questions:

- What is the conversion ratio of this technique?
- What percentage of your business comes from this approach?
- How many transactions does this technique generate for you annually?
- How much does it cost you to use this marketing service to generate leads?
- How many sellers have you gained?
- How many buyers have you gained from this approach?
- How much time do you need to invest to set up this technique and maintain it?
- Have you included the value of your time in that equation?
- What is your net profit from this activity after all your costs are subtracted?

From asking these types of questions for over 13 years, I have found that most people don't have the answers. I began asking these questions in about my third year in the real estate business. I did this because I was the type of person who wanted to do better. In many cases, I would implement strategies touted by other agents and not get anywhere near the results the they claimed. I developed this list of questions and discovered that very few agents could actually answer them. Many speakers and trainers fell into this category as well. Be careful! Some did know the answers, however, and those are the people I respect even today.

Track Your Success

You must track a series of numbers each day. You need to track contracts, leads, and especially appointments. I also believe that it is highly effective to track your contacts by categories. You need to be able to see the difference in results in each area you are prospecting. You will see different lead volume and number of appointments depending on whether you are calling past clients, expireds, or call capture leads. You need to understand the ratios of your results by sources.

Daily Disciplines	Contacts		Leads	Appts	Activity	
	Face to Face	Phone				
Past clients sphere					Total contacts	
					Number of hours prospecting	
Expireds					Leads generated	
					Listing appts set	
FSBO					Listing appts gone on	
					Listings taken	
Calling around listings and sales					Listings canceled or expired	
					Listings (I turned down)	
Door knocking					Listings (I didn't get)	
					Price reductions	
Cold calling					Listings sold	
Current lead follow-up					Buyer appts. set	
					Buyer interviews	
Goals					Buyer contracts	
Totals					Qualified showings	
					Offers written	
					Buyer sales	
					Transaction fallout	
					Listings closed	
					Buyers closed	
					Commission paid out	

Rate your day (0–10)

Why I rated it this way: _____

_____

_____

_____

_____

_____

_____

_____

"The daily disciplines lead to success. Don't neglect to do them today."—Dirk Zeller

©2006 Real Estate Champions, Inc.

Figure 6.2 Champion Agent Daily Tracking Form

To have a Champion Agent's business, you must also understand the ratios of listing presentations to listings taken and buyer interviews to buyer contracts (signed agreements stating an exclusive right to represent). In a changing marketplace, your conversion numbers can be variable and can change to a lower number. It might take more leads to generate an appointment. You have to be able to watch for that and make the necessary adjustments.

Figure 6.2 is a comprehensive tracking form that is easy to use. Tally your efforts while you are prospecting. (The only flaw in the form is that it won't dial the phone for you!)

C H A P T E R

Leads Are Your Lifeblood

The creation, control, and conversion of leads determine the revenue and success of your business. In this chapter, I focus on the control and conversion of leads. Most speakers, trainers, coaches, and authors focus a lot of their time on the creation of leads. They try to sell you their "lead-generation system"—the system that creates thousands of leads for you to work! And we have all heard of these new third-party Internet companies that, in most areas, are charging agents lots of money for low-quality, low-conversion-rate leads. The only people who are making money out of this deal are these Internet companies.

> **Champion Rule:** *Creating leads is easy! It's managing and converting them that pose a challenge.*

Manage, Convert, and Gain Commitment from Your Leads

The real barrier in the equation isn't lead creation, as everyone believes. It's in the management, conversion, and commitment of the leads. If you are an agent reading this and don't have enough leads right now, you might think I am wrong. Bear with me as I present the evidence and truth.

There are literally thousands of ways for agents to generate leads. The list is really endless, with new avenues being created all the time. We have farming, cold calling, direct mail, expireds, direct response advertising, FSBOs, pay-per-click, calling our sphere, our Web site, calling past clients, Realtor.com, calling current clients, relocation referrals, strategic alliances, open houses, interactive voice response (IVR) systems . . . you get the idea. Each method has its own ratio of success attached to it.

I know agents who generate all (or the bulk) of their business from only one of these sources, not from a combination. I had a friend in Portland who sold as many houses as I did . . . more than 150 a year. He could connect over 80 percent of his sales to open houses. He did them every Saturday and Sunday. He was a master at meeting the people, connecting with them, and converting them to clients. I would rather have my skin eaten off by ants than do open houses, but it worked for him. The problem is not lead creation.

I get magic lead-generation schemes daily via e-mail, as you no doubt do, too. I received one the other day from one of those "magic guys" who is an agent and speaker in Canada. He was touting his latest protégé, who did 60 transactions a year and generated over 1,200 leads a month. This all happened in his third year in the business. (By my third year in the business, I was doing over 100 transactions, so I wasn't that impressed. I realize, however, that the average agent would be frothing at the mouth for 1,200 leads a month.) The whole focus was to promote this speaker's direct response advertising system, which, if followed, would create 1,200 leads a month.

Champion Calculation

I did what any good coach would do: I grabbed my calculator as I read the glowing copy of his marketing piece. This "new superstar" agent generates over 14,400 leads a year! That means he has to invest his time and resources to manage, track, call, mail, e-mail, and try to convert over 14,400 leads annually. If the claims of that lead volume are true, that's a lot of leads to properly process. The key word being *properly* process. The net result, in his case, of 14,400 leads is a mere 60 transactions. That represents a conversion rate of 0.004167. That is less than one-half of 1 percent! In other words, he has to talk with, mail to, e-mail to, send information to, track, and manage 240 people to get one person to buy from this magical, easy, instant-lead-generation system.

Good Leads, Not Just *Any* Leads

An intelligent person comes to one of two conclusions (or a combination of both). The first is that the quality of leads is poor (keep in mind that conversion rate is a function of the quality of the leads). The cost of conversion runs so high that, by the time the advertising and marketing expenses are paid to generate 240 leads and run them through a lead follow-up process to get one transaction, there is little (if any) net profit left. The other conclusion is that the leads are better than his one-half of 1 percent personal conversion rate and that this agent, like most, doesn't know how to control, convert, and commit the leads. It is also quite likely a combination of both.

═══════════════════════

I have a client in Toronto, Canada, who is one of the best agents in North America. He has built a wonderful business with a large volume of production and a solid team. He has 11 buyer's agents who work for him. Soon after we began working together, we evaluated the numbers and ratios of his buyer's agents from the previous year. In that year, 5,537 of the team-generated leads indicated some level of interest to buy. They closed 276 transactions on the buyer side from those leads. Again, I instantly reached for my calculator and found that their conversion ratio was less than 5 percent.

During our discussion, I asked my client what he needed to do to increase his sales by the desired 100 units in the next year. (I didn't share with him the conversion number I had just calculated.) He said, "I will need to increase my leads by roughly 30 percent." That would be the natural response from most agents, even great ones. However, why process, manage, pay to create, mail, e-mail, and invest staff time to deal with 30 percent more leads when there is a better way? When I asked him if there was another way, he was stumped. I said to him, "That's why you pay me the big bucks!" I shared with him that if we raised the conversion ratio a little less than 2 percent, he could add 100 units to his sales volume without the additional cost to generate another 1,661 leads.

═══════════════════════

This agent's situation was certainly much better than the "magic guy" example, but it isn't where we should be as salespeople. To have that many leads with that low of a conversion rate is really unacceptable. (My client agreed.) The truth is, most agents don't know the number of leads they generate, much less the conversion percentage of those leads. They have no idea what is really working in their business because they don't source or track their leads well.

Champion Rule:	*Each lead costs money to create.*

Leads Cost Money

Don't think for a moment that there is not a cost attached to each and every lead generated. There are costs to acquire that lead in advertising, marketing, your time, and so on. No matter the source of your lead, there is a cost. You can determine your hard costs to generate a lead by tracking the dollars invested to create leads and dividing that by the number of leads you create annually. That's just the per-lead cost to create it. Then, to convert that lead, you have to manage it, track it, call it, and send stuff to it.

Just think of the investment you have in each lead—and my client thought he needed 1,611 more of them. Actually, all we had to do was increase his conversion rate by 2 percent to reach his goal. It was a measly 2 percent! We could and did do that—and more.

I had him give me one more number that clinched it. I asked him for the conversion rate of his team's buyer interviews versus their closed buyer transactions. In other words, how many interviews did they conduct and how many sales did they make? The worst buyer's agent had a 46 percent close rate; the best buyer's agent had a 68 percent close rate. All the others were somewhere in between. So the team had a less than 5 percent conversion rate for leads, yet a close rate above 50 percent, on average, once they had face-to-face prospects. The barrier for most agents isn't lead generation, it's lead conversion from the initial contact to the face-to-face meeting.

I would venture to say that wherever you are in your career today (whether you are a new agent, struggling, or trying to break through to the Champion level), you can easily achieve a 50 percent conversion rate once you are face-to-face with a buyer or seller. Leads are the lifeblood of your business, but managing, controlling, and converting them to face-to-face meetings is the heart muscle of your business. (See Figure 7.1.)

The ability to define, categorize, systemize, follow-up, control, manage, process, convert, and commit the lead is far more valuable and far more challenging than creating it in the first place.

Lead Conversion

The first step to higher lead conversion is developing a better definition of what a lead is. What's the criterion of a lead for you? Is it a specific time frame or level of motivation? Is this a subjective or a predetermined scale you use? For most agents, a lead is considered any human being who can fog a mirror when it's held up to his or her mouth—basically, anybody and everybody. Such a broad category precludes ever reaching the Champion Agent level.

Champion Rule: *The leads you have in your database are in other agents' databases as well. Whoever calls them and meets with them first wins the game.*

©2006 Real Estate Champions, Inc.

Figure 7.1 Lead Mastery Sales Cycle Flowchart

Too many of us are investing our time and money trying to convince any and every lead to turn into a good lead. In effect, we say, "Oh, please, Mister Lead, if I work with you long enough, won't you turn into a good lead, because I really don't want to have to prospect, and I need to make my mortgage payment next month." Are you trying to turn bad leads into good leads, or are you looking for good leads? It's almost as if we are trying to water dead plants in hopes of resurrecting them. They are dead . . . move on! What is the quality of your leads right now? What would someone pay to buy your leads? If the answer is "not much" . . . then, Houston, we have a problem.

Competitive Marketplace

This, my friends, is the truth of our business. For some reason, many agents haven't come to grips with this concept. We think somehow we are the only agent who knows about this prospect's desire to buy or sell. This is particularly true of agents who work exclusively by referral. You are making a huge mistake in today's competitive market if you feel that you have the inside track or noncompetition track. Couldn't another friend have referred them to someone else? Isn't it possible that they searched the Internet and got information from other agents? Could they have been out to an open house?

Lead Follow-Up

Effective lead follow-up is like threshing wheat at harvest in ancient times. Threshing is, essentially, separating the wheat from the chaff. The good kernels of wheat would be removed and used for food, while the chaff would be blown away in the wind. If you aren't actively threshing your leads, you will become complacent. Too many leads can cause lead complacency. Too many leads can be a bad thing. You did read that right. Too many leads can be bad!

An overabundance of leads can initiate complacency in your prospecting. You can stop or slow the flow of new leads by reducing your prospecting because you feel comfortable that you have a certain number of leads (50, 100, 1,000, whatever the number may be). You may feel that you don't need to prospect today because you have enough. However, how much chaff do you have? It's going to take a lot of effort to find out.

―――――――――――――

When I started working with a particular client a few years ago, I asked him how many leads he had who wanted to buy and sell in the next six months. He said he had 247 that fit into that category. He was proud of himself, yet I found out he had not talked with them in a while, and he hadn't been prospecting because of this volume of leads. His attitude was, "I don't need to; I have 247 leads."

I asked him to call all 247 in the next two weeks and request an appointment. If they were not ready to list or buy, he was to set an appointment with them anyway to move the relationship along, so he could secure them as future clients. Two weeks later, the first thing out of his mouth before hello was, "I have 59 leads." He dumped over 182 leads that were junk. He realized he needed to prospect to create new leads every day.

―――――――――――――

Seven Rules for Lead Follow-Up

1. *Lead follow-up is really a disqualification process.* Your objective should be to disqualify people from doing business with you by evaluating their probability of conversion against a predetermined set of standards and criteria. You have to be willing to let go of poor leads to invest your time in creating, securing, and converting good ones.

2. *A no is as good as a yes.* The truth is, there are only three possible responses that a prospect can express. Those responses are yes, no, and maybe. The killer time and energy waster is *maybe.* We often beat ourselves up when we don't convert a high enough percentage of maybes. However, I would rather get a no today than a maybe. In my studies, most low-grade maybes eventually turn into nos. People need to be able to say no, and then we can move on. A no is as good as a yes, because the uncertainty in both cases is removed.

3. *A low-probability prospect is worse than no prospect at all.* When you have low-probability prospects, you work them in hopes of changing them. When you have no prospects, you go out and search for new ones. When you seek you will find. The part most people forget to do is seek.

4. *Don't waste your resources on low-probability prospects.* You invest large amounts of time, money, energy, and emotion to work with your leads. Some leads require more of these resources to convert than others. The lowest-probability prospects are the worst.

5. *Remove the lead and terminate the conversation if you can't gain movement or commitment from the prospect.* If you are not moving the prospect closer to a face-to-face appointment, you are losing the game. If you know that the timing isn't right to book the appointment now, get off the phone. If there is some motivation, call back in a few days or a week and try again. Being on the phone with someone for 20 minutes to book an appointment is too long. The longer the call goes on beyond 5 to 10 minutes, the lower the chance you will secure the appointment.

6. *Invest time only in high-probability prospects.* The most significant cost in an agent's business isn't the broker, advertising, marketing, car, or anything else. It's the opportunity cost of investing time in the wrong person and forgoing the income you could have earned by working with someone else who would have generated a commission check. The opportunity cost is the largest cost in your business.

7. *When people think that you are willing to take no as an answer, they are willing to talk with you.* Consumers fear being talked into buying something from a salesperson. They believe that trainers teach salespeople verbal judo in order to pin them to the mat. The best approach is to let the prospect know up front that it's okay to say no. You won't be offended if the right answer for the prospect is no. Your scripts must be designed to give the prospect the ability to say no early in the conversation.

Objectives of Lead Follow-Up

Determine the value of the lead.   It boils down to how much, how soon, and how much effort. The amount of effort contains two parts. How much effort is needed to get the lead to the committed-client level, and how much effort is needed to serve the prospect to a high level of satisfaction so that he or she buys and is delighted with your service?

Determine the need, want, and ability to afford your service.   Does the prospect have a demonstrated need? Is there a gap between what he or she wants and the current home situation? Is the prospect seeking assistance? Is there a desire to change, or is it a want or wish? Does the prospect have the ability to proceed? (This usually relates to financial equity, down payment, credit score, and employment.) Does the prospect want someone's help?

Too often, we as agents try to determine the interest of the prospect. Don't be fooled into thinking that interest has any value to you as a salesperson. The prospect's level of interest is meaningless. What matters is this: Does the prospect need it and want it, and can the prospect afford to take action?

Champion Example

I have interest in securing more real estate. I am always looking to buy more. My interest is in securing property for 70 percent or less of fair market value. How valuable is my interest to you now? I would be happy if you called me to tell me about properties you have that meet that criteria. (The truth is if you find that type of opportunity, you'd better be buying it yourself, not selling it to me.)

When someone says he or she is interested, it's a short way to say, "If you could sell my home for $50,000 above market value and find me a home to buy for $50,000 below market value, I would let you represent me on those transactions."

Categorize the lead.   This is where a lot of agents stumble. They don't have a clean categorization process. They don't have the ability to see the inventory of leads they currently have in their possession. Most agents categorize leads based on time frame. I think that is the right approach, but it is only half the equation. You might create categories (e.g., A leads could be those who will act in 30 days or less, B leads those who will act in 30 to 90 days). You could can create four or five categories like these.

Commitment. The real question, beyond time frame, has not been factored into this typical type of system. The real question is about *commitment.* How committed is this person to working with you? How committed are your leads to giving you at least an interview to represent their interests? Committed to me means that I would bet big money on these people. I would bet my car, my house, all of my possessions that they would give me an interview or that they would list or buy with me. Someone in that category has great value to me and my business. However, not everyone is in that category.

Probability. The next category would be those who will *probably* do business with me. A probability is something that happens 51 percent or more of the time. I know there's a wide

Urgency to take action   (A, B, C, D)
Commitment to you   (1, 2, 3)

A—Will take action within 30 days
    1—Committed to you
    2—Probably with you
    3—Possibly with you

B—Will probably take action within 30–120 days
    1—Committed to you
    2—Probably with you
    3—Possibly with you

C—Will probably take action within 120–360 days
    1—Committed to you
    2—Probably with you
    3—Possibly with you

D—Will possibly take action sometime
    1—Committed to you
    2—Probably with you
    3—Possibly with you

<u>Committed</u> means you would bet big money on it
<u>Probably</u> means better than 51% chance of it
<u>Possibly</u> means 1% to 50% chance of it

    Follow-up activity should be based on accurate assessment of conversion probability
©2006 Real Estate Champions, Inc.

Figure 7.2 Accurately Assessing Prospect Conversion Probability

gap between 51 percent and the committed level of 98 percent. People make a lot of money on probabilities, because the odds are in their favor. Casinos play the probability game, and so should you.

Possibility.   The last category is a *possibility,* which is something that is a 50/50 chance or less. It could be only a 1 percent chance—still a possibility, but you'd better have a plan B if you are going to operate with such low odds.

Figure 7.2 will help you assess the likelihood of your prospect conversion. Your follow-up plans need to be designed on your ability to accurately assess the conversion probability of the prospect. If you can combine the typical agent's letter-based time frame categorization (A, B, C, D, etc.) with the commitment scale (1 being committed to you, 2 being probably with you, 3 being possibly with you), you will have a process that will enable you to maximize the return on your time, energy, and effort to increase your conversion rate and income. By tracking these different categories of leads, you will achieve a clear picture of the health of your business. To have a healthy business, you must have a reasonable level of leads in each category. You need to cultivate leads upward from long-term leads to short-term. You need to move leads from the possibility level to the probability level quickly. If you can't move them to at least the probability level quickly, the odds are too long; refer them to another agent (who is willing to invest time and accept the high burnout rate on these leads).

C H A P T E R

Who Wants Referrals?
I Do, I Do!

Every salesperson I have ever met wants to build a referral-based business. Too often, what he or she really wants is to build an *easy* business. While building a referral-based business is the best approach to long-term sales success, doing it right and for maximum benefit and reward is far from a work-free existence. You can do nothing but send mail to your clients and earn a reasonable income if your database is large enough. However, you're not tapping into the full extent of the business that is available by executing a Champion Agent's referral strategy.

Three Golden Rules of Referrals

In order to rise to the Champion Agent level, you must build or generate at least 30 percent of your revenue from referrals. You can easily do that by providing outstanding service, segmenting your databases, and leveraging your referral relationships.

Provide Outstanding Service So You Are Referable

There is a direct connection between service and referrals. Outstanding service is really the first step to generating referrals. (It doesn't guarantee you will get referrals, but you won't get referrals without it.)

There is a unique problem in the real estate industry with the way we are paid for the services we provide. Much of the service we provide to consumers is not tangible. We do it behind the scenes, without them ever knowing it. Champion Agents invest time to know the marketplace and to increase their skill. Consumers never see that. They only know when an agent falls short, because the service level drops.

Assess your client's service needs.   To achieve referability, you must service the client after the sale. You must be in constant communication with your past clients and sphere through mail, e-mail, phone, and in person. You can't neglect raising your referability by methods such as after-sale service of market trends reports, interest rate updates, and regular valuation services (at least every few years) of how their home has appreciated.

One of the ways to increase referrals is to determine the prospect's and client's expectations early. Our job as salespeople is to explore. Explore the client's needs, wants, desires, and expectations. Most agents spend too much time trying to pinpoint clients' tangible (i.e., home) wants and needs and not enough time determining their intangible (i.e., service) wants. Who defines outstanding customer service? In the end, the customers and clients do! Most agents think a client merely wants to buy a home or to sell a house. Those end results may be the finish line, but there are a number of ways to arrive there. If they are looking to arrive in service style, you'd better sell them Mercedes-level service. If they are more utilitarian buyers and sellers, Kia-level service will do. Here are some effective questions to ask to assess their service wants and needs:

- What do you expect from the agent you choose to work with?
- What are the top three services I could provide that would add value when working with you?
- How frequently and by what method do you want me to communicate with you? (According to a number of studies by NAR, the most common complaint from consumers about agents is frequency of communication. Find out how often you need to talk with your clients.)
- If you've worked with other agents in the past, what did you like best about them, and what did you like least?

The never-ending thank you.   One small nicety is to tell your clients thank you. When was the last time your insurance agent, attorney, dry cleaner, or even the gas station attendant said thank you when you used their services? All consumers (including real estate agents and our clients) have lots of people to choose from to perform the service required.

Put your thanks in handwritten thank you notes. These clients are the people who put gas in your car, shoes on your kids' feet, dollars in your retirement account, and provide memorable vacations with your family. Because of our rushed lives, instant world of e-mail, mailboxes stuffed with junk, and the no-call list, the handwritten thank you note carries more power than ever before. Don't neglect to use one of the most powerful marketing techniques available . . . the handwritten thank you note.

Segment Your Database: Mine for Gold

You need to identify the people with the highest referral potential. Don't waste your resources by treating everyone in your database the same. Divide your database info into four segments, not by source but by probability of referral, by the level of connection you had with the client and the likelihood of regular referrals from the client. Evaluate the people in your database first by these following traits:

- People who previously have sent you referrals—even if those referrals didn't create a commission check
- People you liked to work with and who really liked you
- People who understand your need for business referrals
- People who were delighted with your service

People who get an affirmative response in the majority of these questions should be considered your top-tier referral sources. You might call that group the Platinum Club. This is your best group of referral alliances and referral partners. The key to this group is regular, personal interaction with you.

I believe that establishing a monthly mailing or e-mail newsletter should be done for all of the people in your past client or sphere database. The baseline of mailing or e-mailing something to everyone monthly is really a minimum standard. In addition, sending a quarterly market trends report establishes your position as an expert they can go to for real estate advice. All levels of people in your database need these services. The personal interaction from you (frequency of calls and handwritten notes, birthday cards, anniversary cards, Christmas cards, calendars, and all other forms of marketing and personal promotion) is how you differentiate among the four levels of clients and sphere.

Platinum-level clients. The Platinum Club is the highest level. I recommend a call at least every other month to this group, but once a month is even better. Call them until you reach them or call and leave messages at least three times for that month. Most agents are painfully inconsistent in executing calls to their past clients and sphere. (Earlier, you learned about the four rules of business expansion. This is clearly rule 1—protecting what you've got.)

Gold-level clients. Your second tier of Gold Club clients are the people who answered about half of your questions affirmatively. You will have to work over an extended period of time to rev up their referrals. This group will usually produce about half the referrals of the Platinum Club.

Your contact frequency with this group should be quarterly. Talking with them or leaving a voice-mail message to update them or just to say hello will be effective. Leaving a voice mail for the people in this group is acceptable for up to 50 percent of your calls in a year; however, remember that the Gold-level group is still a solid source of referrals.

Silver-level clients.   These people provide less than a 50 percent possibility of getting a referral. This group may refer someday, but the jury is still out regarding when and if. Nonetheless, these people still deserve your attention and follow-up.

You need to understand that their excitement will be muted. They might be people who struggle to give referrals to anyone, no matter what the quality of service. Often, they can be demanding in their expectation of service, and that puts the brakes on their willingness to share referrals with others.

Bronze-level clients.   This is the catch-all bucket for the rest. The referral value is minuscule, but you could do another transaction with them in the future. With the average consumer moving every eight years, if you have 40 people in this category, you should expect five transactions a year from this group. They are probably worth the mail and e-mail contact. You might make one personal call a year to check in with them.

Leverage Your Referral Relationships

Too many agents are "secret agents" to the people they know. You need to establish referral relationships with the people in church, at the athletic club, and at the kids' sports events. You need to leverage the relationships you have by communicating what you do. In your everyday life, you come in frequent contact with people you can add to your contact list.

As you move forward, set a high standard for the quality of your service and communication with these new people. In addition, set a low standard for a quick payoff. You have to plant, water, and protect these acquaintances before you can expect a referral garden. You must be willing to be both persistent and patient.

Generate Referrals from People You Know

Some of us view asking for referrals as bothering a client. You need to approach the referral process with the correct mindset, the right skills, and the proper timing. Some of selling is being there at the right time. The same is true for referrals.

Respect the Referral Process

My friend Bill Cates, the "referral coach" and author of the book *Ultimate Referrals,* taught me this: *Referrals are hallowed territory.* You are entering the domain of another person's most valued relationships. You are asking for access to his or her most intimate personal space and relationships. This is holy ground you are asking to tread on.

Don't merely use a throwaway line like "oh, by the way" before you ask for the referral. This tactic cheapens the referral process rather than raising it to the high level of honor and respect it deserves. The client can see right through this cheap technique. A quality referral request should take at least 5 minutes, and 10 would be better. I learned from Bill Cates to frame the referral request with the statement, "I have a very important question to ask you." This technique will force a pause, build anticipation, and set the tone for a valuable conversation.

Ask for Help

A referral is a request for assistance. You are asking your past clients, current clients, and sphere for help. "I value your help" or "I need your help" are key phrases to open the referral floodgate.

Ask Permission

You want to ask permission to explore people they know who might benefit from your service. You are asking permission to access areas of their life. You are trying to discover friends and associates you might be able to help. You can ask permission to explore using a script like this one:

> *"I'm delighted that I've been able to serve you. I am wondering about others you might know in your life who would also benefit from my service. Could we explore for a few minutes who else we might be able to serve?"*

The final segment of the script is the Champion segment. It is telling them you need a little time together to probe and think about who they know. Too often, we bring up the subject and then give our source the chore of thinking up names. Most people who are referral sources or referral alliances don't want to work that hard. They will work that hard with you, but not alone. Be willing to come alongside and help them. This will increase the quality, quantity, and frequency of the referrals you receive.

Be Specific

This rule is the most frequently forgotten. We have been taught to make a general referral request. We use general language like, "Who do you know that might want to buy or sell real estate?" This approach is akin to the department store clerk who asks, "May I help you?" The clerk, well over 90 percent of the time, receives what is called the "reflex no." It's the automated response we use when we, as consumers, are on autopilot. Let me give you a hint, autopilot customers are not good for salespeople. An autopilot or reflex response to that clerk would be, "No, just looking." How many times have you said that to clerks to get rid of them?

Coach's Tip: *We coach our Champion Agents to collect a profile on each client in key areas. This accomplishes two things. First, it gives you questions and areas to discuss during your personal calls to them. I get asked all the time, "Okay, I will call my clients and past clients, but what do I say?" Treat them like a friend, and see how they are doing. Then tell them something relevant in the real estate marketplace like interest rate increases, inventory level changes, appreciation results, investment opportunities. It's easier to talk with people when you know their interests.*

Focus the referral request by narrowing the field of choices. If you give people the whole world to choose from, it's easier for them to say no. Explore with them in niches or areas of their lives in which they have relationships. Ask them about people in their immediate family, their small group at church, the people in their department at work, Bobby's soccer team, Susie's second-grade class. If they are involved in social service organizations or clubs, have them pull out the roster and invest some time talking about the names on the list.

Figure 8.1 is a form we use with our coaching clients: 19 questions to ask your referral sources (over time) to increase intimacy. When you ask them about certain areas of their lives, it's easier to explore and create referrals in that area. You will feel more comfortable asking for referrals, *and* they will feel more comfortable sharing referrals.

If you really want to be a Champion, I have one more step for you. Have your computer technician program these fields into your database management software with space to type in responses. When you are talking with the client, you can record the responses in your CRM program. Doing this will increase the ease of use dramatically.

Your assistants and buyer's agents can access the information as well. You can train them to use the information to create a connection with the client while they are servicing them. Imagine the warm feelings you as a client would have about selecting the right agent and team to represent your interests when the listing coordinator asks how Bobby's soccer

Our desire is to provide ongoing value and service to our clients. That commitment extends far beyond the closing of our initial transaction. We firmly believe we are in a long-term service relationship with each of our clients. We are focused on being a service provider for you and your family for life. With that in mind, we would ask you to spend a few minutes completing our Platinum Client Profile. We look forward to providing you, your family and friends our Platinum service for life.

Date_____

Customer

1. Customer's name? _____

   Does s/he use nickname?_____

2. Company name?_____

3. Company address? _____

   Home address? _____

4. Telephone numbers? (Which is best to reach at?)

   Business: _____   Home: _____

5. Date of birth?_____

   Place of birth? _____

   Hometown? _____

Education

6. High school?_____

   Year graduated _____

   Attend college? Which one? _____

   Year graduated _____

7. Did you belong to any college fraternity/sorority? If so, which one?_____

   _____

8. Did you participate in sports? _____

   _____

Family

9. Spouse's name and occupation?_____

   _____

10. Spouse's education?_____

    _____

©2006 Real Estate Champions, Inc.

Figure 8.1 Real Estate Champions Client Profile

11. What are spouse's interests? _____

_____

12. When is your anniversary? _____

13. Do you have children? If yes, names/ages? _____

_____

_____

_____

14. What are your children's education levels? _____

_____

_____

_____

15. Children's interests? (hobbies, problems, etc.) _____

_____

_____

_____

Special Interests

16. Do you belong to any clubs, fraternal associations, or service clubs? (Masons, Kiwanis, etc.)

_____

17. Are you active in your community? How? _____

_____

Lifestyle

18. What is your favorite place for lunch? _____

_____

What is your favorite place for dinner? _____

_____

19. Do you enjoy spectator sports? If so, which sports and teams? _____

_____

_____

©2006 Real Estate Champions, Inc.

Figure 8.1 Real Estate Champions Client Profile *(Continued)*

team is doing or, a year after the move, when you call to inquire about a misplaced document, asks if you have been playing much golf. The typical client appreciates this kind of personal interest.

Create Your Referral Strategy

There should be a well-defined and well-developed strategy for each segment of your business. For example, if you currently generate a lot of business from referrals, or hope to, you must spend the time to create and implement your strategy.

Most agents rely too heavily on the mailing strategy: mailers such as calendars, recipe cards, football schedules, and other so called items of value. Marketing for referrals through what I call the "trash-and-trinket strategy" is only marginally effective. It falls far short of the personal phone calls or visits that allow you to make a person-to-person request for referrals. When creating your referral strategy, you must realize that people send referrals for a number of reasons that are personal to them. The following two reasons are usually high on most people's lists of reasons:

1. *Trust and friendship.* Most people are willing to help people that they trust and like. If you have done a wonderful job for them, they will send you future business if you ask. Share your goals and vision for your business with these people, and they will help you even more. If they can catch your passion and enthusiasm and see how they can help you with your dreams, you will create a valuable referral source. You can elevate them to a level where they feel a vested interest in helping you achieve more success.

2. *Desire to be Champions for others.* When you deliver world-class service and the outcome or result meets or exceeds the expectations of the client, your benefit beyond the commission you earn is that you create clients who are willing to champion or promote your business. These people know the quality of your performance and service firsthand. They know the service quality that their family and friends will receive is very high. They become heroes to those people for connecting the parties together.

Your Strategy Must Be Balanced

Another strategy that many agents are trying to achieve is a 100 percent referral-based business. That strategy seems to be very popular currently. We profess to be "by referral only," as though that adds cachet and enhances our worth or value in the marketplace. Let me be honest, that stance comes from the sales trainers who teach referrals as a marketing strategy in order to sell more tickets to their seminars. If that is a primary focus of your business strategy, there is danger lurking.

Relying entirely on referrals for new clients is a very narrow, exclusive, and unbalanced approach to business. You leave yourself, your business, and your revenue extremely vulnerable to the changes in the marketplace. When real estate is appreciating at a rapid rate and home equity is growing quickly, it's easy to generate a lot of referrals.

However, when the markets return to normal levels or below, referral volume will drop dramatically, because everyone in the world isn't a potential buyer or seller. This same phenomenon happened in the late 1990s, with the dot-com stocks. Everyone was talking about how much money they were making on Internet stocks; everyone had a piece of the dot-com explosion. Then the bottom fell out, and everyone moved back to the blue chip stocks. Referrals will increase when people want to sell and buy more for the frenzy of investment purposes than for a home to live in. We the market normalizes the referral numbers will decrease.

It's a poor business decision to put all your eggs in one basket. Solid businesses have multiple lead generation areas and multiple customer types to whom they sell their products and services. If you don't have some level of diversity, something bad can (and probably will) happen. Look at Delphi industries in 2005. A large multi-billion-dollar company that manufactures automotive parts, Delphi's primary client is General Motors. General Motors accounts for over 70 percent of Delphi's gross sales receipts. When GM fell on hard times, Delphi had to declare bankruptcy, because its biggest source of business revenue dropped significantly. The parallel between Delphi and the 100 percent referral agent is startling.

If your referrals decline, you won't have other prospecting or marketing systems in place. The trouble you will experience will come fast. The referral gurus don't bother to reveal these truths, because it would be bad for their business. Your strategy must be balanced.

Strategy Must Be Customer-Focused

Finally, your strategy must focus on sellers. The 100 percent referral strategy without a seller focus as well will tip your business to the buyer side. You will end up with more transactions from buyers than sellers. You will generate more buyer leads and buyer transactions through referral sources. Most consumers view agents as people who drive customers around in cars to sell a house. They don't view us as salespeople who represent their interests in the sale, marketing, exposure, and market evaluation to maximize equity to clients.

I have analyzed hundred of agents' businesses and tracked their numbers. When you evaluate the referral segment of the business, it produces more buyers than sellers by at least two to one, sometimes approaching four or five to one. To become a Champion Agent with the earnings and quality of life you want, you can't have four or five buyers to one seller—or even two to one. You must begin to focus your referral requests to securing sellers. The referral pillar of your business should be the strongest and should create the best-quality leads and the most transactions over all other sources. (But it can't be the only source, as many agents are trying to make it.)

Evaluate the Value of Your Prospects, Clients, and Sphere

Besides segmenting your database into the Platinum, Gold, Silver, and Bronze levels, you must evaluate other areas to ensure you are maximizing your referral sources.

The Couple

In a typical real estate transaction, you represent the interests of a husband and wife. You also represent other couple-related people. Most transactions involve two buyers and two sellers. The fact that there are two people on each side of the transaction is significant. It creates two past clients whom you personally represented. You must call, interact, and ask for referrals from both of them. If you talk to only one, which happens most of the time, you could be getting far less than 50 percent of the referrals these couples have.

If you examine the value of a couple, one person will generally have more value than the other. For example, my referral value is significantly less than Joan's. I know a lot of people, but they are all over the country. My career and business allow me to meet high-powered people like you everywhere in the world, but fewer in Bend, Oregon, where I live. Joan, on the other hand, volunteers at Wesley's school, leads a Tuesday morning group Bible study in our church, and is a leader of women's ministries in our church, which serves nearly 500 women. It seems to me she knows everyone. I am constantly being introduced to people in my town as Joan's husband. It's great! Anonymity has it's privileges. I am about as worthless to a local real estate agent as one can be for referrals. If agents talk with me instead of Joan, they are missing out on a whole lot of business. I shouldn't be ignored, but to talk with me every month or every quarter would be a waste.

As agents, we need to evaluate the value of each person in the couple and make sure we are calling based on his or her value. In addition, with the divorce rate exceeding 50 percent, we need to build a relationship with both people. You don't want to lose a listing because you are viewed as strictly the wife's agent or strictly the husband's agent.

The Behavioral Style

Our client's behavioral style determines the quality and quantity of the leads. Some behavioral styles are more introverted than extroverted. Some have almost unreachable standards for service; others are much more lax. Some people, because of their behavioral style, are people-oriented, and some people are task- or objective-oriented.

Coach's Tip: *To better understand how to recognize people's behavioral style and "read" them through their body language, tone, pace of speech, and even the words they use in talking, go to our Web site at www.RealEstate Champions.com; we have a number of programs that specialize in this area. You will raise your sales performance by 25 to 50 percent by knowing how to behaviorally align your prospecting, lead follow-up, and presentations. You may also take a free behavioral assessment to help you understand your own behavioral style at www.RealEstate Champions.com/DISC.*

The best referral source is a high influencer. They are people-oriented; they know more people than anyone else. They seek the limelight and champion their friends and service providers to their other friends. In their world, *everyone* is a friend, some of whom they just haven't met yet. These types create the greatest quality and volume of leads.

Influential Positions

You need to evaluate your referral strategy based on your clients' positions in their company and organizations they belong to. For example, a human resources director of a large company is an extremely influential and valuable person to generate referrals. To be able to know the people who are transferring in or out, or people who receive promotions, would definitely add dollars to your pocket. You need to understand that the influential positions of referral sources can increase the volume of referrals.

Work Your List for Revenue

The most effective strategy in sales is to send, call, and see. You should be sending something at least monthly. Call your sources on a set schedule based on the category. See them periodically in person to enhance the relationship. A Champion technique is to coordinate these activities. Too many agents send out their monthly mail in bulk. The problem with that is, by the end of the month, when you are making your final calls, the clients have no idea what you sent them. They don't remember.

> **Champion Rule:** *Mail out this week only to those you can call next week.*

You want to coordinate a one-two punch to your clients. This ensures a better bang for the marketing dollar and better return on investment for the call. It will also create an opening for the phone call in case you are challenged by how to begin.

> **Champion Rule:** *Build referral relationships with your current clients.*

Current Customers Are Your Best Source of Referrals

Current clients are the most forgotten source of referrals. We often wait to establish the referral relationship until a few weeks after we are down the road with them. You can get referrals the night you list the home. I have done it a handful of times. In a marketplace that is challenging and tough, where the client will probably realize less profit then they had hoped, get the referrals now. Later they may not be happy with the outcome, through no fault of your own. The market might dictate the negative feelings. It's never too early to begin building referral relationships. You can start during the first meeting or phone call with any prospect, using a script such as:

> *"Fred, I build my business primarily based on referrals from clients. The benefit to you is my focus will always be to give you the best service possible. The reason is I want to earn the honor to talk with you in the future about who you know that would benefit from my service. The only way I deserve to have that conversation is based on the job I do for you. I know that if you are delighted with my service, you will want to help me and your friends out."*

Ask them for referrals during the course of the transaction. Practically every conversation in their life is about the home they are buying or selling. They are talking about real estate as much as we are. Don't neglect to call them a number of times right after the closing. The most fertile time for referrals is from the time they decide to buy or sell up until around 45 to 60 days after the close.

> **Coach's Tip:** *Call them at least four times in the first thirty days after they close. Remember, in their view, every call you made up until closing was because you wanted to get paid. Every call after you close is because you care.*

| **Champion Rule:** | *Implement a strategy to upgrade your referrals.* |

Explode Your Referral Business

Developing a strategy to upgrade your referrals can really explode your referral business. Most salespeople get the name and contact information and then try to get off the phone immediately to call the prospect. That is a significant mistake. Follow these steps to increase the odds of your success.

Immediately thank the referral source.   Assure your sources of the quality service their referral will receive. You are giving them your personal guarantee. Before the close of the business, today, handwrite a thank you note. You can use gifts or other inducements as well, but with the handwritten note, you don't necessarily need them.

Determine the quality or level of the referral.   You are trying to increase the probability of the referral. The first step is to secure more information before you make the first call. The first call is the point at which you will win these people over or not. Determine which of these four categories the referral will be.

> *C level.* This referral is the coldest variety. The conversion rate is at the lowest level. These referral sources have given only the name and phone number of a potential prospect. They have not allowed you to use their name to create an opening or connection.

> *B level.* I would describe this referral as lukewarm. The odds are improving, but still probably less than 50/50 conversion. These referrals have given you the prospect's name and phone number, and they have given you one thing the C level did not: permission to use their name as the referral source to open the door. That certainly helps the connection on the first call.

> *A level.* You are getting warmer with this referral. Again, you have the prospect's name and number, but you have also been granted permission to use the name of your referral source to open the dialogue door. The best part is that these sources give you time to ask questions. They are willing to give you 5 or 10 minutes to explore the referred individual, to probe and help increase the odds of connecting with the prospect.

> *AA level.* This is the level to shoot for. It's the Cadillac of referrals. It has all that the A level has and more. You have all the information that you have with an A, but these referral sources are willing to open the door for you themselves. They are willing to make an introduction call personally for you. This call doesn't replace your call.

It only makes it easier to call and raises the chance of a quicker positive result. You might find that a really effective referral source can set up a lunch or breakfast meeting with everyone involved.

Explore the following questions to increase your conversion odds of connecting with the referral individual. Invest time with the referral source. (This will take you only 5 to 10 minutes, but will be well worth the time.)

- How would you describe your relationship?
- How do you know this person?
- Is there anything that you can see that we have in common?
- What type of a personality will I encounter?
- What organizations does this person belong to?
- What are a few of this person's personal interests?

Thank your referral source again.   Once you have secured as much information as possible, again offer your assurance that you'll provide the same level of quality service that your referral source has received from you in the past.

Referrals Are Not Complicated

Success is simple; it's not complicated. Referrals aren't a complex system or strategy. Success in referrals is achieved through consistency of the fundamental process of client connection and client service. The truth about success is that sometimes it's better to hear something you have heard before but are not doing than to hear about something new. Make the commitment to execute the fundamentals in your referral section of your business. That objective will create the growth you desire.

It's Easy Street on the Internet

The Internet is one of the fastest-changing aspects in the real estate industry. There has been a massive shift in the marketing of properties away from print advertising to the Internet. We have seen a tidal wave of new businesses (good and bad) that have entered the real estate arena to help agents with the Internet.

However, here I want to share my view of the Internet technology explosion and what a Champion Agent must look for, evaluate, and implement to maintain a growing dominant position. I am not an Internet expert. I don't think I have to be, and neither should you. Having a reasonable level of knowledge about the Internet and hiring or working with the best people will get you there.

Coach's Tip: *If you want the best people on your side to really teach you to be effective in the cyberworld, the best place to go is the Real Estate Cyber Society, which has brought the greatest Internet strategies in the real estate area under one banner. This organization is the best and can be found at www.REcyber.com.*

The Internet as a Tool

The Internet is a great tool, and that is all it is—a tool. For some agents, it is an essential tool for their business success. For others, it is a very minor piece of the puzzle. There are a lot of ways to generate revenue in this business, and the Internet is one of those ways.

Use the Internet to generate leads that you can drive to a fundamental sales channel. Getting prospects to reveal their full contact information so that it takes the form of an inquiry is paramount. This allows you to call them back, which also raises the conversion ratios substantially. Additionally, you have that 90-day window of opportunity for future phone contact within the confines of the no-call laws. Most agents are chasing a lot of low-probability prospects through the Internet. They have an e-mail address and are sending property match searches daily. They have them on an electronic newsletter list. All of those methods are automated, so limited time is invested. However, limited reward is created as well.

The Internet was supposed to be the easy, miracle way to earn money. We are praying for miracle traffic to our site, miracle conversion of the leads, and miracle commission checks. We have people in the real estate arena selling the "miracle" everyday. Most agents' Web sites are little more than an electronic business card.

Generate Internet Prospects and Profits

The two main issues you face with the Internet are quality and quantity issues. You want to drive visitors to your site so you can increase the odds of generating leads from it. You want to increase the quality of the prospects so you can separate the really good buyers and sellers from all the rest. You want to achieve a reasonable conversion rate, which is much higher than the 0.5 to 1 percent you are now seeing via the Web.

There is a delicate balancing act in terms of quality and quantity. If you had to choose one, which would you choose to do first—quality or quantity? Before you select, let me tell you the truth of the Internet. The volume of traffic is important. At the end of the day, the one who has the most visitors usually wins. You may build a beautiful Web site, but you have to drive traffic to make money with the Internet.

Once you have traffic, you have to convince people to stay and leave a trail. You need for them to at least leave a trail of bread crumbs: their first name and e-mail address. You could send a couple thousand people to your site monthly and end up with two or three prospects. I am not talking about clients; I am talking only about prospects. You now have to do the work of moving them up the loyalty ladder to becoming a client by converting them from visitors to buyers.

You can do this by offering a free report, a newsletter, or something that a buyer or seller would deem valuable enough to give you at least their first name and e-mail address. You need to walk them up each step of the conversion track. With each level or step they take, your probability of earning a commission check grows. The object is to move the visitors to prospects, prospects to clients, and clients to referral sources. (See Figure 9.1.)

©2006 Real Estate Champions, Inc.

Figure 9.1 Conversion Track

The more complete contact information you can get people to leave, the higher the probability you can move them up to the client stage. More information increases the opportunity of moving them to a fundamental sales channel of send, call, see.

Third-Party Lead-Generation Companies

Third-party lead-generation companies are the biggest threat to agents. We need to drive them out of business. These interlopers are, in effect, marketing for your customers and selling them back to you or another agent in the marketplace. The approach of these "lead terrorists" is to cybersquat in the key areas on the Web—whether that's through search engine optimization techniques, pay-per-click advertising, or strategic links. If you go to any highly used search phrase like "Portland, Oregon, Real Estate" or "Denver, Colorado, Real Estate," you will see these third-party companies taking four, five, or even six of the top 10 positions in the search engines. In effect, we have allowed these interlopers to hold us hostage far too long. The major real estate brands, in the past year, have recognized how these lead kidnappers are affecting our business and we are starting to address the issue to take back the Internet leads. These lead-generation companies may seem to be our friends, but they are really our foes.

By working with these people, we are giving them credibility. In some cases, we are paying $100 apiece for a lead that usually has a very low conversion rate. If it took you even 25 leads to generate a transaction (actually, the numbers are probably higher), you would be investing $2,500 in that third-party interloper to get a transaction. If the gross commission for that transaction was $8,000, which would be a high average commission for most agents, you basically paid a 31 percent referral fee. The truth is, it's actually much worse than that.

It's worse because, when an agent sends you a referral, you both share in the risk. The other agent doesn't get paid until you get paid. Most interlopers charge by the lead or area. They want their money up front, whether it works or not. Some even require contracts. You are the one who is taking all the risk to work these leads, which are marginal at best.

Having to work 25 leads to convert one transaction (and that would be a good conversion rate) makes for very long odds. You would have better odds than that working FSBOs or expireds. You have to amortize all the costs: marketing, your efforts to do a competitive market analysis, or CMA (for one of these companies, you have to provide a house value to the prospective seller), and your time. Think of how long it takes to do a decent CMA and multiply that by 25 for just one commission check. It's called no net profit . . . "Big hat, no cattle."

Internet Strategies That Work

The first step to finding an Internet strategy that works for you is to establish which strategies you might have at your disposal. At the current time, I believe there are three viable strategies for real estate agents.

Company Image (Branding) Web Sites

Branding is a fairly standard term to marketers of all types. It basically means that you'd like to establish a memorable brand for your potential prospects and customers. Ideally, you'd like all of the people in your given market to think about you when they think about buying or selling a home.

There are a few factors associated with branding, however, that don't make it the best solution for 99.99 percent of real estate agents. First of all, it is *very* expensive. Second, it takes a very, *very* long time to establish. Finally, it is almost impossible to quantify the effectiveness of branding. All three of these difficulties are contrary to what most people think the Internet is all about—and rightly so. Branding, therefore, is not a very good choice for an agent on several fronts. However, I would actually suggest that every agent participate, to some extent, on a main company Web site that has the typical business card feel.

On the Internet, you can have a Web site up and running within days or even minutes for the cost of dinner with a loved one, and it will give you all kinds of data about your visitors. Basic requirements for this type of site would be a nice look, company logo, professionally placed photos of agents, bios of the agents, and several means of contact for the visitor. The main purpose of this type of Web site it to make it easy to reach you. Visitors to this site will likely be people who have your letterhead and want to contact you. You should send a lot of traffic there because its sole purpose is to show that you are legitimate and help the prospect or customer get in contact with you.

Property Information Web Sites

These types of sites are focused solely on one property and can be very effective in systematizing the sales process of individual properties. You can purchase these sites for as little as $30 per month for three individual addresses, or you can spend up to $99 per month per address. You must treat these sites as part of a sales and marketing process.

Let's say you have a house listed at 123 Main Street. You fire up one of these sites, and it allows you to include a virtual tour of the home, all the particulars about the home, all of your contact information, and many more details. The site, by itself, really has no value, but if you run a classified ad in the newspaper talking about the home and include the 123MainStreet.com link, now you've gotten somewhere.

The problem with these sites is that the prospect may make a negative decision based on a bad photo on the virtual tour or the fact that the paint color was wrong. You can't answer a prospect's objections, and you may never have the opportunity to even know his or her name.

So, these sites can be a valuable way for you to gain exposure for your properties, but the lead volume will likely be small—albeit, the leads will likely be good ones. Use this type of site as *part* of your arsenal, to gain exposure for specific properties.

Lead-Generation Web Sites

One of the biggest problems with the activities we find ourselves involved in as real estate agents is that we often forget why we are doing them. If I had only one choice for what a Web site would do for me, it would be to generate leads—not some leads, but a ton of them; not any leads, but very qualified (ready-to-do-business-with-me) leads.

This brings me to my favorite kind of Web site, the lead-generation Web site. The sole purpose of this site is to generate a large volume of a specific type of lead, whether for buyers or sellers.

This Web site is designed for a very targeted audience. This could be buyers and/or sellers of homes in Anytown, USA, or it could just be buyers and/or sellers in general. The narrower your focus, the more targeted your niche, the better. The best choice among the prior examples would be a site dedicated to *only* buyers or *only* sellers in Anytown, USA. How about buyer?

For buyers, you need to have the site loaded with content that is extremely valuable to only your target prospect. Let's say our site is geared toward buyers in Anytown, USA. The Web site must be focused solely on things that (1) are very valuable to buyers in Anytown, USA, and (2) will help buyers in Anytown, USA, to accomplish their objective, which is to buy a home in Anytown, USA.

The Art of Persuasion

One thing that I have to touch on lightly is that there is also an element of persuasion that must take place. Having high-value content for a targeted audience isn't enough by itself. You must, through persuasive sales copy and Web conversion elements, persuade the folks who visit your Web site to become prospects. For this, I recommend that you contract a good copywriter—preferably one who has Web site design experience. You can find them online at www.elance.com or any other contract labor source. The key is to find one that is good at persuasive copywriting and design for the Internet; those are the prerequisites for hiring. A great copywriter could make you hundreds or thousands of dollars for every dollar you spend. I know; I have one of the best on my staff.

Get the Customer to Interact

The goal is to interact with the visitors and have them leave a trail. You also want them to come back to your site again and again. They become more valuable with each return visit. It also increases the odds that they will leave a more recognizable trail.

Offer free reports.   Again, get them to take information that is valuable by offering free reports. Offer access to information (e.g., "The 10 Mistakes Sellers Make When Selling a Home"). Such a report lists mistakes and solutions for solving them. Someone who pulls that type of a report is at least considering a sale. Another report (e.g., "How to Guarantee You Get Your Home Sold and for the Highest Price Possible!") could lead them through the steps to ensure the sale at a top-dollar sales price. There are similar reports on the buyer's side as well.

> **Coach's Tip:** You *can get various free reports through most direct marketing companies. If you need some to get started, I have placed a handful on my Web site at www.RealEstateChampions .com/FreeReports.*

You are trying to generate a volume of leads at this point. Free reports are a good first point of contact. There are thousands of reports already produced, so don't sit down to write one.

Offer free newsletters. Free newsletters are also a very effective means of communication. There is immense power in having an e-mail list of people who read your material regularly. Your job is to provide value in that newsletter. I encourage you to do a newsletter monthly. Start with a generic version or template version.

Offer a consistent message. The ability to consistently communicate with an audience is extremely valuable. Some of my marketing results come from the consistency of the message delivery, as well as the message that is delivered. It's easier for an agent to be consistent if he or she starts with a template newsletter. Test it; evaluate how much or how little work it is, and see whether your people like it and read it. Then work up to a hybrid or combination newsletter, in which some material is your own and some is from a template. If that goes well, create your own newsletter.

Expand Your Reach in Cyberspace

If you sell real estate in a resort area, linking with agents who sell resort real estate in other areas can drive traffic. Linking with resort Web sites, tourism Web sites, and local chambers of commerce can help to drive traffic to your site. The objective is to link strategically to *increase your Web site traffic.*

Another strategy is to link to other sites and sources to *increase your search engine ranking.* There is a difference between quality and quantity. Search engines give weight to the relevancy of a link. If you go out and link to anyone and everyone, it probably will not be very beneficial. Your links should be focused on real estate and/or on your specific market area.

Search Engine Optimization

The goal for every agent should be to have a Web site that is optimized for the search engines. The value of being ranked high in the search engines continues to grow.

The major search engines of Google, Yahoo!, and MSN represent about 90 percent of all Internet search traffic. If you aren't ranked with them, you won't be found. If you are not on the front page with them, you won't be found. Most people do not go beyond the first page when they type in a particular search. In fact, even the first page is astounding. If you are number one on a search engine, you can expect to get about 40 percent of the people to click your link. If you are number two through number five, you can expect to share the next 40 percent. The rest go to the remainder of the first page. It pays to be number one. The next four ranked sites have to share the same traffic that the number one ranked site gets all to itself.

A word of caution—before you run out and hire someone to implement search engine optimization for your site, be careful! Implementing SEO strategy is tricky business. You need to make sure you are working with a reputable firm that will stand behind its work. You also can't have the philosophy of once and done—fix it once and it will last forever. Effective SEO strategy is never-ending. Everyone is fighting for that front-page position. It changes each day, so you have to work to maintain your ranking.

Coach's Tip: *If you're like me and recognize the value in finding a company that can sort through the techno-jive and deliver a turnkey solution so you can focus on what you do best (sell real estate), then I highly recommend visiting www.RealEstate WebsiteSEO.com. Say you're a referral from Dirk's book and that I sent you, and you'll not only get preferential treatment, you'll get a better price on this site's services.*

You also want to make sure that the SEO firm is using reputable techniques. A lot of firms use what the industry calls *black-hat tactics.* The problem with this strategy is that it's very short term. Once search engines find out you used black-hat tactics, they won't just drop your ranking, they will likely ban you. By that time, the SEO company has your money and you probably can't find them. Another trick is that SEO companies get you ranked in terms that no one searches for and that last only as long as it takes for you to figure out that you have zero Web traffic.

Pay Per Click, Not Pay Per Prospect

More and more agents are getting into pay-per-click as an answer to their online marketing. Pay-per-click advertising on the search engines and other sources can be effective, or it can be a bust. Most search engines have pay-per-click areas on the right-hand side of their Web site. People bid for the spots on a pay-per-click basis, which can range from a few cents to a few dollars each. The truth is, only about 10 percent of searchers go to the pay-per-click section. The vast majority of people use a search engine to search a specific phrase and then select the top-ranked sites to click on.

Keep in mind, you are not paying per prospect but *per click.* A click doesn't mean that you are going to get anything. Pay-per-click can be used effectively if you know the conversion numbers of your Web site, meaning you know how many people take a free report, sign up for your newsletter, ask for more information, identify themselves as a lead, or are willing to book an appointment with you once they get to the Web site. To make pay-per-click profitable, you need to know your numbers, both online and through your standard sales process. Until then, you will only be guessing whether it works and is profitable.

10

Creating Leads through Interactive Voice Response Systems

With the explosion of technology over the past 15 years, we have seen many new lead-generation systems come and go. However, interactive voice response (IVR) systems have stood the test of time in the past 10 years. They have become an important source of leads for Champion Agents. This type of system, when employed correctly, can quickly become part of your lead triad.

IVR Technology

Interactive voice response is a system that captures the phone number of an inbound caller to a predetermined phone number. The phone number is usually a toll-free number, and because you are paying for the call, you have a right to their phone number.

Within the toll-free number are extensions that are voice-mail boxes where you can record messages that the caller can access. You advertise your toll-free number everywhere you would normally advertise and market. This includes such things as your mailings, Web site, classified ads, and FSBOs or expireds campaigns. The goal is to create lead traffic in your system so you can capture phone numbers to call. More people will access information about homes if they can do it anonymously.

One of the reasons the Internet has had such explosive growth is that it allows prospects to be stealthy. The problem with stealthy prospects is that they are hard to convert. The conversion ratios on stealthy prospects without phone numbers is pretty dismal. You need to focus on creating leads that you can then transfer to a fundamental sales channel of calling, and IVR is one of the best technologies available to remove the stealth barrier between you and your prospects. Go to the website www.callcapturesuccess.com to look more closely at specific IVR services.

In addition, IVR produces more leads, because most prospects don't understand that they may get a call from a salesperson. The key word is *may.* I know too many agents who have IVR technology and call the leads back inconsistently at best. You won't convert leads without a call.

Leverage Leads

The volume of leads you generate from an ad in the newspaper or home magazine will usually increase fivefold when you use IVR technology. For example, if you would normally receive 5 calls on an ad, you will receive 25 when using an IVR system. All your ads direct prospects to the 800 number and the code. More people will call the recorded message because they think they won't have to talk with an agent. Using home magazines is also very effective with call-capture technology. The home magazine that has a one-month shelf life will often see a greater increase than the fivefold we see with classified ads. It is not uncommon for agents who have high-single-digit inventories of homes to get a couple hundred calls a month to their IVR system with the right marketing approach.

The system also generates leads and opportunities while you sleep. It's like having a 24-hour marketing department that churns out leads for you to follow up. More leads and 24-hour service sounds too good to be true. Of course, there are obstacles as well; it's not all rosy, but the benefits are significant.

A call-capture or IVR system is also valuable in the sense that it allows you to create leverage by accessing people on the federal do-not-call registry when these "do-not-call" prospects call your system about a home, your free reports, podcasts, or general real estate information. You can secure their number with the system. You then fall under the 90-day inquiry period provision of the law. This inquiry period allows you to contact the prospect for up to 90 days after the call was first made, even if the prospect is on the no-call list.

Specifically targeting people on the do-not-call registry is an effective strategy, because you know they are having limited personal contact with real estate agents. When you connect with a high-probability source like expireds, you have created a wonderful combination to generate listings. You are combining limited-access strategy with a high-probability prospect. You won't have much competition for the business, and you will be working with a prospect who has a demonstrated need.

By using the IVR technology, you also alleviate one hassle of the no-call registry—having to document that they called you first. Your IVR system takes care of noting when the first call was made. A word of caution when working people on the registry—the 90-day inquiry period can be cut short if they tell you not to call again. If they do that, you can't call them until they engage you again through your IVR system.

Work Out the Kinks

I think the biggest mistake agents make with the IVR technology is not contacting all the people who called in. We get busy, and we fail to schedule the time to return a prospect's call. It's as though the prospect called the office inquiring about a property, the reception-ist took a handwritten message, and we just don't call them back. I doubt you would do that, but countless agents, every day, fail to call their IVR leads.

One of the challenges with using IVR technology in your marketing is that the volume of leads increases without your being able to address the quality of the lead. If you ran a standard marketing page in a home magazine directing prospects to call you for more infor-mation, the number of callers would be less than with the IVR, but the quality would be higher. When people call a real estate agent's office, they are expecting to talk with a sales agent. The likelihood of them not being represented by an agent when they call in is very high. Your conversion ratio on that type of a lead should be very high as well. Ad calls and sign calls generate a higher probability (there I go again using that word *probability!*) of making the sale.

If you are driving everyone from your ads and signs to your IVR number, you are com-bining into one large pool of warm and cold leads most of the people who would have picked up the phone and called you directly. The only way to find those golden, high-probability leads is to call everyone who uses your IVR system. I required my buyer's agent to call them all—no matter what. I watched and monitored her progress in this area. I didn't want to lose the easy ones. They can get mixed in with the more challenging ones.

You must be careful not to focus solely on buyers who call in. Some buyers must sell as well. I have seen agents who secured the relationship with a buyer, but lost the buyer's listing because they forgot to ask for it. People will be calling who want to sell as well, especially if you integrate in your direct mail to sellers a call to action—to order your free market update report, or your strategy to achieve top market value for their home, or the 10 mistakes most sellers make when selling their home. All of these are drawing cards for sell-ers to call your IVR system. These are especially helpful when you are marketing to a tar-geted area, such as non-owner-occupied properties, first-time home buyers through rental lists, or any market you can segment. It's equally effective for expireds that are on the do not call list registry. If you can cause them to make an inquiry that allows you to call them back, you may be the only one who can follow up on them via phone.

Another mistake agents make is to leave long, rambling messages about their properties. For most of the IVR systems, you are charged by the minute. The longer your message, the more money you will spend to create the lead, whose number is captured in the first few seconds. A 10-minute message will only run up your monthly service bill.

Responsiveness Reaps Revenue

Calling all of the inquires back improves your odds. Calling them back close to the time they called you will improve your results as well. Getting a faxed printout of yesterday's or this week's captured numbers dramatically diminishes the return. Make sure you subscribe to a system that has an instant notification system. That way, when a phone number has been captured, the phone number and voice-mail box are sent to you instantly via your pager or your cell phone. E-mail notification is better, but falls far short of the cell phone pager notification. What if you are not at a computer to be able to retrieve the e-mail message? (If you use a BlackBerry or Treo, e-mail notification might work for you, since you carry that access with you.)

The best rule to follow in responsiveness is to call people back in less than 15 minutes, which increases the chance they are still at the phone number they called from. Do anything you can to raise your reach percentage. Act quickly!

A portion of these people might be startled by your quick response. In most cases, they are not expecting you to call. A number of techniques are effective in getting prospects to open up. Once you call them back, my favorite technique is what I call the *customer service call.* You approach them softly: "This is a customer service call to the person who recently called our real estate information line. Were you the person who called? How did you like the service? Did you get all of the information you needed?"

Once you get through those early questions, just move into a standard buyer script to convert the lead and book a face-to-face appointment. I really like the customer service call approach. It is softer and you will produce fewer negative responses, such as, "How the heck did you get my number?"

Creating leads through interactive voice response is an excellent way to increase leads generated and lead sources. It's also an effective strategy to help your buyer's agents increase their business. You produce more leads, so they can increase their income and skill. I would recommend the company at www.callcapturesuccess.com to serve your IVR needs. Most Champion Agents who are building a team and have buyer's agents swear by the value of their IVR system.

PART III

CHAMPION SALES PRESENTATIONS

11

The Champion Listing Presentation

Champion Agents use their listing presentation as the cornerstone of their business. Their sales and delivery enable them to separate themselves from the pack of imposters. They are able to convey their competitive points of difference and why they should be selected.

A little over 18 months ago, I created a teleseminar program titled "How to Get the Listing in a Tight Listing Market." We sold close to 400 seats to this program. As I was building the program, I determined that if the agents had better listing presentations, they would prospect more and prospect more consistently. Certainly, more prospecting would lead to more listings in any marketplace. Also, if their listing presentations were better, the agents would secure some of the listings they were currently losing to other agents.

In my effort to give more value to the program, I offered (off-the-cuff, which my staff went into a panic about) to listen to the listing presentation of anyone who would tape it and send it to me. I didn't care whether they role-played it with a friend or did it in front of a legitimate seller. If they sent me a tape, I would listen to it, critique it, and give them an hour with me personally coaching them about how to dramatically improve their presentation. My staff expected an onslaught of tapes to hit our office over the next two weeks. We had an office pool going. I won! I said I would get five of them, and I got four. Think about it: almost 400 people on the call, and only four people had the courage to challenge themselves to become better. I have found that Champion Agents are the people who are most honest with themselves. There is nothing more honest than taping your listing presentation. These tapes were from great agents; some of them were top agents in their marketplace. Here's the truth: their presentations were awful.

The Greatest Show on Earth

Your listing presentation can make or break your career. If it's really good, it shouldn't bother you to go toe-to-toe with any top agent in the marketplace. I felt confident that, even if another agent had the inside track through a referral, if I executed my preparation before the appointment, knew the stats of the other agents, clearly understood the client's expectations, and followed my presentation structure, I couldn't be beat. When I did lose, it was because an agent made a bad business decision to radically overprice or undercommission the property.

Making your presentation worth watching isn't about a snazzy PowerPoint presentation or taking a picture beforehand and bringing prospects a flyer. It isn't about recording a call-capture message about their property ahead of time so they can hear it at the listing presentation or creating a special Web site to show them their home. Those are all gimmicks agents use to win the listing against a good, average, or even poor agent. When you are a Champion Agent, none of these gimmicks stand a chance against you.

Prelisting Package

Preparation for the listing process is where you will win or lose the listing. It's what you do before you walk in the door that carries the most weight. If you prepare properly and have solid skills, you will win more than your fair share. A Champion Agent has better preparation than other agents.

Just as championship teams in any sport win because of preparation, you will win the listing based on your preparation. Championship teams win *before* a game. You will take listings based on the way you practice, prepare yourself, and prepare the seller. Preparing the seller means sending out information ahead of time in a prelisting package.

Package Pointers

I built my first prelisting package in 1992. Mind you, it was not pretty because it didn't have to be. I was the only one doing it in my marketplace. By the time I added a video in early 1994, my prelisting package had gone through half a dozen revisions.

The presale or prelisting package is an essential tool in today's marketplace, but most agents have not taken the time to construct one. The package gives you an opportunity to sell the prospect before you ever walk through the door. It also shows the prospect you are organized and professional.

The prelisting package is similar to a stockbroker's prospectus on a stock you are considering for purchase. The seller is investing his or her time in you. Just as the prospectus tells you about the track record of the stock, the trends, overall market information, and proposed future return, your prelisting package serves the same purpose.

Create an effective template.   Your package needs to be automated. You must be able to print it easily on a laser printer or have a printer do a large quantity at one time. It is best to print your prelisting package in-house. This allows you to customize it for the individual seller. It also allows you to make small adjustments easily.

Offer dynamic delivery.   Most consumers favor the phrase "right away" when used by a salesperson. The faster you provide a valuable service, the more value the consumer places on your service. You want to deliver the package as quickly as possible, so use an outside courier service, which will usually deliver your package within a couple of hours for a nominal fee. I had my field coordinator deliver the packages. Personal delivery makes a strong and lasting impression.

Enhance your credibility.   This is where you have a chance to presell yourself before you walk through the door. You should include a personal bio, along with your credentials. Remember to tie in the benefits and not just the fact that you have a Graduate Realtor Institute (GRI), a Certified Residential Specialist (CRS), or any other credentials. You have to show the client the benefit of a CRS or GRI designation. Use statistical evidence regarding your success. Use the comparison of average list price to sale price of the local real estate board against your success. Include your average days on the market compared to the board, and insert three to five testimonials. Testimonials are powerful ways to express the results you have achieved for other clients. The best way to use testimonials is to target them to the person you are presenting to. For example, if you are doing a listing presentation for expireds, use testimonials from previous expired clients with whom you had success. This will position you as a successful problem solver and results-oriented agent.

Use charts and graphs.   Here you need to start educating your prospects on two things:

1. The significance of pricing their home properly
2. The fact that you are different from the other agents in the marketplace

This section should be straightforward and easy to understand. I encourage the use of charts and graphs that show the contrast between days on the market and showing activity or even days on the market and reduction in sale price. You need to create a strong correlation between selling and market time. You can easily acquire these types of graphs from your broker, NAR, or other agents.

Preview paperwork.   If you enclose a few of the documents that prospects need to fill out, even if they list with someone else, you have created an advantage. I always include the property disclosure forms, the lead-based paint disclosure form, and any other forms that are necessary. In most states, sellers have to provide these forms to the buyer, even if they sell FSBOs. Encourage your prospect to complete the forms. This information is important for you to know at the listing appointment. Some of their answers could affect the value of the property. Telling that to the seller has increased the number of people who fill them out before I walk in the door.

Coach's Tip: *When you arrive for your appointment, and the forms are filled out, you know three important things: (1) your prospect follows directions well; (2) your prospect has a reasonable amount of motivation to sell; and (3) your prospect is seriously considering listing with you.*

Introduce your pricing philosophy. You want to start by warning sellers of the dangers and pitfalls of overpricing. This gives you a strong advantage over other agents, since you are not originally bringing up the bad news. There are effective videos on the market about pricing property. You might consider investing in a few to prepare your client. You might, as I did, produce your own prelisting video that highlights your credentials, benefits, dangers of overpricing, and the service you provide.

Position yourself.   This section focuses on your position in the marketplace, or your company's position. List your training and formal education. Make sure to tie in the benefit to the prospect. Remember, to your prospect, GRI is a bunch of letters at the end of your name.

Included here are two highly effective forms that you may want to add to your prelisting package. Figure 11.1 is the Realtor Pledge and Survey Form. This form is used to back up your qualifying to make sure prospects are giving you consistent answers. You will also know, in advance, the real areas of concern. Your job is to make sure they fill it out before you arrive. If you arrive and they have not taken the time to fill it out, then ask them to fill it out while you take a look at the home.

The point of this form is for prospects to tell you their concerns so you can address them in your presentation. If their concerns are high enough to be designated a 5, you are going to probably see that concern voiced in the form of an objection before you can close. Wouldn't it be nice to know what you are up against in trying to make the sale?

Figure 11.2 is a series of questions you want the sellers to ask any agent they are considering. These are questions that agents should know the answers to but usually don't. By giving these questions to the seller, you are setting the stage for a large percentage of the

I am here to provide you the service that you desire. I will always put your interest first before anyone else. To provide you the best and most professional job I would like to know your concerns, so we can jointly achieve the desired result. Please take a few minutes to complete the survey below.

Concerns about selling your home	Not concerned				Very concerned
Communication with Realtor	1	2	3	4	5
Buyer qualifications	1	2	3	4	5
Multiple Listing Service	1	2	3	4	5
Marketing of your property	1	2	3	4	5
Advertising	1	2	3	4	5
Open house	1	2	3	4	5
Selling commission	1	2	3	4	5
Possible unforeseen problems	1	2	3	4	5
Systematic process to the sale	1	2	3	4	5
Time of possession	1	2	3	4	5
Pride of your property	1	2	3	4	5
Closing costs	1	2	3	4	5
Security of your home	1	2	3	4	5
Salability	1	2	3	4	5
Negotiating the contract	1	2	3	4	5
Repairs after the inspection	1	2	3	4	5

©2006 Real Estate Champions, Inc.

Figure 11.1 Realtor Pledge and Survey

agents they might be considering to fail the test. Agents who can't answer the questions, or worse, try to wing it, will look pretty foolish. Strongly encourage sellers to ask the questions of each agent who interviews for the job of selling their home.

Showcase your strategic team. Show prospects they have more people on their team than just you. Illustrate how you provide more value through great vendors who provide exceptional service to all your clients. You have many people you direct on each transaction; put them fully on your team: your lender, title company

Coach's Tip: *Be sure you have the answers to these questions. If you calculate your own results and have a really poor number for one of the questions, chop that question from the list. For example, if you had a poor year last year, drop question 7 from your list.*

1.	How long have you been a licensed Realtor?
2.	Do you work as a full-time Realtor?
3.	Do you have assistants that work for you?
4.	How many homes did you list last year that sold?
5.	How many homes did you list last year that failed to sell?
6.	How many of the listings you took did you actually sell yourself?
7.	How many transactions did you do last year?
8.	What was your average list price to sale price for your listings?
9.	What is the real estate board average list price to sale price?
10.	What are the average days your listing has been on the market?
11.	What are the real estate board average days on the market?
12.	Where do you advertise and how often?
13.	How do you communicate with sellers and how often?
14.	Why should I hire you?

©2006 Real Estate Champions, Inc.

Figure 11.2 Seller Questionnaire

representative, escrow closer, attorney, termite inspector, home inspector, roofer, home maintenance person, and any assistant or buyer's agent who works with you.

The prelisting package can have a powerful impression on any client or prospect. It can be a strong presentation before you even meet or speak with the sellers. Another advantage—it will reduce the amount of time you need to invest at their home.

Qualify Client *before* the Presentation

Preparation also means qualifying the seller before you make the presentation. It separates the best salespeople from all the others. (See Figure 11.3 for an example of a prelisting letter.) The more information you have going into the listing appointment, the higher the likelihood you will achieve success. Success to me in the listing process is defined by the following:

- Getting the home listed at the appointment
- Getting it listed at the right price that will cause it to sell
- Getting a long enough term on the listing so you are guaranteed a sale
- Establishing expectations in the seller so you are assured to underpromise and overdeliver

Dear _____,

I am looking forward to our appointment on _____ at _____. I may be calling you for additional information about your property. This will help us to jointly establish the correct value of your property, since pricing is extremely important to the sale of your home.

I would also appreciate your taking the time to fill out the enclosed survey and disclosure forms. This will enable me to provide you with the service you deserve and desire. You will notice that I have included some questions to ask any agent you are considering to represent you. Selecting the right agent to represent you can often mean the difference between having a solid agent or simply a For Sale sign.

©2006 Real Estate Champions, Inc.

Figure 11.3 Prelisting Letter

You have to look at the qualifying part of the listing presentation process as the diagnosis. You must find out as much information as possible to be able to do the proper prescription. Many agents go in without a clue about the diagnosis. It means they are on the edge of malpractice—they are just distributing pills.

To properly diagnose the appointment you need to know:

1. How the customer is going to make the decision
2. When the customer is going to make the decision
3. Whether the prospect has the capacity to move forward
4. What the prospect wants
5. What the prospect needs
6. The prospect's authority to move forward
7. The amount of motivation or desire to do it
8. How a successful relationship with you will be determined
9. Anyone else under consideration

All these areas must be covered in the qualifying or questioning stage before you go out to meet with the prospect. The answers either raise or lower the probability of your success in securing the listing and help establish the framework for a long-term successful relationship between you and your client. Figure 11.4 is a qualifying survey that will enable you to prepare for an appointment. I will give you some of the *why* behind the questions so you are less likely to omit any of them. It is through extensive testing and analysis in changing the questions and changing the order of the questions over the past 16 years in real estate sales, training, and coaching that I am able to give you my best advice. Use it.

The first four questions are time frame and motivation questions. One of the keys to selling is being there at the right time. You have only one opportunity to make a presenta-

Hi, _____, this is _____ calling for _____ at _____. Are you and your spouse both going to be there? Before I come out, there are some questions I need to ask. Is this a good time for me to ask?

1. Where are you hoping to move to?
2. How soon are you hoping to be there? (Motivation)
3. Tell me about your perfect time frame. When do you want this move to happen?
4. Is there anything that would cause you not to make this move?
5. How many properties have you sold in the past?
6. When was your last sales experience?
7. What was your experience with that sale?
8. How did you select the agent you worked with?
9. What did you like best that your agent did?
10. What did you like least?
11. How much do you want to list your home for? (Number/Motivation)
12. Are you planning on making another investment in another house? How much are you hoping to put down on the next property?
13. Are you expecting that entire down payment to come from the proceeds of this house, or are you going to put down additional funds?

I desire, as a professional agent, to give you all the information you need to make the best decision for your family. I always do a net sheet for my clients so they know the *true* amount they are going to net from the sale of their home. To do that, I need to know more information about your current property.

14. How much do you owe on the property?
15. Have you ever thought about selling it yourself?
16. Are you interviewing any other agents?
17. Please describe your home for me.

_____ Bedrooms _____ Square feet
_____ Bathrooms _____ Type of home

Yard, landscape _____
Condition of property _____

18. Are you planning to list your home with me when I come out on ____?
19. Did you receive the package of information we sent you?
20. Did you fill out the information that was in the packet? We sent a number of disclosure forms.

Because my desire is to create long-term successful service relationships with my clients, I need to ask you a few questions with regard to service and your expectation of service.

21. What is your expectation of the agent you choose?
22. What are the specific services that you want from me?
23. What would it take for you to be confident that our service will meet your requirements?
24. How will you measure success in our relationship?
25. If I provide you _____ and _____ and _____, what will you do?
26. Do you have any final questions that you need answered before I come out?

©2006 Real Estate Champions, Inc.

Figure 11.4 Listing Prospect Prequalifying Questions

tion. You have to make sure the prospects are ready to make a decision. If you are there too early, you won't be able to close and secure the contract.

The next six questions are what I would describe as experience questions. I want to know how educated prospects are in the process of selling a home. I want to know if they have had previous experience, good or bad, so I know their frame of mind during the appointment. If they have had a bad experience, I want to be able to assure them that it won't happen again and that I don't do those things in my business. If it was a good experience, I want to assure them that I do those things, too.

The next set of questions (concluding with "Are you planning on listing your home when I come out on _____?") I call the "guts questions." I call them that because you have to have guts to ask them. Too many agents shy away from asking tough questions. A Champion Agent asks the guts questions, even if he or she is uncomfortable doing it.

How much do you want to list your home for? You have to ask that question. You need to know their view of the marketplace and of the value of their home. I canceled about 20 percent of the appointments I booked before I even exited my office because of this question. The difference between the home value (my price) and their imaginary value was so vast that we would never have worked well together. If I couldn't get them to consider my viewpoint on the high end, which would be in terms of value plus 5 percent, I canceled the appointment. It saved me from wasting time better spent with my family. It also saved me from beating myself up later because I didn't or couldn't close the deal. (If your closing ratio on your appointments is low, it could be that you are not rejecting the unqualified appointments.)

Are you interviewing other agents? This is another big-time guts question that must be asked. Not knowing who you are up against is poor preparation. Can you imagine an NFL or a college football team not knowing who they will play next week? You have to know who else your prospects are considering. If they won't give you people's names, ask them for the companies they are considering. Once you get that information, ask them for the agent's name again, using the company name to open the discussion.

Sellers need to be able to completely evaluate the track record of all agents who are competing for their business. I want to be able to show them that comparison. If I don't do it, nobody will. If I knew who the other agents were, I could pull up their listings, sales, pendings, and expireds. I could show them the vast difference in production, experience, probability of success, and money in their pocket by selecting me. I did not denigrate my competition; that is unprofessional. I merely exposed the truth of the reported numbers and led the client to the logical conclusion. The only way to complete that type of preparation was to know who I was up against.

Are you planning to list your house with me when I come out on _____? This is a guts question as well. I need to know prospects' intentions. If they say no, I need to know why.

I need to understand their terms and conditions in advance of their listing with me during that appointment. What's the probability of me listing the home that day? I want to move the odds in my favor to secure the listing at that time.

Champion Rule:	*Play to win.*

Winning is taking the listing the day you are there, not a week later.

Champion Rule:	*There is no second place.*

You are in a game where you aren't paid for second place. If you do all the work I have outlined and you don't get the listing, you don't get paid. At that point, it doesn't matter if you are their second, third, or fourth choice. All of them receive zero compensation.

You must get the listing fully executed while you are sitting in front of the sellers. I don't believe in the "I'll be back" listing concept. You're not Arnold Schwarzenegger. You have to understand the stark reality of the business that we are in. To reach the pinnacle of real estate sales, you have to understand these two rules.

The final series of questions are expectation questions. I want to know what they expect from me. I want to know their standards and how I will be judged. My goal is to know how to "sell" them at the presentation. I have said this a few times in the book—it's a lot easier to sell people what they want to buy than what you want to sell. With these questions, I will know what changes I need to make in my presentation so I really connect with them. I can build credibility and trust easier if I know what they want.

The second-to-last question is the summation close question. It basically asks, "If I provide you with what you want, what will you do?" I am merely pushing their "hot buttons" and gaining an agreement that, if I do those things, they will work with me. I can refer back to it in the listing presentation if they are hesitant to sign the listing agreement. I can point out, in a nice way, the fact that we already had an agreement in principle the other day when we talked on the phone. I can use this question's response on the listing presentation to my advantage. Here's an example script:

> *"Bob and Mary, when we talked the other day, you said if I provided a complete marketing plan and showed success generally and in this neighborhood specifically, we would work together. I am a little confused. I think I have done that. Is there something else I missed?"*

Four Characteristics of a Champion Agent's Presentation

Numerous studies have shown that your tone and body language account for over 90 percent of your presentation's effectiveness. The words you select account for less than 10 percent of your effectiveness. If you're focusing on finding the right words, as most salespeople are, you are not focusing on the areas of your presentation that are most important. If you don't know what to say, all you can do is focus on the words to say. If you know what to say, you can begin to focus on your tone and body language.

Conviction

Webster defines *conviction* as "a fixed or firm belief." I'd add that there is nothing more compelling than conviction. Your unshakable belief that you are the right person for the job and can accomplish the task will set you apart from the competition. Your conviction in the value of prospects' homes will earn their trust, even if your price is lower than that of other agents. Your bedrock belief about where the marketplace is headed, backed by statistics that prove your belief and conviction, sells you and shows them why they should do business with you. People are attracted to people who have conviction. They trust, admire, and respect people with conviction, even when they don't agree with them.

Enthusiasm

There is an old saying: enthusiasm sells. Sellers want to work with agents who are enthusiastic about their home. If you don't like (or don't express enthusiasm about) their property, you reduce your ability to secure the listing. If the market is tough or changing, you have to be honest; you can't hide market realities. Any agent can demonstrate excitement about the opportunity to list the home and represent the seller's interests. However, a Champion Agent is enthusiastic enough to make sure the home is priced right in order to sell it.

Confidence

I know that my edge as a new agent was my confidence. I am not completely sure where that confidence came from, besides athletics. I was new to the game of real estate, but I was confident I was the best agent for the seller. You need to tap into victories you have had in the past. Those are so valuable. As you increase your confidence in preparation, it allows you to prepare with more passion because of your expectation of winning.

Assertiveness

One of the single biggest mistakes of non-Champion performers is not wanting to be seen as too pushy or aggressive. Most wimp out before the close. One way to overcome this is to tell clients up front that you are going to ask for the business. That way, they expect you to do it. They are not surprised when you ask them to sign the contract. It also sets you up, in advance, for when you get to the end of your presentation. You'd better ask for the order because you said you would.

Going for the close or asking for the order is not pushy. If you don't have enough confidence in your service, skill, and value, you should get out of the business. Your confidence will sell. As a real estate agent, your job is to persuade prospects that you have the best service and the best value. The best value is not price, but by factoring in all the benefits of your service, you present the best value. Your job is to link your benefits with their service expectations. Then ask them to act now so you can help them.

As I said earlier, if you are having trouble with the final close, tell the prospect it's coming in advance. This helps your probability more than anything else. Early in the presentation explain, "At the end of my presentation tonight, provided we're all in agreement, we'll finalize the paperwork so I can begin to work for you right away. Doesn't that make sense?" Laying a closing foundation will come in handy if you encounter resistance or objections at the time of the close. If that happens, consider one of these scripts:

> *"This should be no surprise. I told you I would ask for your business. You want me to follow through on what I commit to you, don't you?"*

> *"I'm proving to you right now that I follow through, right?"*

> *"Listen, Mr. and Mrs. Seller, homes are sold, not bought. The reason conversion of leads is so low is because many agents lack assertiveness with the buyer. So my question is: Do you want an agent that you know for sure will ask every buyer to buy or an agent you* hope *will do that? Which gives you more comfort?"*

Create the Structure for Success

When I finally arrive at the home, I want to have completed all of my work ahead of time. I want to walk in the door fully prepared and with the expectation of success. My belief is that you establish a flow to your actual presentation and stick with it. Don't change the structure or allow clients to do so. If they want to talk about something out of order, ask them politely if you could go over that later, in a segment of the presentation where you normally address that concern. You are trying to deflect the objections to later (or never) and keep your rhythm and flow of the presentation.

Many of you are reading this and saying, "I don't want to operate that way. I don't feel comfortable doing a canned presentation." I am not talking about a *canned* presentation. I am talking about a *planned* presentation. The first segment must be to inform the client of the time frame this presentation will take. Just employing this one technique will shorten an hour-long presentation to 45 minutes. If prospects know you will take 45 minutes, that's what it will take. Then move on to reviewing the qualifying questions. Remember to ask both decision makers if they agree with your notes from the other day. This technique clarifies the goals and objectives and builds trust, because you cared enough to ask, record their responses, and make certain that you got it right. You are also engaging the person who didn't get a chance to talk with you earlier.

Discover Needs and Move into Presentation

Once you confirm the questions and understand their needs and expectations, you are ready for the crucial stage of the presentation. You are going to share with them why they should hire you. This segment, for most agents, drones on much too long. All you need to do is have about four to six key benefits of why someone should hire you. The ones you select to give them should align with what they said they expect from you in the qualifying questions. Remember, they told you exactly how to sell them.

Why Hire You? Begin Closing

At the end of the why-they-should-hire-you segment, you need to insert trial closes. You may be thinking you can't do that; they don't know the price of the home. My friends, the price of the home should be immaterial in their decision. People who select an agent to represent their interests based on the price the agent places on the home (the price they feel the home is worth) are selecting the wrong agent. The price an agent puts on a home is not the determining factor of whether he or she is a good agent. Price is the determining factor of whether the home will sell. That's why trial closes at this stage are paramount. You want to at least build a little "yes" momentum and potentially get the contract signed at this stage.

Price (value) counseling. You must then move into the price counseling segment, whether you have secured the signature or not. The truth is, you need to remove the word *price* from your dialogue when talking about their home. What you are really discussing with the sellers is the *value* of the home. The value of their home today is based on the inventory of homes for sale, inventory of available buyers, location, condition, and the scarcity of similar properties. Our discussion is centered on the comps, which we all have been taught by our broker. It is also centered on your market trends report that we discussed in Chapter 5, "Building Credibility and Trust." Use the market trends report to show the competitive nature of the marketplace and how it will affect the value of their property. A discussion of the law of supply and demand could also be used to further illustrate the condition of the marketplace.

After the value counseling, then and only then ask for an agreement on the value. You don't want to proceed with another step until you have an agreement on the value of the home. You might have to stay there all day, but once you get it, you can move on to a net sheet and trial close, again. You need to determine whether this net figure is enough for them to accomplish their goal. If not, how far off are you? Can they borrow a little more? Can they live with a little less? Can you adjust the interest rate by using a different loan program? Can you get the seller of the home they are buying to participate in closing costs? Do they just need to bite the bullet and sell for less than they had hoped? In order to walk out of the listing presentation with the contract signed, you can't leave this problem unsolved. Once you solve it, another opening is created for a Champion to close.

Marketing information can weaken your presentation. You will notice that, up until this point, I have not mentioned anything regarding my marketing plan, which should have been in my presentation package. I have not talked about marketing or what I will do. If my why-they-should-hire-me segment is strong, the marketing discussion is unnecessary. In fact, the discussion of marketing only weakens an agent's presentation. Someone will always have a better Web site or snazzier flyer or be willing to run more ads or hold more open houses. The truth is, if you get them to price it competitively, it will sell. You can't keep a good listing a secret. Agents can sniff out good property at a fair value and a fair price. The home will sell, and the marketing will be immaterial.

> **Coach's Tip:** *If you have to go into marketing, keep it short. The only reason to go into marketing is if you haven't secured the signatures at this time. In the last five years of my real estate career, I had over 120 listing presentations per year. That's over 600 listing presentations in that time. I could count on one hand the number of times I talked about marketing.*

Final Close

Once you reach this stage, you are down to objection handling and closing. That's really all there is left. Continue to pause, acknowledge, explore, isolate, answer, and close. We all make three presentations in any selling situation. The first presentation is when we are on the way to the appointment. The second one is the real one in front of the seller, and the third is on the way home, replaying the tape of what happened. The real objective is to make the best one the real one. For most people, the best one takes place on the way home.

Five Steps to Improve Your Listing Presentation

To really take your listing presentation to the highest level, you need to follow these guidelines and steps for the next 60 days. The longer you wait, the longer it will take for you to reach the Champion Agent level. These steps will make you a Champion in a short time frame.

1. *Practice your listing presentation once a day for the next 60 days.* Your ability to go through the presentation frequently will make the difference. If you do your presentation only a few times a year or even a few times a month, it will be noticed.

2. *Role-play your qualifying questions twice a day for the next 60 days.* If you have those questions nailed down in your mind and ready for your delivery, your confidence will go through the roof.

3. *Work on the major objections on the listing side of the business for 30 minutes each day for the next 60 days.*

- I want you to think it over.
- I want a shorter listing period.
- I want you to cut your commission.
- Another agent will list it at a higher price.
- I need to net ____.
- I don't want to give it away.
- I want to do a few fix-ups before I list.
- I want to talk with a few other agents.
- You don't sell homes in my area.
- I have never heard of your company before.

4. *Tape your listing presentation and listen to it.* This is the best way to know what you are really saying early in your coaching career. The universal truth I learned by listening to over 50 listing presentations on tape is that we talk more than we listen. Over 80 percent of

the presentation is usually the agent talking. The seller should be talking 80 percent of the time, not the agent.

5. *Evaluate your performance after every presentation.* Be honest with yourself about how you did, but don't be too hard. Ask yourself the following questions and write down the responses. You will learn from your mistakes and improve, instead of making the same mistake over and over again (as most people do).

- What are two or three things I did well?
- Did I listen to the client's concerns?
- How much of the time did I talk?
- How much of the time did my client talk?
- Did I stay on track during the presentation?
- What objections caused me problems?
- What is the one area I need to improve on?
- What did my client get most excited about?
- What steps do I need to take to stay on track better?
- What could I have done differently to get the listing?

Being a Champion Agent starts with having a Champion listing presentation. The preparation beforehand is the area I believe most agents really need to focus on. If you go into a presentation with more information than your competitors, you will win 80 percent of the time—even if another agent is there because of a referral.

12

Why Should Someone Hire You?

This is the fundamental question faced by every agent, every day, and by every person they meet. Why should I do business with you over the hundreds or even thousands of agents I could choose from? What makes you different from someone else I could select who might be cheaper? In order to not only survive but thrive in the competitive world of real estate sales, you have to be able to answer the basic question for consumers, "Why should I hire you?"

WII FM Radio

Everyone in life, especially those we do business with, is tuned into WII FM radio 24 hours a day, seven days a week. WII FM radio stands for "What's in it for me?" One of the more significant mistakes that salespeople make is not being tuned into their client's frequency. We are constantly selling with a narrow-minded, egotistical, and grandstanding focus. All of our sales presentations and services need to be turned to the benefit of our clients. Our prospect can have the extreme attitude of "So what? Who cares?" Our job is to show them what's in it for them.

To be a Champion Agent, you need to know what prospects, customers, and clients want. What services do they want you to provide? What standard or measure is the client going to use to determine whether good service and good, or even great value has been received? What are the ultimate goals that you will be helping to achieve? If everything could be perfect, what would that look like for your client?

These are the types of questions and information you need to be able to formulate and service strategically to enable you to exceed their expectations. It also clearly uncovers clients' "hot buttons," which will help you sell your services. (It's much easier to sell to someone what they want to buy than what you want to sell them.)

Consumer's Mindset

Consumers in most markets have a unique mindset about real estate agents. At times, the mindset is market-driven. When everything is selling quickly, many consumers don't feel they need an agent. Their view is that they can save the fee by choosing "for sale by owner" (FSBO). Another view is that the home will sell easily, so why pay an agent a full fee to generate the sale?

When the market is more challenging, consumers begin to see our value as professionals. We move beyond the necessary evil in a real estate transaction. We can hold the key to unlock the door of their wants and dreams. We always had that key, even in a robust market. It's our duty, as professionals, to inform them of our value and give them reasons to hire us.

We Are Paid Too Much

The public sees agents driving expensive cars and often living in better homes than they do. They see the outward appearance of wealth in fancy cars, fancy clothes, and a nice home. What they fail to realize is that most agents are living beyond their means to achieve this outwardly successful appearance.

The consumer doesn't understand the essential risk/reward connection in real estate sales. This is a profession without base salary, car allowance, health insurance, or retirement plan—a profession without a guaranteed income of any kind.

The Work Is Easy

Too many consumers perceive that we pound a sign in the ground and wait for a home to sell. Much of the work we do as real estate agents is behind the scenes. It isn't recognized or seen as work. The perception is that we plant the sign in the ground and wait for a commission check. I am not sure we will ever be able to fully change this perception, because the consumer will never see the behind-the-scenes work a good agent does.

It's almost as though we are stage managers in a Broadway production. The actors and orchestra conductor receive the applause and accolades from the audience. They get to take their bows and recognition. You never see the director or stage manager get a round of applause. The show would not go on without them, but they gain little recognition for their important role.

We Are Not Professional

Their view is that we don't need an advanced degree—almost anyone can acquire a real estate license. There is some truth to the view that anyone can get a license. Becoming a licensed agent doesn't mean you will be a good agent. It certainly doesn't mean that you will be a Champion Agent.

Practically everyone knows of agents they don't respect. They might have done business with such an agent in the past and were dissatisfied. Maybe they have a close relative, high school buddy, or family friend they think is a bad agent. The basic philosophy is, if so-and-so is an agent, they must all be just like him.

It's a Show-Me Business

You have to demonstrate to your prospects and clients that you add value and are worth your fee. Too many agents don't like to be labeled as salespeople. A Champion Agent is proud that he or she is a salesperson. Honestly, I grow weary of agents telling me that they are marketing experts, service consultants, client care consultants, and on and on. We create all these fancy, fictitious titles to make us feel better, so we don't have to call ourselves what we are . . . salespeople!

Champion Rule:	*Champion Rule: You are a salesperson!*

Be proud of your sales heritage. Your ability to acknowledge and enhance a sales philosophy to attract and convert prospects into clients will determine your income.

What Do You Sell?

When I ask that question in public, I get a wide variety of answers. I most often hear "ourselves," "service," "professionalism," "houses," and "the dream of home ownership." All those are minor features of our service. In terms of our product, I think that, in order to be highly profitable and respected, we sell two things:

1. Our time
2. Our knowledge

These are our two primary assets. Any other response you could possibly come up with fits under these two classifications. These are tangible assets you trade for the money you earn.

Time

For years, we primarily sold access to consumers. We did this in two ways. We used our personal bank of time in large quantities to show we cared about our prospects. We would tell them we were available 24 hours a day, seven days a week. "You just call, and I will be there." "I am there for you."

Many agents are still stuck in this trap. New agents sell accessibility because they have limited skills and knowledge. The problem is, when you gain the skills and knowledge, you are too scared to take the professional approach to business. I believe there's a larger group of 24/7 agents than ever before.

Access does not equate to value. It's also not a way to differentiate yourself from other agents. You look like everyone else when you do that. A Champion Agent doesn't tread the same path as all other agents. A Champion Agent's time has tremendous value.

My competitors in real estate sales were always trying to paint a picture of me as unreachable, unapproachable, and too busy, that their 24/7 access was superior to my professional office hours approach to business. I was quick to point out that if their approach was indeed better, then their results should also be better . . . which they weren't. They also connected access with a higher level of concern or care. Yuk! I care so much for my clients that I take time off so my family life is sound, so I'm recharged for the next week of work, and so I will do the best job for my clients.

Categorize Your Clients

Champion Agents don't have enough time to work with everyone they come in contact with. They are focused on working with only the highest level of people they can provide service to. By working with only the highest level, it saves them time. The time saved can then be spent on another person. There are really three categories of people you can invest your time in: (1) prospects, (2) customers, and (3) clients.

Prospects.   These are people in whom you are investing your time with the hope of moving them to clients. Prospects need to be evaluated based on their level of probability of generating a commission check. To this end, there are four key evaluation questions:

1. *How much will it take?* How much time will you have to invest? How long a time frame will it be? The amount of time might be the same, but one prospect will commit and buy or sell now. Another will be six months away. The one who is six months away

has less value. I didn't say *no* value, I said *less*. Too many things can change in six months.

2. *How much effort will it take?* What kind of energy and effort will you expend to transform this prospect into a client? Just as many other Champion Agents do, I prefer working with sellers because of how long and how much effort it takes. I found the control, time frame, and effort was significantly less to represent the seller rather than the buyer.

3. *What are the odds of them becoming a client?* The Champion Agent evaluates the odds continually. Low-odds prospects create low-odds commission checks. Are your odds better than 50/50? If they aren't, you will need to question whether you should proceed forward in servicing.

4. *What is the long-term residual value?* The purpose of a real estate practice is to generate long-term residual value from your past clients and sphere—to provide a service level that encourages repeat and referral business. Some people have lower long-term residual value because of their behavioral style, sphere-of-influence size, types of jobs, and outside interests. The question should be, "Is this person an AAA referral source or a D-level referral source?"

Too many agents provide too much service to prospects in hopes they will miraculously become clients. My view is that prospects are worthy of limited amounts of service. The length, duration, and quantity of the service you provide to them must be limited. You will notice I didn't say *quality* of the service. My belief is that the quality of the service must be at the highest level. The adjustments come in how long they will receive this high-quality service. If you degrade the quality of your service, you will look just like all the other agents vying for their business. The quality must be at the level you would provide for any client. The key question is, "Do you want to continue receiving this market knowledge, responsiveness, and expert counsel long term?" If the answer is yes, that person must become a client.

Your job in sales is to attract prospects and convince them to become clients. The natural tendency is for them to want to remain prospects if their motivation is low. If their motivation is midrange, they want to become customers. If their motivation is high, and you have tangible benefits that point them to why they should hire you, they will want to become clients.

Customers. I am going to be bold in my stance with customers. Customers have limited value. In a service business, customers can pay the current bills, but that's it. A customer has limited residual value. You can earn a commission check if all the factors are aligned in terms of time frame, motivation, and market conditions. If you are an agent who has plateaued at a production level for the past few years, it's generally because you have been working with too many customers, not enough prospects, and not driving the prospects to client status. It's easy to get into the habit of working only with customers; you don't have to prospect as much. It feels like you are making progress, but you are only treading water.

I also believe it is more difficult to move a customer to a client position than it is to move a prospect to client. Prospects, if handled correctly, know they will lose quality services if they don't commit to exclusivity. Provided that they want your high-quality services, you can move them to an exclusive client relationship in a short period of time. The customer has been receiving the valuable services for a long period of time and has not been asked to make a decision of exclusivity. The customer becomes confused when, all of a sudden, you change the rules. Most people who hang out at the customer level will never make an exclusive commitment to you. (In most cases, they are unwilling to commit to anyone.)

Clients. These people have exchanged commitments with you, preferably in written contract form. They expect counsel, guidance, service, and the fiduciary duties of an agent. They are willing to trade commitments of loyalty and exclusivity because of the advantages you create for them in the marketplace. You provide them with representation, counsel, knowledge, interpretation of the knowledge, analysis, and greater equity or money. They know they have the edge over the competition of other buyers and sellers because they are working with you.

Because the selling game in real estate has changed significantly in the past 10 years, the advent of the Internet has lessened the monopoly of MLS information. The consumer has access to just about the same real estate information in local markets as do the agents. The media has been on a rampage in the past half-dozen years about how we should be charging less and because our value is diminished due to technology changes in information about houses for sales, transaction management advancements, and the propagation of discount real estate models. Working with clients today is more important than ever before in the history of real estate sales. How you position your time and knowledge and connect them to value will determine whether you achieve a Champion Agent's production and quality of life.

Our Knowledge

This area really separates Champion Agents from everyone else. Champion Agents sell their knowledge and, specifically, the value of their knowledge more effectively than even great agents do. This is the arena that needs dramatic improvement. Intelligent people who are forward thinkers will pay for knowledge. You fit into that category because you invested in this book. One of the fastest ways to increase your leverage, earnings, and quality of life is to use other people's knowledge to get you there.

If you can clearly demonstrate for prospects that your knowledge gives them an advantage in the marketplace, your prospects will be more likely to decide to use you as a service provider. Most agents are unable to convey how their knowledge creates an advantage for the client. If they are able to create some kind of inside track to the client, it's relationally based. Too many agents rely too much on the relational connection rather than "expert" connection. A Champion Agent works to establish both.

Knowledge creates benefits for clients.   Champion Agents' knowledge creates quantifiable benefits for their clients. By empirically proving your advantages to prospects, customers, and clients, you raise the probability of your success.

A Champion Agent's knowledge provides these benefits to clients:

- More money for the sale of their home
- More efficient, less hassle transaction
- Better strategic positioning of their properties to attract more buyers
- Stronger property demonstration to enhance value and sale price for sellers
- Effective price versus value counseling

All of these services translate into dollars in your client's pocket. All are achieved through the value of your knowledge and skill. That's what separates the Champion Agent from the others.

Two Reasons to Hire You as an Agent

When you evaluate why someone should hire you, you really have only two options. You can sell features of your service or you can sell the benefits the client will receive.

When I listen to agents sell their services, most spend far more time discussing features than the benefits or the outcome the client will receive: the features of years in the business, membership in the Million-Dollar Club, a certain company production award, number of homes sold, sales volume, and all features of the agent's service. Most agents use these exclusively to answer the nagging question, "Why should I hire you?" The problem is that these are merely features of your service. A certain level of production or years in the business doesn't leap out at the prospect as a benefit.

You have to be able to connect the benefit of security, reduced risk, smooth transaction, higher probability of sale, and high sales price to the feature we provide. Then, and only then, will you be the agent who is able to defend and increase your value and answer the question of why someone should hire you.

Benefits of Working with an Agent

Most agents talk about their marketing services, ads, and Web sites. Those are merely features of their service. Many even describe the hits, unique visitors, or ranking of their or their company's Web sites. The problem is, for most sellers, you are speaking a foreign language. You might as well be speaking in French. What does this mean to them? What is the benefit they receive? How does that create an advantage for them? Why is this information so important? Most agents talk about features of their service rather than the benefits the clients receive.

I frequently ask two questions at seminars. The first you have already been exposed to: Why should I hire you? I get immediate feedback on this question, usually responses like *customer services, size of company, communication, follow-up, experience,* and *honesty and integrity.* I want you to look at this list. How do you feel about these items? Do they separate you from the others who are interviewing for the job to represent someone's interest? What do you think?

―――――――――

I was doing a training session for a company, and the corporate trainer came up to me and said that he felt I missed something in my discussion of why someone should hire me. He felt I really missed an important point of emphasizing honesty and integrity, because I didn't mention them as something to say in a listing presentation or buyer interview. The reason I didn't is because I don't think it is a competitive advantage or a reason why someone should hire you. Now, before you draw the wrong conclusion, read on. I do think that honesty and integrity are paramount characteristics to being a Champion Agent. When do customers or clients really find out whether the agent they selected lacks honesty and integrity? Usually, after it's too late. It's after an agency relationship has been consummated. They have to be working with the agent to really find out.

Another reason is that many people have differing views or standards about honesty and integrity. The threshold is different for each one of us. We had a president a few years ago who claimed, "I did not have sexual relations with that woman." For many of us, myself included, that whole fiasco in our history was caused by a lack of honesty and integrity on his part. I can say that my definition of what constitutes sex is clearly different than his. I think his wife had a different definition as well. I am not making a political statement here. I am merely trying to illustrate a truth—that honesty *and* integrity *are subjective terms.*

My last point, which I made to this corporate trainer, is you would not be making a presentation to the buyers or sellers if they didn't feel you had honesty and integrity. To exclaim during the presentation that they should hire you because you have honesty and integrity is a wasted argument. If a prospect thought you lacked those characteristics, he or she wouldn't have allowed you to make a presentation. Would you knowingly interview a representative such as an attorney, a financial planner, an accountant, or a real estate agent if you knew that person lacked honesty and integrity? Of course not, and neither would your prospects.

If you say that your honesty and integrity is greater than that of another agent your prospect is considering, you have just denigrated your argument that you have honesty and integrity. The honesty-and-integrity argument is weak, and you will lose this position more often than not.

The reasons listed by most agents as advantages to hiring them are too nebulous. They offer no proof and no real tangible benefit to the seller. They also repeat what all other agents are saying. To be a Champion Agent and join the Champion Performer ranks, you have to be different. Being the same means that you have no reason for prospects to hire you over the cheaper option. Being the same allows them to select Uncle Fred, or the agent referred from their boss, or the discount guy down the street. If you are the same, your value is reduced. The reason that Luciano Pavarotti, Michael Jordan, Lance Armstrong, Jack Welch, Jim Carrey, and Oprah Winfrey are paid at the highest levels in their fields is because they are different. They can explain why they are different and why they are worth the extra investment of money. They are not ordinary. They are not the same as the rest of the people in their fields.

To help differentiate yourself, think about the following questions:

> **Coach's Tip:** *As the owner of various businesses for more than 20 years, I have discovered a rule that has proven truthful throughout my career: the more someone talks about personal honesty and integrity, the lower the level of honesty and integrity that person possesses. People who do business and live life with honesty and integrity don't go around talking about it.*

What is it that I do? Each agent's answer will be slightly different. You must know what you do and be able to articulate that in a compelling way to your prospects and customers in order to create clients.

What am I good at? What are the skills and services you provide that are top notch? What are the specific things you do better than others? I used to emphasize sales skills and the value of them to my clients. It was something that I possessed in terms of skills that few others possessed at any level.

What skills and services make me unique? What are the skills, services, strategies, tactics, and philosophies of the marketplace, your business, and working with clients that make you stand out? You are trying to be unique in an industry of over 1.4 million individual competitors nationwide.

Why should anybody care what I have to say? What do prospects, customers, or clients receive from you, and why is it important to them? Does your expert status exceed most in the marketplace?

With the changes that are occurring in consumer demands in the real estate industry, what will make people think you are the best at what you do 5 to 10 years from now? Champions Agents build their business and strategy for the long run. They work to create competitive advantages that they can develop into a decisive advantage for many years. That doesn't mean adjustments in strategy and tactics don't occur. It means that these adjustments consist of fine-tuning rather than wholesale changes. It also means their core values and core purpose for their business are adhered to. Those bedrock beliefs don't change due to seasonality or market conditions. A Champion Agent is able to show specific value that is tangible to the client.

Demonstrate Your Professional Value

Champion Agents can convey the six key rules that equate to professional value to any prospect or client. They are able to drive home the key points to raise their value to the prospect.

We Don't Sell Properties

We are salespeople, but we are really selling something other than a property. What we really sell to the marketplace is our knowledge. Our knowledge is better and more complete than our competitor's, which enables us to charge a higher fee for our service. Why is one attorney worth $500 an hour while another is worth only $100 an hour? It's a 60-minute hour for both. Assuming they can accomplish a similar volume of work, why pay the higher price? The answer is obvious—different levels of knowledge and skill. Why are real estate agents any different?

We sell our time. Just as doctors, dentists, attorneys, or accountants sell their time, we also sell our time. Because our fees are in a general range, the real variable to profitability is the amount of time required to earn our fees. If we can accomplish our clients' goals to their satisfaction in less time, we can increase our revenue and net profit.

We sell our service. The purpose of a service business is to provide service in return for compensation. We often forget that last part—*for compensation.* We won't be in business long term without the ability to charge enough to cover our business expenses, personal living expenses, recreation expenses, retirement savings expenses, taxes, children's college funds, and investment savings. We often barely cover our costs and sometimes come up very short when we discount our fees.

We broker transactions. We do not so much "sell homes" as we do represent the interests of people by advocating for their position in the marketplace or a particular transaction.

Key Service Business Requirements

The fact that we provide service and receive compensation is certainly the most important thing. Good service businesses go beyond that level, though. They check back after the sale. They might even survey their clients to see how they did and how to improve their service.

Sell Yourself First

Sell your services, benefits, and value first. The first step is to believe in your value. If you don't believe it, you can't sell it. I often ask agents what knowledge, skill, or production level they need to acquire or achieve before they will achieve an unshakeable belief in their service or value. The more you can quantify that, the easier it will be to attain. You have to know the target before you have any chance of hitting it.

Deal with the Competition Challenge

The real estate business is an extremely competitive business. With new competitors entering and advancing daily, we need to be prepared for competition. Some of these competitors will try to attract customers through discounted fees. Some will overpromise sales price and marketing exposure but will then ultimately underdeliver.

are key competitors?
- Who has more market share than you?
- Who has more name recognition than you?
- Who has market share similar to yours?
- Who has equal or better statistical results?

This evaluation should be made based on company statistics, as well as individual statistics and analysis.

Understand what your competitors are offering. Before every listing presentation, you should know exactly who you are up against, what those agents and companies offer, and what their stats are in the marketplace. If you can acquire your competitors' prelisting package, marketing brochures, or anything that will clue you in to how they promote and communicate their value and service, you will raise your preparedness for the appointment.

Be competitive: Competition creates success. By checking out your competition, you will be able to present an offer that is in direct competition for the business. If, for example, you are charging 9 percent to sell a home, when the market average is 6 percent, you are not competitive enough to secure business. Charging an additional 1 percent as a premium service fee over the competition may allow you to reasonably prove the value. You don't necessarily have to match the price others charge if your service is different. You will make a more effective presentation when you are competitive.

Most people don't want to engage in a competitive environment because they are uncomfortable. They also recognize that it's difficult. They will have to work harder to improve their skills, activities, knowledge, mental focus, and mental attitude. Most people don't want to work that hard.

My response is always the same, "Don't wish it were easier; make yourself better." Take on the challenges that most won't in order to make yourself a more skillful real estate agent. Work through the short-term challenges to access the long-term opportunities.

Beating the Competition

Champion Agents have figured out that being specific and deliberate in terms of what they offer, the benefits the clients receive only from them, and the value they bring to the marketplace allows them to beat the competition. If you offer generic services, you must compete on price. Webster's dictionary defines *generic* as "nonproprietary, any product or service that can be sold without a brand name." It's something that anyone can do or provide. An example would be the fact that any agent can put a home in MLS. When you move away from generic to unique, you can compete on value and service and avoid price.

By clearly knowing your competitive points of difference and effectively communicating those differences, you are able to draw a stronger distinction from the competition. In essence, you can beat the competition. You can then communicate the quantity and the quality of your benefits.

The Professional Difference

You need to sum up the differences so that prospects clearly understand the following:

- All companies are not the same.
- All salespeople are not the same.
- Your differences create advantages for your clients.
- Significant or beneficial difference creates greater value.
- Here are my beneficial differences.

Champion Agents convey these points to show, without question, that they are a different type of agent than this prospect has ever seen. In a nice way, they are saying, "Don't be foolish by taking the risk of achieving a worse result by using another agent."

Create a Competitive Advantage

A Champion must show that, in terms of net dollars, the client will make more money. Being able to sell to the client's inherent greed factor creates an advantage. The discount agents are selling to the greed factor through fee structure reduction. You have to engage in this game as well, but by using truth in net dollars.

The Champion Agent's Big 3

The successful businessperson raises the value and enlarges the whole pie. You can demonstrate more money from the sale by what we at Real Estate Champions call the *Big 3*. We have been teaching the Big 3 for almost a decade.

1. Average list price to sales price ratio
2. Average days on the market
3. Average listings sold versus listings taken

All of these are tangible, empirical ways to show sellers and buyers why they should hire you. Each one of these figures or ratios has tremendous power to convey value. One reason they have so much power is that few agents actually know their stats. Most agents are also unfamiliar with the marketplace stats. If you can prove that clients will earn a higher net in

ckets through average list price to sales price, you win. If you can prove that clients
.ake one less home payment on a home they don't want to own through average days
.e market, you win. If you can prove that the client has greater odds of accomplishing a
: because of your listings sold versus listings taken percentage, you win. These key sta-
.tics are what Champion Agents use to create differentiation and competitive advantages.

> 1. "Wouldn't you agree that the real result you are looking for is more
> net dollars in your pocket from the sale of your home? So, if I could
> prove to you that you will realize a larger net through my representa-
> tion, we would have a basis for doing business together, is that right?"

> 2. "Mr. Smith, right now in the marketplace, the average list price to
> sale price is _____ percent. My average list price to sale price is
> _____ percent. That means that you will put an extra _____ percent in
> your pocket by being represented by me compared to any other agent
> you are consulting. That's an extra $_____ based on the value of your
> home. Is that something that you are interested in?"

> 3. "Mr. Smith, the current days on the market for homes is _____. My
> days on the market, or time to sale, is _____. That reduction in market
> time is of huge benefit to you. It creates increased activity and show-
> ings on your home. It increases the probability of offers and good
> offers. It reduces your mortgage payments on a home that you don't
> want to own any longer. Do you see how this benefits you"

Create an Efficient Transaction

You can prove efficiency through client surveys, true closing percentages, and communication systems that you use to keep all parties in the transaction informed. The goal is to
save your client stress and money: the stress of not knowing whether an agent has done the
job and money delayed in closing fees, extra moving costs, interim rentals, and additional
living expenses. Studies show that less than 16 percent of consumers return to their previous agents; that stat demonstrates that clients aren't overwhelmingly thrilled with our ser-

vice. It also speaks to our after-sale service. Most consumers are merely satisfied with service as agents. In a recent survey by NAR, 69 percent of the people surveyed said the were satisfied with their real estate agent. Satisfied to me would probably be a C grade. I hard to create loyalty to an agent or brand when customers and clients are merely satisfie with our service.

> *"Do you, Mr. Seller, want to take the risk of extra stress and frustration in this transaction from an ordinary agent? An agent who, based on the stats, will lead you to do business with them again less than 16 percent of the time?"*

Realize that, if the transaction isn't efficient and timely, your client could also lose the opportunity to lock in a low interest rate. Typically, a 0.5 percent increase in rate would cost buyers close to $50,000 over the life of a 30-year mortgage. That is a considerable risk attached to a lot of money by choosing the wrong agent.

> *1. "Mr. Smith, it's a fact that only 16 percent of consumers return to an agent who worked with them previously. That statistic demonstrates that the efficiency level is low and the stress level is high for the customer. Well over _____ percent of my transactions are with repeat clients and the referrals they send my way. This difference, and my personal guarantee, creates a better, smoother transition for you into your new home. Do you see how this creates an advantage for you?"*

> *2. "Mr. Smith, a negative to an emotional, nonefficient transaction is that the buyer and seller can be at odds. That increases the probability of more costly repair negotiations, late closures, and last-minute demands to closing. We can save you money through a more efficient transaction process. Doesn't that make sense?"*

> . "Mr. Smith, the truth is, if the transaction isn't efficient and timely, the closing could be late. With the volatility of current interest rates, this could cost you in the long run over the life of your loan. Because we close over ____ percent of our transactions on time, we can ensure these costs don't happen to you. For a typical person, a ½ percent increase in rate equals close to $50,000 in extra payments over the life of a 30-year mortgage. Do you want to take that kind of risk with another agent?"

Positioning Strategy

As a result of your positioning strategy, can you prove that you produce more leads or more meaningful ad calls, sign calls, or Internet inquiries? Does this increase of leads generate more showing activity or more buyer consultations? Does the way in which you position the property within the real estate agent community result in more showings to more buyers? The first step is to prove to the client that your positioning strategy generates more showing activity. A Champion Agent generates more showing activity than other agents in the marketplace.

Do you have an inventory advantage that creates more showings as well? On average, I carried around 30 listings at any one time. It enabled me to cross-market my properties effectively with a wider reach to generate more showings than many other agents in the marketplace. Increased quantity of leads creates more opportunity for the seller. More leads generate more showings. More showings increase the probability of selling the home. The increased showings can also lead to a higher potential sales price for a high-demand home.

Law of Supply and Demand

The law of supply and demand drives real estate sales and real estate values in any marketplace. It drives appreciation, investment, and activity. It can also drive list price to sales price ratios, days on the market, and listings sold versus listings taken ratios for most agents. Champion Agents will always filter their strategy and positioning through the law of supply and demand. They will end up with far superior stats than other agents. They will counsel their prospects, customers, and clients on the influence of supply and demand in the marketplace. This is especially true when the marketplace is shifting.

When there is a shift from a seller's market (low inventory and high demand) to a neutral marketplace, Champion Agents will show inventory levels, sales price ratios, and sales per month and will counsel their clients based on the current market and where it is heading. Our job, as Champion Agents, is to inform our clients of the current and emerging market conditions. The law of supply and demand controls the frenzy in sellers' markets and the slow cautiousness in a heavy buyers' marketplace.

By knowing and tracking the marketplace, you can better position your clients to achieve the best results in the current marketplace. Your job is to clearly communicate how the law of supply and demand will affect each of your clients and how it is impossible to achieve significant results contrary to the law of supply and demand. Agents who are promising contrary results either don't really understand the marketplace, are overly optimistic and delusional, or lack the skill to be able to really represent their interest at the highest level. This will become very obvious to prospects if your discussion about the law of supply and demand is delivered with conviction and power. You need to tell the sellers and buyers that marketplaces heat up and explode because demand is greater than supply . . . it's that simple! When supply increases and demand falls, the activity level goes in the other direction.

> *1. "Mr. Smith, since we position your home more strategically, we increase the number of agents who actually show your home. With the increased showings, we can increase the buyers and potential offers. This creates more buzz on your home, which equates to more dollars in your pocket. Doesn't that appeal to you?"*

> *2. "Mr. Smith, one of my primary jobs is to enhance the demand for your home. Real estate at its core is a supply and demand business. My job is to increase the demand for your home over the competition in the marketplace. One way to know if an agent is successful at accomplishing that is to compare the statistics of listings sold versus listings taken. The broad average right now is ____ percent of homes actually sell. My average is over ____ percent. Would you agree that we are more effective at positioning your home?"*

Strong Property Demonstration

As a Champion Agent, you need to demonstrate the value of the property to two groups before selling the home. First, you demonstrate the value of the property to consumers when you show the property to them. You must be able to demonstrate the value, benefits, and features of the property as it relates to what else they could acquire in the marketplace.

By having intimate knowledge of the other competing homes in the marketplace, you can draw a contrast between your house and others. This is especially valuable to your sellers in homogeneous neighborhoods. When dealing with properties of similar or identical floor plans, the amenities or customization of the seller creates a greater leverage point for property demonstration. By demonstrating the superior yard, finish work, appliances, or granite countertops, you can increase or enhance the resale price and resale value for your clients.

Being able to communicate this to a buyer increases the emotional connection between the home and the buyer. It causes the client not to discount certain features and to achieve an accurate comparison between the home you're representing and other homes in competition for this buyer.

You need to demonstrate the value of the home to a second party: the co-op agent. Your job is to demonstrate value because that agent is working to negotiate your client down on behalf of his or her client, the buyer. The co-op agent's objective is to secure the home for his or her client and to accomplish that result with less money invested.

You can demonstrate or build value through property comparison. A Champion Agent needs to keep abreast of the competition in the marketplace at all times. One of the best techniques is to define the difference between the seller and the buyer.

Champion Calculation

Say if, for example, $5,000 separates the two parties; if you are representing the seller, it is in fact $5,000. To the buyers, it isn't $5,000, in most cases, unless they are paying cash. For most buyers, it means borrowing another $5,000. And at a 7 percent interest rate, it's $350 a year, or $87.50 a quarter, or $29 a month, or less than a dollar a day. It's really a minimal difference on the part of the purchaser. Your ability to demonstrate the value of the property and break down with this technique is paramount to achieving Champion-level status as an agent. The key question to ask your client is, "Are you willing to turn off the seller or get beat out by another offer to save a few dollars a month?"

1. "Mr. Smith, often buyers are down to two or three houses they are trying to decide among. With new competition coming on the market daily, it's important to move when you get on a buyer's short list. The agent can mean the difference between getting an offer or no offer, through their ability to demonstrate value and benefits of your home. Is that what you are looking for?"

> 2. *"Mr. Smith, when an agent is writing an offer on behalf of a buyer, or when we are negotiating with a buyer, it is imperative that your agent can demonstrate the value of your property compared to the competition. It is clear that I have that skill given my average list price versus sales price is ____ percent higher than the other agents. Do you see the benefit to you in that?"*

Effective Price versus Value Counseling

Many national marketplaces have shifted considerably in the past 12 months. The skill of *price/value counseling* has become even more essential in the past five years. The fundamental mistake that most agents are guilty of is using the wrong terminology. The buzzword most agents use is *price* or *price of the home.* This is incorrect. It's not about price; it's about *value.* The first step in effective price/value discussion is to use the word *value* instead of *price.* You need to focus the client on the value of the home today, in today's marketplace and market conditions.

When you look at price and the influence of price, it's really fundamentally connected to marketing. Raising or lowering the price of something creates a layer or smaller pool of potential purchasers, based on how the potential purchasers perceive the value. We all make our buying decisions based on value. The job of a Champion Agent is to position the property relatively close to its value to widen the pool of prospective purchasers.

As an example, a 10-year-old BMW 7 Series car has a certain value. You can price it at $100,000, but the real value of the car is substantially less than that. In fact, the *Kelly Blue Book* value is right around $15,000. What are the odds, if you were to price this car at $100,000 or $50,000 or even $25,000, that you would receive even close to those figures? As they say in Texas, "Slim to none, and slim just left town."

Too many agents still believe that price and value are interchangeable, but they are not. Value relates to actual worth—the amount of money one could expect to receive in the free market. It doesn't matter what the value was last year, last month, or even last week. Value is determined by the conditions and influences of the current marketplace. Too often, sellers get hung up on faulty thinking when the marketplace shifts against them, so to speak. They don't want to view the reality that their home, worth $750,000 a year ago, is today, based on supply and demand, worth only $680,000. Value is extended by the scarcity of something and the ease of replacement with similar, equal, or better products or service. In essence, this all correlates to the law of supply and demand.

> *1. "Mr. Smith, many agents are more concerned with securing your listing rather than having a real conversation about the value of your property. They talk in terms of price, not value. They will get you all worked up about the price and set you up for the big surprise. The question is, do you want the truth now or later?"*

> *2. "Mr. Smith, let's agree to talk in terms of value—what your house is worth. Once we agree on that, we can talk about price, which is really a marketing strategy. Is that agreeable to you?"*

Client Receives Benefits by Working with You

The truth is revealed up front. You don't operate by taking the listing and beating clients up on the price at a later date. This is a tactic that far too many agents employ and will be clearly reflected in their Big 3 numbers. If agents take listings above fair market value, their Big 3 numbers will be worse than the board average.

1. *Continuity of "real" dollars.* I firmly believe that clients expect to receive a specific net in their pocket, which they have predetermined in their mind based on the initial list price of the home. They make assumptions and plans based on that net dollar number. A Champion Agent gives the client realistic numbers of dollars that they can expect.

2. *More competitive positioning of the property.* Champion Agents are diligent about the competitive positioning of their clients. Too many agents are surprised by a change or adjustment in the marketplace. It is rare for a marketplace to change overnight. It only seems that way to most agents and sellers because of the lack of analysis, tracking, and preparation on the part of agents. Markets often experience a correction when inventory levels rise. If that is linked to a drop in sales numbers, the correction comes more swiftly, and the correction is larger.

3. *Creating aggressive buyers through value positioning.* Aggressive buyers lead to good offers, bidding for a seller's home, and a stronger negotiating position for the seller. All of these offer clear benefits to your sellers and lead to more money in their pockets. Skills in counseling effective price versus value are demonstrated only by Champion Agents.

"Why Should I Hire You" Exercise

Before I conclude the discussion on why someone should hire you, I want to help you uncover a few reasons, benefits, and strategies that are *unique* to you, that are unique to your custom approach to the real estate business.

1. List the 10 ways in which you add value when working with your clients.
2. Create a list of 10 things that differentiate you from your competition. (How are you positioning yourself?)
3. What benefits do your clients receive from your specific lists?

"Here is why you should hire me. Here are the benefits you will receive that are exclusive to me. I am worth what I charge; just ask me why." Being able to definitively assert these statements will enable you to climb the mountain of success to the Champion Agent level.

13

Protecting Your Commission

Champion Agents have the mindset and sales skills to be able to defend their value in the marketplace. One of the most significant challenges facing agents is the constant downward pressure on real estate fees over the past few years. There has been an erosion of fees charged by agents and companies of epic proportions.

Recently, I went out to dinner with friends, one of whom happened to be a very good real estate agent in Bend, Oregon (where I live). I was expressing my views on the scourge of discounting and commission cutting in the industry and in our town. I was obviously being forceful about it, because I got the business from my wife, Joan, when we left. I was stunned when I turned to the other agent in the group, and he didn't agree that discounting his fee was an error. My mouth hit the floor.

Understand Your Own Value

Champion Agents understand their worth and don't need to adjust their fees to attract clients. There are millions of prospects you can work with if you are willing to work for free. The number of potential prospects is unlimited. I could book myself to speak every day of every year if I were willing to speak for a lower fee or, in essence, give away my intellectual property for free. It doesn't take much skill to attract clients and prospects if your sole selling point is price-related.

The purpose of a service business is to provide service for compensation, and real estate agents are in a service business. I assume that we all are providing some level of service that is valuable to consumers in the marketplace. The key issue then becomes one of fair compensation.

The discounters' main strategy is to declare that we are all the same, that we all provide the same level of service, that there is no difference between discounters and full-commission brokers. I would call that the Southwest Airlines argument or the Charles Schwab argument. Extrapolating that theory to real estate is ludicrous.

The media has latched onto this issue of fees and trumpeted it from coast to coast. They purport to protecting the consumer from the big, bad real estate agents . . . ridiculous. They often use the analogy of the financial services industry or insurance industry to illustrate their point of how fees have decreased based on the technological advances in the world. To compare a stock transaction, life insurance policy, or airline seat from LA to Boston with the services of a real estate agent is comical and inaccurate.

If you decide to buy 1,000 shares of Microsoft stock, those 1,000 shares are exactly the same whether you purchase them from Merrill Lynch, Charles Schwab, or any other brokerage firm—or do it yourself online. The shares of Microsoft are truly a commodity. An airline ticket for a trip from Los Angeles to Boston is just a seat on a plane leaving on a certain day at a certain time from one location to another. There are subtle differences between Southwest, United, and American Airlines, but it's merely an airplane seat or a commodity. However, although many consumers view our service as a commodity, and discounters try to portray our service as a commodity . . . it's *not*.

Homes Are Not Commodities

Any home that you buy could never be equated to apples, an airline seat, or 1,000 shares of Microsoft. A home has differences in location, school district, finish work, lot size, decorating, emotional appeal, prestige, amenities, floor plan, placement on the lot, landscaping, color scheme—the list is really endless. All of these factors converge to determine sales price, future appreciation, and demand for the home. A home has far too many variables to be considered a commodity. All of those variables need to be evaluated by someone—either the purchaser or the seller or the agent selected to represent their interests.

Value of Service

As agents, the service model we use individually is not a commodity, either. There are differences between agents in sales skills, marketing skills, demonstrating-the-property skills, negotiation skills, value and pricing skills, and communication skills. There are differences in market knowledge, transaction process knowledge, and inventory knowledge. There are differences in strategy, philosophy, and track record of results. All of these differences create greater value for some agents' services than for others. The way a Champion Agent combats the erosion of fees is by not lowering fees to compete and instead raising the personal conviction of the value of his or her service in the marketplace.

Whenever price is the question, value is the answer. When consumers question your price or fee for service, they are really questioning the value. They are essentially saying, "I don't see the value for the fee you charge." You don't win by then lowering your fee to compete. Most agents provide more value to the consumers than we give ourselves credit for. We have never really attached or defined the value for each of the services we provide to our clients. The barrier that exists before you can become a Champion Agent who can charge an upper-level fee for your service is *belief.* You must believe that your service far exceeds the cost.

One way to enhance your mindset is through regular affirmations of your value. Being able to say and believe in your value is one of the initial steps to higher fees and less price competition.

Affirmations of your value

1. I am absolutely worth what I charge.   You have to believe it yourself before you can convince others. Do you believe this statement to your core?

2. My value is measurably greater than my competitor's.   The key word is *measurably.* Is there a scale or measurement that can prove through empirical evidence or data that you sell the home in less time or for more money? Can you prove factually, not subjectively, that you are better and that you provide more value?

3. The value of my services clearly exceeds my cost.   If you can show and define the value of each component of your service in dollars or percentage of sales price and then compare it to the actual cost, you can tip the scales in your favor.

4. I don't give away my hard-earned and well-deserved fees.   To reach the Champion level in earnings, you have to stop giving away your fees. When you adjust your fees, you are merely adjusting your net profit. All of the commission fees you fail to collect are revenue that would have flowed straight to the bottom line. You are giving away your net profit . . . that's all! Consider the following factors:

Risk. What consumers, and even agents, fail to recognize is the risk-to-reward relationship in our business model. We, as an industry, could charge lower fees if some of the risks were shifted to the seller or buyer. Because we are assuming all of the risks, our fees need to reflect that. We risk our time, energy, money, knowledge, and emotion with an expected return when the home sells or the buyer buys. What if the home doesn't sell or the buyer doesn't buy? We have to amortize the cost of our service over fewer transactions. This raises the costs of our service on a per-transaction basis, thereby reducing our net profit.

Expenses. Even if a full fee is acquired at closing, we have paid for all of our time, living expenses, marketing, and advertising dollars out of our own pocket. Additionally, in most cases we do not receive 100 percent of the total commission; we split the fee with another co-op agent. Our broker receives some of the compensation as a percentage of the commission or a desk fee. We then need to account for our expenses in marketing, advertising, pro rata share of car, insurance, gas, errors and omissions (E&O) insurance, cell phone, Internet site, assistant's salary, and all other fixed costs for our business.

Taxes. We also need to pay our taxes. Since we are, in effect, self-employed, we pay the employer and employee section of the payroll taxes, FICA, Medicare, and so on. The tax rate is usually 15 percent total for self-employed people. We must then pay our federal and state withholding amounts, which can be up to 33 percent for federal and often up to 10 percent for the state. Many of us pay in excess of 50 percent of our net income, after expenses, to taxes. When you calculate actual net dollars earned, it's easy to see why you don't want to give away your hard-earned and well-deserved fees.

5. I firmly believe that cut-rate fees accompany cut-rate service. It is not possible to provide more service for less money. When the cost of service goes down, the service goes down as well. Discounters have to cut something out. Southwest Airlines is often used as the model for discount fee success. Its cheaper tickets are accompanied by cut-rate service. You get peanuts to eat. You can't buy a snack on board. You don't know where you are going to sit until you compete with others for the best seats. There is no option for an upgrade for the frequent flyer group. Southwest flies smaller planes, only 737s. It has zero wide-body or two-aisle aircraft in its fleet. This lowers comfort for flyers on longer cross-country flights. There is no entertainment on board (except the flight attendants). Cut-rate fees always accompany cut-rate service. Most consumers, when working with a real estate agent who offers discounts, don't think they will receive cut-rate service. They expect to receive high levels of service for low levels of fees. In the end, life and business don't work that way.

6. In the end, you get what you pay for. We don't usually beat the system, although we all secretly wish we could. We get what we pay for. There is a reason that a Mercedes sells for far more than a Kia. The question is, do you want a car to get from point *A* to point *B*? A

Kia will do that. In real estate sales, your safety, future appreciation, current sales price, and net dollars at closing could be compromised by selecting the discount agent.

The Four Ps of Marketing

One of the challenges for salespeople is selling in generalities when consumers really want specifics. If you stay in the generalities, you will lose. You need to show the consumers specifically what they will receive when working with you: what specific results they can expect in sales price, net proceeds, time frame, communication, and additional services—and how your approach differs from the competition. You need to show them what type of guarantee you offer, if any. The commodity mindset that consumers possess demands the specifics. If they don't receive them, it makes their decision to select the cheapest alternative a foregone conclusion.

Anyone who has ever taken a college-level marketing course probably remembers the four Ps of marketing. These four factors make up the elements of marketing: *product* (or service), *promotion, price,* and *place* (delivery system). When people apply a discounting strategy to their business, they are really trying to apply a marketing formula to attract more opportunity. This is true of any business in the world.

Product

For example, let's say you own a pizza parlor. Your sales are lower than you would like. What do most pizza parlor owners do? They use one or a combination of a few of the four Ps of marketing to increase sales.

As a pizza parlor owner, your product is pizza. You might offer salads, soda, and beer, but pizza is your revenue stream. There is not a lot you can do to change pizza. It is dough, some type of sauce (usually tomato-based), with cheese and other toppings added. Pizza Hut is always trying new types of pizza to expand sales, but other than changing a few toppings, pizza today is very similar to what it was 20 years ago.

As a real estate agent, what changes can you make in service? I believe there are numerous options and differences in services you can provide. The core problem is that prospects don't see them because you have never bothered to really show them. There is a huge opportunity for us here . . . unlike the pizza parlor owner.

Promotion

For the pizza parlor owner, this is the area shown frequently to consumers. Promotions include coupons in the newspaper, direct mail coupons, TV commercials, radio ads, and charity promotions, the most common of which are coupons of some type.

As an agent, you can increase your marketing promotion through newsletters, direct mail, farming, sending all kinds of things to your past clients and sphere, bus bench blurbs, and shopping cart ad copy. Some of these techniques produce results at a much higher level than others. You can spend any amount of money on promotions.

Price

Pizza parlor owners use this one extensively. It is often linked to a promotion—"get $2.00 off on your next purchase."

Agents often use price breaks to attract more business. We feel that, by lowering our fee or giving the appearance that we are willing to consider a lower fee, we attract more people. One challenge with this strategy is that repeat or referred clients will expect the fee to remain the same for future business. As an example, the auto industry tried to increase sales after 9/11 through 0 percent financing. By offering no-cost financing to their best customers, they increased sales. Almost five year later, they are still stuck using 0 percent financing on vehicles to generate sales. One short-term pricing strategy to fix sales has led to catastrophic results five years later. They can't seem to break away from giving away free money to finance their cars. Most of the automobile manufacturers make more money financing vehicles than they make on the sale of the vehicles (or they used to!). They promoted away their profit margins.

Place (Delivery System)

If you have a good business location, there is little reason to change. You might consider expanding to another market area. You can do this geographically, as a pizza parlor might.

As a real estate agent, you could also do this by market segment rather than geographically. You could start a farm; work expireds or FSBOs; create strategic alliances with lenders, probate attorneys, family law attorneys, and financial planners. Your place of business, in terms of market segment, is unlimited. The most obvious way to expand business is through increased advertising and reduction in the price. What is the easiest is not always the best.

Core Marketing Message

To be effective in marketing ourselves while still protecting our value and fees in the marketplace, there are three core marketing messages we need to establish.

You Are a Business

The first is the fact that you are in the business. Too many people forget that you are a real estate agent. A Champion Agent uses repetition of the message to drive a point home. Don't leave to chance or luck the possibility that people will remember you when it comes time for them or their friends to buy or sell.

> **Coach's Tip:** *Protect your commission through your service first and foremost by raising the value and perceived value the consumer receives. If you need more leads, rather than marketing discounts, focus on promotion or expanding your place of business. Look at attracting and creating new lead sources rather than marketing a reduced pricing strategy to increase potential clients.*

You Are Good at Your Job

The second message is that you are good at what you do—that you possess skills, abilities, and knowledge that few agents possess. You have to be cautious about how you convey this message. You don't want to come across as arrogant or self-absorbed, yet you do need to exude the confidence of a successful salesperson. Prove your value and the fact that you are a good real estate agent to each person you come in contact with.

Selecting the Right Representative Is Important

Third, you need to demonstrate that it is really important for the client to select the right representative. The people doing the discounting are trying to convince sellers and buyers that we are all the same. We must mobilize and explain to people that an agent can have a large effect on sales price and the smooth transition of the transaction. An agent can have a positive influence on the short- and long-term equity position.

Improve Your Skills and Marketplace Knowledge: Do Not Discount Your Fees

The natural tendency is for agents to lower their fees in competitive marketplaces where listings are tough to acquire. When the competition is fierce, rather than improving knowledge, skill, attitude, or activities to compensate for the increased competition, we lower fees to attract and secure more prospects. Champion Agents apply the opposite approach; they work to increase their activities, to increase their leads, and to increase lead sources. They focus on raising their skills and knowledge to create more recognizable differences between themselves and the competition. This allows Champion Agents to convert prospects to clients in higher volume despite their higher commission rates. Finally, they control and improve their attitude so they can increase the number of prospects and the conversion rate.

Too many agents figure that their work will be less strenuous, that they will exert less effort to achieve a specific sale. They hope that the property will sell in a week or a few days, and they equate the shorter time frame to quicker and cheaper marketing, thus justifying a reduction in fees. I have never heard of doctors lowering the cost of surgery because the operation took less time than they expected. The charge is based on the procedure. In some cases they take less time and in others more time to complete the surgery. They don't rebate the easier ones, because they know they may have a really tough one in the next few weeks.

If we get in the habit of discounting or rebating fees because one sale is easier or quicker than another, we will lose in the long run. There is no way of telling how difficult or easy a transaction will be to complete until you have fully closed the transaction and are looking back. You cannot predict whether a sale will occur quickly and easily. There are always transactions during the course of the year that you do not make a profit on because of the difficulty and stress associated with them.

I know what it's like to try to defend my value and fee structure. I know what it feels like to be face-to-face with a tough seller and to be asked to cut my commission rate. I have faced that request hundreds of times; prospects say that another agent will do it for less money. I have also had both buyers and sellers, during negotiation, expect me to cut my fee or to participate in buying and selling the home through a fee reduction.

Myth 1. *Champion Agents who never cut their commission aren't being asked to as often as other agents.* It isn't that they are asked less frequently to reduce their fee; it's that Champion Agents just won't do it. They choose not to play that game. They have the personal integrity, sales skills, and mental strength to be able to defend their value and not give away their hard-earned and well-deserved fees and profit. The truth is that high-volume Champion Agents are asked to reduce their fee *more* frequently than other agents. That's because they put themselves in more selling situations, which raises the likelihood of the subject coming up more frequently in the course of business.

Myth 2. *A little adjustment in my fee won't hurt.* The minute you consider the option of a fee adjustment, you have opened Pandora's box. You have started down the slippery slope. Most agents are willing to adjust a little, but they shouldn't. They will be unable to stop once they start.

I believe the fees you charge affect your self-esteem and self-confidence. By cutting your fees, you are sabotaging yourself. When you accept less, you start to feel that you aren't worth as much, that your value is diminished. I know few people who feel like Champions when they walk away having adjusted their fee downward. In fact, most of them feel poorly. Some will even beat themselves up over being weak. This whole negative mindset will affect your future performance. It will create a negative self-image and negative expectation when you are faced with the tough situation again.

In addition, some people feel guilty because they are giving preferential treatment to one person over another. You may feel as though you are taking advantage of the client who is willing to pay you a full fee. We can feel unethical about changing our fees, because we know deep down inside that one of our clients is getting a raw deal. We turn ourselves into the equivalent of a car salesperson.

Consumers have always rated car salespeople at the lowest levels on the respect chain. The reason is twofold. First is the high-pressure, hot-box technique often used to sell cars. The second is because they know others are buying the same car for less, which seems unfair. This is especially true for women. Women, on average, buy the same cars for more money than do men. The same car will sell for various prices for different people, even in the same day. Do you want that to be your reputation as an agent?

No Two-Deal Philosophy

Each transaction takes its own individual effort, work, knowledge, and expertise. Your surgeon doesn't offer you a discount on the second operation. I had surgery in college to remove a cyst on my tailbone. The doctor didn't get it all the first time, so a year later, I had to do it all over again. My parents paid for the second operation even though the surgery wasn't completely successful the first time. This volume-discount philosophy occurs only when you don't clearly express your value in each individual transaction.

A few years ago, my father sold the family home that I grew up in. He also bought a condo in downtown Portland to live in. He knew which building he wanted to live in. I flew up to look at all the condo choices he had in that building. In a few hours, we settled on the right one for him. My father, his real estate agent, and I discussed how the offer needed to be constructed and presented. Once that was agreed to, I watched in horror as the agent, who was a good agent, slipped into his listing-presentation mode right there in the condo. He proceeded to talk about listing my father's home. He concluded his 10-minute discussion by stating that he would charge 1 percent less than his normal fee if Dad would buy and sell through him. He gave away 1 percent, or 33 percent of his gross fee, and probably over 70 percent in profit, within 10 minutes, and he wasn't even doing a real listing presentation! He didn't have the paperwork, didn't have the value of the home figured out, hadn't evaluated the marketplace, didn't know the services that my father wanted. He just gave away his hard-earned dollars before my father even asked.

The truth is, my father would never have asked for a reduction in fee. I had done a few previous transactions with my father involving investment property and development land. As his agent, I never offered a reduced fee, and he never asked. I never offered because I was worth every penny of the fees I charged. This agent, who is prominent in the Portland market, gave away about $4,000 in commission at the drop of a hat. I would estimate he gives away between $75,000 and $100,000 a year in net profit because of his rebate philosophy. He has probably given away in excess of $1 million in commissions in his 15-year career!

The only good news is that I get lots of mileage out of telling how even seemingly successful agents are not always Champion Agents. A Champion Agent would never operate that way! The list of available prospects and customers is unlimited if you are willing to work for free or at a substantial discount. It doesn't take any particular skill to attract people as prospects if you discount.

Real Objections to Your Fee

There are only two viable objections to your commission rate. You either haven't established value for your service or the seller or buyer has a fear that you haven't addressed properly. These client fears are real and must be eliminated before you can secure a representation contract from a buyer or seller.

1. *Fear of making the wrong decision.* You must probe to understand the root of this fear. It could be a previous bad experience with a real estate agent. It could also be that the client feels the need to talk with parents or friends. A commission reduction, even if asked for, will not alleviate this fear. The client still won't sign unless you deal with the "wrong decision" fear. Having an understanding of that fear, and giving reassurance that you will do everything to make sure the fear will never be realized, handles it for most people.

2. *Fear of making any decision.* Some people are paralyzed by decisions. They brood, steam, and toss and turn all night about decisions. The perceived risk is significant. You have to lower the risk in their mind. An easy-exit listing agreement, whereby they can void the listing quickly, will provide more relief than fee reduction. These people want to think about it. We need to find out what they need to think about. In order to secure them as

clients, you have to isolate the fear and walk them through the situations and challenges that come to mind, overcoming each one.

3. *Fear of change.* Commission reduction really won't help with these people, either. We often try to motivate them based on the monetary deal. We have to sell the benefits of change. Identify the worst-case situation to prove to them that there is a limited downside. Personal reassurance of the next steps and of the protection and security you are offering will work well. You might even build a sense of urgency based on the marketplace, interest rates, or the fear of loss. Convince them that the window of opportunity is open now and might not be as favorable a few months down the road.

4. *Fear of being cheated.* For some people, this one can take aim at your fees for service. We must build value for our service to show that, because of our skills and strategy, they will end up with a high sales price, more potential buyers viewing their home, a higher probability of a sale, better negotiations, and a smoother transaction with less risk. Because they are receiving all of those benefits, the value is enhanced, so the fees don't need to be lower. You have to demonstrate clearly that, even though they are paying more, they are getting more value.

5. *Fear of looking bad to others.* Most people want social acceptance by others. Other friends and neighbors will talk about how they worked on an agent to reduce the fee. It's like a badge of honor in the community. Some people use it as the litmus test to make decisions, because the social recognition is so important. The way to combat this is, again, with value.

6. *Fear of acting without sufficient knowledge or reflection.* Too often, agents attack this problem with fee reductions, trying to create a decision now. The best defense for this fear is a good offense. Know how they typically make decisions of this magnitude. What is their decision process? Know the timing of when they want to buy or sell. Some of selling is being in front of the prospect at the right time. There is no substitute for correct timing of your presentation.

All of these fears are born out of a heightened feeling of risk. They are really not commission-based concerns. Focus on assuming the risk yourself or removing it. Then, give your prospects strong reassurances that they are making the right decision and that they should make it now. Don't concentrate on your cost of service; focus on reassurance and work to pinpoint the client's fears and remove them.

When you give up commission, you end up working harder for less money. Your clients and prospects respect you less. They feel in greater control of the relationship and the transaction. They will usually start to take greater advantage of that control and extract more from you. It's like the old saying, "Give them an inch, and they take a mile."

There have been hundreds, even thousands, of studies done over the years about buying trends. In all of these surveys, when people decide on a product or service, the price of the product usually comes in as the fifth or sixth most important factor in their decision. We often treat the price as the number one factor, not the fifth.

Theory of Self-Exclusion

I know what some of you are thinking. Some of you are tapped into the theory of self-exclusion. The theory of self-exclusion says that your marketplace, your competition, your services, and your customers are so different that a full commission arrangement could never happen. That simply is not true. Even in high-priced marketplaces, agents are getting full fees. I have had clients in Beaver Creek, Colorado, Lake Tahoe, California, and Destin, Florida, where the average sales price is north of $1 million. These markets, by and large, have little discounting by any agent. If those markets and agents convince their sellers of their value, why not you?

> **Coach's Tip:** *Your career success hinges on your conviction and belief in your personal value. You must have the attitude that "I am worth more than the competition . . . ask me why!"*

Attitude and Expectation

There are two key concepts that will lead to success in your life. These concepts control the successful outcome of your business, marriage, and many other areas of life. Although you may have incredible talent and skill in life, you will fail if you do not master these two concepts, and vice versa. Even if you have only limited talent and skill, you will win if you live by these two concepts. These two concepts determine your future: *attitude* and *expectation*.

If you have a positive, forward-looking attitude, you will accomplish great things. How is *your* attitude? Does it need improvement? Are you positive and upbeat? If you have the attitude that every challenge or obstacle leads to new opportunity, success is all but guaranteed. Thomas Edison was said to have worked on creating the electric lightbulb because darkness interfered with his ability to conduct further experiments. He wanted to be able to work long into the night. Edison could have moaned about the darkness—though that would not have done any good. He used his attitude and solved a problem of darkness.

Build a Positive Attitude

Start building your attitude today. Convince yourself that you are the best agent anyone could hire. You yourself have to be convinced before anyone else will be convinced. The attitude you bring when faced with commission objections will help you handle them and get the contract signed. The attitude that you take when you have a problem transaction will make the difference between a deal closing or falling through.

One technique to improve your attitude is by using affirmations. Affirmations drive positive mental pictures into your subconscious mind. Here are some affirmations:

> **Coach's Tip:** *Say, read, rehearse, and internalize your affirmations daily. Put them on a few 3 × 5 cards. Put one on your mirror, so you can see it each morning when you get ready for work. Put it on the visor of your car and computer screen—anywhere you will see it and be reminded to say it a few times a day. To sell your value, you have to believe in it first.*

- I am a great salesperson.
- I am skilled at handling objections and getting the contract signed.
- People do business with me because I am positive, knowledgeable, and professional.
- I earn _____ [you fill the blank].
- I am a great spouse.

Expect to Be Successful

The second power word is *expectation*. If you don't expect to win, you will not win. If you go on a listing and expect to take it at your price and commission, you will. If you go expecting a fight on commission and your price, you will receive that also. Make sure to set the positive expectation of success before the appointment with a prospect or client. You also need to set a positive expectation before every call you make. Expectation is the gateway to confidence. The first step to having unshakeable confidence is to believe that you are the agent for the job, that you are a Champion Agent. If your expectation is strong

Champion Example

Many years ago, Henry Ford went to his engineers and told them to build him an eight-cylinder engine. They said it could not be done. Ford plainly told them to go do it and report back in 90 days. After 90 days, they reported back to Ford. They had spent the whole 90 days figuring out why an eight-cylinder engine was impossible. In the meeting with Ford, they spent their time trying to convince him it could not be done. Ford's attitude and expectation of an eight-cylinder engine was stronger than the engineers' attitude and expectation that it could not be done. (We all know who won in the end!)

enough, people will come around to your way of thinking. You just need to be stronger in will and mental focus than your clients, prospects, and other agents.

Your expectation will create your reality. You have to expect before you can receive. You need to expect that people and situations will enable you to create the future you desire. Expectation does not mean you don't have to work. You will work harder than before to develop the outcome you desire. Expectation of success takes away the fear of failure.

> *"Winning is not a sometime thing; it's an all-time thing.*
> *You don't have to win once in awhile,*
> *you don't do things right once in awhile,*
> *you do them right all the time.*
> *Winning is a habit; unfortunately, so is losing."*
> *—Vince Lombardi*

The Value of Professional Service

This can be summed up in a simple equation:

$$\text{Value} = \text{benefits} - \text{cost}$$

Figure 13.1 shows pie charts representing this equation. The value of your service must exceed the clearly defined benefits a client or prospect will receive after subtracting the cost of the service. The problem for most agents is that the benefits of doing business with them are not clearly conveyed to the client, so the cost looks significant and the value looks minute. With limited defined benefits, it will be impossible to defend your fee structure.

Fee Counseling

Champion Agents follow a structure when discussing their fees for service.

Never discuss fees over the phone.   We are often asked what we charge in commission on the phone. You will automatically lose if you give an answer to this question that remotely resembles a number or percentage of sales price.

Prospects may cross you off immediately as a possible service provider based on fee, not value, or they could use your number to secure an even lower commission rate from someone else. You lose every time . . . guaranteed.

The best response to that question over the phone is "it depends." The response "it depends" doesn't commit you to either a full fee or a discounted fee. It doesn't eliminate

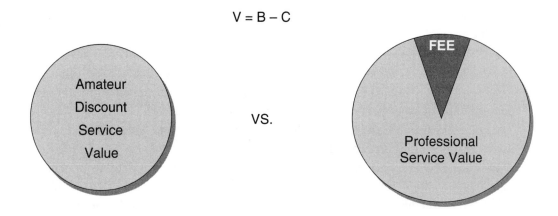

$$V = B - C$$

Some Value = Net Loss = Loss of Business

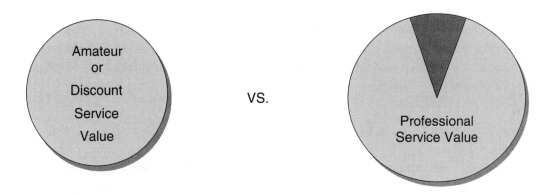

More Value = More Net = More Business

Figure 13.1 The Value of Professional Service

you as a possible listing agent. You will need to explain to prospects what it depends *on*. It depends on:

1. *The competitiveness of the marketplace segment the prospects are in.* You want reasonable odds of earning a fee. A listing in a highly competitive market segment might demand more of your time, energy, and dollars to create a sale.
2. *The price they want for the home.* If they want to overprice and undercommission the home, again, your odds of earning any fee get pretty long.
3. *Their expectation of service.* What do the sellers expect from you in terms of marketing, communication, time invested, and results? The sellers may want extensive advertising and marketing, even though they are searching for a reduced-fee arrangement. Maybe they desire and expect multiple open houses per month, conducted by you personally. Their expectations, in terms of sales price and days on the market, could be outlandish based on the current and emerging market trends.
4. *The anticipated return on investment of your resources.* You invest resources to create every sale. What is your estimate of time, energy, dollars, and emotions against the projected return? (It's hard to evaluate that without interviewing the seller, evaluating the competition and market trends, and understanding the condition of the property.)
5. *The condition of the property.* The property condition can influence the days on the market, eventual sales price, and whether the home actually sells. Even a Champion Agent can't make a prudent decision in most cases without evaluating the condition of the property.

Never discuss commission before you have fully explained your services.   Often, the commission discussion will be moved to the front of the listing presentation by potential sellers. They want to know what you will be charging them. The problem is that they have no idea, at this juncture, how to compare your services to those another agent is offering, or even how your services compare with their expectations. They haven't been told by you that, based on the marketplace, they must have certain services to achieve what they desire in a sale. Champion Agents do not allow a seller to move the commission discussion ahead of their explanation of services and value.

Always demonstrate your value and benefits before discussing a fee structure. Clearly explain the benefits of doing business with you. Being able to quantify the value of your services in dollars or percentage of sales price can help quantify the value you bring to the table. When price is the question, value is the answer.

Never show desperation. You may currently have zero listings and zero buyers. You may be down to your last $100 in your checking account, with your house and car payments overdue. The minute people sense you are desperate, only two things can happen, and both are bad:

> **Coach's Tip:** *Value = benefits – cost. Without explaining benefits before you discuss price, you run the risk that clients will be fixated on the cost of the service and hear nothing about the value. Your job is to increase the value and benefits to such a level that the cost of your service is inconsequential.*

1. They go for the jugular. They sense your need to take the listing at any commission because you are out of inventory. They intensify their focus to grind you down on the commission, costing you even more money.
2. They decide you are desperate and decide that it's not in their best interest to be represented by a desperate agent, even if that agent is willing to take any commission level.

Always demonstrate mutual fairness and the risk you assume. You must demonstrate that you are being fair with people, that you don't receive all the commission because the co-op agent receives about 50 percent, that the broker receives another ____ percent, that your business expenses are ____ percent, that you are self-employed and pay 15 percent self-employment tax, that you pay another ____ percent in federal and ____ percent in state taxes, that the check goes through a lot of hands before you actually receive the money to pay yourself and your bills.

You must tell them that you are assuming all of the risk of expenses to market, advertise, and promote their property to consumers and agents, that you might entertain a fee change provided they write a check for a $5,000 nonrefundable retainer, with the money to be released to you in the next 24 hours. For you to assume all of the risk, as most agents do, while lowering your fee really exposes you to a greater risk, not lower risk.

Always highlight your key points

1. *Market position, market competitiveness, market differentiation.* You can easily do these by driving home the Big 3:
   - Average list price to sales price
   - Average days on the market
   - Average listings sold versus listings taken

These are the statistics of Champion Agents. They use them to create competitive differences between their services and the results of other agents.

2. *Full service, what they receive, and their advantages.* By clearly conveying the advantages, benefits, and favorable odds of working with you, you effectively answer why

someone should hire you: because of the benefits and advantages of your service, philosophy, and results.

3. *No discounted fees.* It fundamentally matters which agent people select to represent their interests. Through strong conviction, you can more skillfully get prospects and clients to realize that you will not discount, that you have strong beliefs in your value and service, and that an agent who will not fight for his or her own income and value will be hard-pressed to fight for the client's sales price and sales equity.

14

Handling Objections Professionally

An unskilled salesperson fears hearing objections, but a Champion Agent views objections as opportunities. It is amazing how an objection raised in the sales process can make most agents look like a deer caught in the headlights: a blank look of disbelief just before the front grille of your car connects with deerskin at full speed. If the deer manages to move at all, it's at the last split second before fatal impact, leaving you to experience a heart-pounding rush of adrenaline for the next 30 minutes. Many agents react to objections the same way that a deer reacts to an oncoming car: they freeze in terror, moving only at the last second before the buyer or seller runs them over.

Often, agents view an objection as a big wall between them and the sale—a wall so tall that they can see no way around, over, under, or through it. But objections are more like a two- or three-foot-high picket fence. There are, in fact, many ways over it . . . or you can just walk down a ways and find the gate.

Objections Are Opportunities

A Champion Agent knows that most objections result from one of two situations: (1) the sellers or buyers have legitimate concerns regarding the property, or (2) they have doubts about your ability to make the sale happen. The first situation is usually price-based. The sellers think that their home is worth more in the marketplace or more than you would recommend.

Price-Based Objection

This is your signal to go back to the price. Explain again the importance of proper pricing. Show that they are today, and will be in the future, the highest bidder for their home. Remove the emotion from the discussion and look at the facts. The more emotion you allow into the discussion, the higher the price the sellers will want. You must have conviction and belief in your price. It is imperative to show that conviction when handling objections effectively. Remember, this is your opportunity to overcome the concern and then ask for the order again. Every objection is an opportunity to close.

Concern about Your Ability to Handle the Sale

The second situation that brings up objections is that your presentation was not good enough, so the seller has concerns about your abilities. This objection stems from your presentation and conviction. When this arises, Champion Agents will go back and focus on the track record and will convince the sellers of their ability to get the job done. Then they will ask for the agreement from the seller. This can be done many ways. I would often ask question such as, "Do you believe I can sell your home?" If they said yes, I would ask for the order. If they said no, I would ask the most important and powerful question in sales: "Why?" It allowed me to get to the bottom of the objection.

An objection arises because you did not convey the confidence that you are the person the seller should hire for the sale of his or her home. You did not make a convincing enough presentation for the buyer to purchase the home through you. The client's desire to work with you is a natural ending to a good presentation. If the presentation is weak, the objections will flow like a river.

Another observation regarding objections is they truly are an opportunity to get a signed contract. When buyers or sellers give you an objection, they are presenting you with an opportunity to close, basically saying, "I like this, but there is one factor I do not like." The buyer might say, "If the home you are showing me had a larger patio, it would be right for me." All you have to do is locate a larger patio and you have made a sale. You must put on your problem-solving hat. If you solve the problem, then you get the opportunity to ask the client to buy.

Without the challenging aspect of selling objections, you would simply be a person with a relatively unchallenging job. The truth is, most of us wouldn't want that. One of the reasons that salespeople are paid so well is because of the objections that people have to purchasing or making a sale. If the challenge of sales objections didn't exist, you would be an order taker. People who take orders aren't paid very well.

The Law of Difficulty

The law of difficulty basically says this: The harder the task, the fewer the people who will try to accomplish it. There is an advantage to the tougher tasks like being a Champion-level objection handler. Most agents will not do the work to perfect the skill. Once you have perfected the skill, you will have limited competition. When most people face a challenging problem or task, they will stop before they even get started. That's why so few agents have the right attitude about objections and the skills to make the sale in spite of the objections or concerns of the prospect.

Become Exceptional in a Specialized Area

There are two ways I have discovered in life to make a lot of money. These are, in essence, two choices we make on how we will approach our business. The first is to be exceptional at something that, fundamentally, no one else can do. The world has become a world of small niches or specialists. We can look to the fields of medicine, law, sports, entertainment, and many other businesses to see evidence of specialists. The medical field started this trend years ago, but the concept has branched into other fields. Being a specialist in real estate niches or skill areas can pay handsomely. I would suggest being a specialist in handling objections. Be prepared for all that comes along. Don't be sidelined, sidetracked, or blindsided by anything a prospect says.

Do Something No One Wants to Do

The second option for high earnings is to do something that no one else wants to do. Some jobs in this world earn large incomes because few people want to do them. For example, working in the oil fields of the Middle East, working on a fishing boat in the Bering Sea, working for an asbestos removal company—all are highly paid but highly unpopular jobs. Salespeople can fall into that category as well. No one likes rejection, especially when you are as close to making a sale as you are when you hear an objection. Mastering objections leads to increased sales, performance, and income.

Champion Rule: *Objections are a gift.*

When a client or prospect expresses an objection, it is merely a request for more information. It's not a *no,* but rather a *not yet* or a *maybe.* The client or prospect is telling you exactly what he or she wants or needs. All you have to do is listen, not panic, probe, respond with an answer, and ask for a commitment. If you can show that you can meet the expressed need, you are more likely to close the sale.

> **Champion Rule:** *Objections are an offensive opportunity in sales, not a defensive position.*

An objection brings an opportunity to resolve an issue in the prospect's mind and then ask for the order. It's really an offensive moment to step boldly forward and make the sale. A Champion Agent starts the objection handling process at the time of qualifying the prospect for an appointment. This effective qualifying process enables the Champion Agent to determine which objections will likely arise during the appointment.

Coach's Tip: *Now is a good time to review this valuable information in Chapter 11, "The Champion Listing Presentation." These questions and thoughts will help you uncover the challenges that await you at the appointment. They will also help you determine if any conditions exist that would prevent the prospect from moving forward.*

Condition versus Objection

A problem arises when agents mistake conditions for objections. Agents often treat a condition as an objection and beat themselves up when they don't close the transaction or get the contract signed. A condition voices a valid reason for the prospect not to move forward. You still need to try all the techniques of handling the objection. You just need to realize that a condition is usually linked to the inability or lack of authority to act now.

Clients might have the desire to move forward with you, but may lack the ability or authority to do so. Ability relates to financial capacity, credit score, and down payment. Those types of issues relate to their ability to act. Authority relates to the ultimate decision maker. Is there anyone else who will be influencing this decision? (Young couples and first-time home buyers often do not have the authority to make a decision without outside guidance, which is usually a parent.)

The most common conditions are lack of money, lack of creditworthiness, and (in the case of a seller) lack of equity. You might not be able to overcome these to make a sale. It is better to know early, before you invest the time in the presentation, if your efforts are guaranteed not to result in a signed contract.

Another condition that is occurring more frequently is a prepayment penalty on a mortgage for a buyer. This clearly could be a condition. My best advice is don't waste your time trying to overcome impossible conditions. Sometimes, you can invest more time than it's worth trying to be the hero. If you are prospecting consistently, you will have more than enough opportunities that do not carry overly burdensome conditions.

Champion Dos and Don'ts of Objection Handling

There is a series of mistakes that prevent most salespeople from reaching the Champion level in their objection handling. In this section, I address the most common mistakes that stunt agents' progress.

1. *Let them be heard.* I have listened to countless agents' presentations. Often, when the client begins to object, the agent leaps into objection-handling mode too soon. Many don't even wait to let the prospect finish the thought. They interrupt,

Coach's Tip: *Be careful not to blur the lines between an objection and condition by becoming emotionally involved. Realize that conditions are often temporary. Circumstances or the market conditions can change. Credit can improve; new loan programs can be created; new children arrive; prepayments can be negotiated. Don't fail to keep in touch with people who have conditions about the possibility of moving forward at some other point in time.*

which is certainly rude to the prospect. It can also cause frustration on the part of the prospects. It's almost as though the agent is hoping to stuff the objection back into their mouth before they even get it out. You need to let prospects express their views and concerns fully.

2. *Argue and lose.* There is a fine balance between *guiding* prospects toward your advantages and the marketplace realities and *arguing* with them. I have, at times, crossed the line into arguing. Almost every time I did, it cost me the transaction or listing. When you feel that you are beginning to be at odds with the prospect, you need to rephrase everything into a question. It moves what might be considered verbal swordplay into a one-person battle. Prospects will be using their swords against themselves.

3. *Shrink it down to size.* You need to shrink any financial objection down to the true size. If it's a commission objection (you want 6 percent and the seller wants to pay 5 percent), you need to shrink it down to the 1 percent difference and not talk about 6 percent and 5 percent commission. If the seller wants to list at $450,000, and you know it needs to be priced at $399,000, you need to talk about $50,000.

You need to use payment, interest rate, inventory levels, list price to sales price, and monthly or even daily cost. The smaller we can make the difference between where prospects want to be and what we think is necessary to achieve their goals and create a reasonable fee for us, the better. That is the key discussion.

Once you have shrunk it down, you can then do a comparison close of the difference: "If [the commission rate, initial list price, etc.] were the same between myself and Agent X, who would you select to represent your interests? So, if I were willing to ____ like Agent X, you would commit to working with me right now . . . correct?"

4. *The "but" of the problem.* The most common error in objection handling is using the word *but.* Using *but* in objection handling is the kiss of death. The *but* negates what you said up until that juncture. Here are some examples:

- "I understand how you feel about my commission, *but* I really feel I am worth it."
- "I hear what you are saying about the list price you want to start at, *but* are you aware of the market conditions?"

Using *but* tells the prospect you really didn't listen to them, and in fact, you don't even care that you didn't listen. It also says, "The things I said to you were said to make you feel comfortable with me. I am just trying to manipulate you to make a sale. I wanted to make you think that I liked you and accepted your thoughts." The *but* says, "I'd agree with you, but you are wrong."

Coach's Tip: *Many salespeople try to substitute* however *for the word* but. *The truth is,* however *is really a dressed up* but. *It's really a but wearing a bowtie. Champion Agents do not negate what they have said previously.*

5. *Get offensive.* I showed earlier that objection handling is really an offensive opportunity. It's not a time to play defense. When you respond to an objection, the final part of the objection should be a question. You should respond to the objection and then ask to proceed forward. Even asking whether there are other questions sets the stage for the close. You can use any question you want: "Shall we get started?" or "Do you want me to handle the sale for you?" or "Shall we do a broker opening this week or next?" or "When can I bring the first buyer through?" There is an unending series of questions that can be asked. You have to get in the mindset that you are going to use objections as a scoring opportunity.

Two C's of Objection Handling

1. *Communication.* Look at your ability to communicate at the Champion Agent level. You need to evaluate your verbal, vocal, and visual communication skills. The vocal and visual are the most powerful when dealing with objections.

Verbal. These are the actual words and phrases you use to communicate to people. The words really don't convey the complete story, since they account for only 7 percent of communication. However, it is hard to think about how best to use the vocal and visual to improve your communication and conversion if you are stuck focusing on the words.

Vocal. This is the tone and pace of your delivery. This carries more weight than the words. We experience 38 percent of our communication using the vocal medium.

Visual. This is what people see when you speak. It's the powerful, subtle head nods, confident posture, and eye-to-eye contact. This form of communication accounts for 55 percent. Your body language conveys how you perceive yourself and the value of your service. If you visually demonstrate that you are the best, the prospect and clients will have more faith in your claim. They can see right through practiced responses that are inconsistent with the body language. The salesperson who exudes confidence and excitement will generate the same feeling in their prospects and clients.

2. *Confidence.* When your confidence goes up, your competence goes up, as well. When you communicate your confidence, and the prospect feels that you are prepared to handle the objections that you might encounter, this will reduce the number of objections they express to you. They will sign more quickly. This confidence must come from the initial contact with the prospect. My question is, what do you need to improve on to dramatically raise your confidence. What skills do you need to practice? What mental attitude do you need to change? Is there knowledge that needs to be acquired?

Respond to Objections

After working with thousands of agents, it is obvious to me that most agents have memorized a few objection-handling scripts but haven't created a pattern to respond to objections. When you watch great golfers prepare for a shot, they have a pattern or preshot routine they follow before they make a swing. There is a six-step pattern that will create your success if you use it repeatedly.

1. Pause.
2. Acknowledge.
3. Explore.
4. Isolate.
5. Answer.
6. Close.

Pause

Take the time to take a breath before you answer an objection. It ensures that you have listened properly and that the client has completed his or her thought. It also keeps you from interrupting.

In the pause, you can also restate the objection to buy yourself additional time. Buying yourself a little time to think is good. It also gives the buyer time to think. I have had situations where, during the pause, the client or spouse answered the objection. (Do not be too proud to accept help from spouses or significant others to make a sale. They know the person's objections and know how to overcome them better than you do.) If you restate the objection incorrectly, the prospect will correct you. It ensures that you are really addressing the right objection.

Acknowledge

This means recognizing there is an issue or concern here. I did not say that you agree. That is completely different than thanking people for bringing it up or thanking them for the question or acknowledging their concern. To say to them, "I see what you mean," or "I understand what you are saying," only acknowledges it. It's a great technique. You are not there to say they are right, unless they are right. You might also praise the prospect by saying, "That's a really good question."

Acknowledgment is a great technique to use when the timing of the objection is wrong. For example, if they ask you about commission before you have reached that place in your presentation where you discuss your fees, you could say, "That's a great question. May I answer that later in my presentation after we discuss my services, please?" or "I understand what you are saying; I have a flow to my presentation that works well for my clients. Would it be okay if I answer your concern when I talk about marketing? My clients have really felt that discussion links in well with your question." The truth is, once you acknowledge and delay the discussion, it rarely comes back up again. You have, in effect, hurdled the objection that was asked too early—through acknowledging it, delaying it, and then ignoring it.

Explore

You need to explore the client's frame of mind. Why is the client feeling or thinking that way? What is causing the concern? You need to probe. "Tell me more about it" or "Why do you feel that way?" are two excellent phrases to use in exploring your prospect's views.

Isolate

This is the one technique that separates good agents from Champion Agents. Most of us jump right into our verbal judo we have been taught by some broker, trainer, or manager. Isolation is the skill that separates Champion Performers from everyone else. It is the access point to get to the bottom-line objection. It creates access to the real reason, concern, or hesitation of the prospect.

Some prospects don't want to reveal the real objection because they know it's their last defense mechanism. Isolation helps you avoid the "I want to think it over" objection that some people use as a last resort. Since an objection is a request for more information, isolation defines the information they need. If we don't isolate, the prospect will dredge up more and more objections once you answer the first one well. You will put yourself in a cycle that will lead to "I want to think it over."

Most agents don't want to probe in the isolation stage because they are afraid of losing the sale. The truth is—you don't *have* the sale, so you can't lose it. When you are scared to isolate, it's because you think you can't afford to lose this potential sale; that's because you don't have enough appointments; that's because you don't have enough leads. You don't have enough leads, because you don't prospect enough. It's a vicious cycle.

> **Coach's Tip:** *Non-Champion agents often think that isolating objections causes even more objections. This is not true. Isolating objections just brings out the ones that are already there so that Champion Agents can respond to them.*

Isolation scripts.   Following are a number of isolation scripts that really work well. Practice and use these before you move on to answering objections.

1. Is that the only reason that holds you back from moving forward with me?
2. Other than that, is there any other reason you can think of that would cause you not to purchase this home?
3. If we could solve the financing issue to your satisfaction, would you go ahead with this home purchase?
4. Suppose that we could find a satisfactory solution to this important concern of yours— would you give me the go-ahead?
5. If this problem did not exist, would you be ready to proceed right now?
6. Is this the only problem that is holding you back?
7. Obviously you must have a reason for saying that. Would you mind if I asked what it is?
8. You obviously feel very strongly about that. What triggers such a strong reaction?
9. Would you mind explaining to me why you feel that way?
10. Before I answer your question, are there any other concerns that are holding you back from enjoying this home?

Answer

Once you have isolated the objection and there are no other concerns (or even if there are 3, 4, or even 10 concerns or objections), you have something to work with. You have an end

Coach's Tip: *You need to have professionally crafted responses to objections, and there are lots of good scripts out there to answer the major objections. If you need some, check into our Objection Handling series with flash cards and workbook. There is even a CD in this series that you can play on your way to your appointments. It can prepare you for the most common objections. Go to www.realestatechampions.com.*

in sight. If you have the proper answers, you will be able to close and get a contract signed. Your answers need to be delivered with power and conviction and be focused on the benefits for your clients.

Close

A closing is really the culmination of a great presentation. That is also true when you are handling an objection with a prospect. You want a successful close because of your conviction and belief in your solution; that is, because of your experience, this is the right path that will ensure their complete satisfaction. You can also do a simple summation close. Simply sum up the benefits of doing business with you and ask them to take action now.

The two reasons I was effective in handling objections were my ability to close (based on belief in myself) and my preparation. I asked the right questions before the presentation and prepared and practiced before I got to the selling moment with a prospect. A Champion Agent understands that handling objections is about mental toughness, preparation, and practice.

15

Making the Case to the Buyer

When a real estate agent begins a career, that person usually works with more buyers than sellers. This pattern, or business mix, can often continue for the agent's entire career. To be a true Champion Agent, your personal mix of business needs to be dominated by sellers. You have to do more transactions on the seller side of the business than the buyer side. Agents who have more transactions on the buyer side of the business end up working harder, having less time control, and having a lower quality of life.

All agents experience the learning curve of moving from struggling new agent working predominantly with buyers to successful agent working with buyers to one who has perfected the buyer side of the business. The next step is to begin moving the business mix from buyers to sellers. To reach the Champion Agent level, you have to move your business through each of these phases, eventually transitioning away from buyers completely and training other agents to work with them on your behalf.

Most agents have never gotten to a high level of proficiency and efficiency with buyers, so they are not equipped to teach others this specialization. Too often, we never learned the skills to conquer the mastery level; or it's been too long ago, and we have forgotten the critical rules, philosophy, and systems to create, secure, service, and generate referrals from the buyers we work with.

The reason I have devoted such a significant segment of this book to buyers, when I believe *listings* are the way to reach Champion Agent status, is not obvious to most people. The truth is, in order to fully leverage their business, Champion Agents eventually build teams that include one or more buyer's agents. Usually, Champion Agents have no system or structure for these buyer's agents to follow to success, so they flounder. Champion Agents become frustrated and usually go through a number of these agents before they get their systems, philosophy, and procedures in order to enable the buyer's agent to be successful. These couple of buyer-focused chapters will help you avoid that cycle.

Three Cs of a Buyer

In order to be considered a prospect, the buyer must possess the three Cs: (1) commitment, (2) compromise, and (3) competitiveness.

Commitment

A Champion Agent expects commitment from the client. Most trainers tell agents to ask buyers, "Are you working with another agent?" That really isn't the right question or wording. The word *working* has a broad connotation. *Working* could mean that they met an agent at an open house, that they are receiving property matches from them, that there is an agent who farms their neighborhood. The word *working* doesn't mean they will buy and sell with that agent. The proper question is, "Are you committed to another agent?" The prospect will either know exactly what you mean or will ask for your definition of committed. Either way, you gain clarity and avoid wasting your time with a prospect who could prove disloyal in the end.

Compromise

A Champion Agent works only with clients who are willing to compromise. If a prospect has the objective of achieving an "I-win-you-lose" type of transaction, your job will be far more difficult as the agent. If the prospect is unwilling to compromise in what is wanted in a home, you will both be looking a long time for the perfect home.

Champion Agents counsel their clients that there are no perfect homes, that most people end up with about 80 percent of what is on their wish list in terms of amenities, that we are working to find the best possible home based on their needs, wants, and desires given the current market conditions and market competition.

Competitiveness

A Champion Agent makes sure the prospect is willing to be competitive. Many buyers are hoping to be the exception rather than the rule. They want to be the one buyer to buy that home at 80 percent of the asking price when the market average is 95 percent. They are unwilling to offer full price to anyone, even when the lack of inventory of homes, large volume of buyers wanting homes, and market conditions dictate otherwise. A prospect or client who is unwilling to be competitive or to take competitive action when the circumstances dictate will increase your time invested, your frustration, lower client satisfaction, and lower the probability of your compensation.

Desperate Agent Model

Too many agents operate with buyers from a mentality of desperation. They use the four-step desperate agent model, applying it over and over again, hoping that the odds will miraculously swing in their favor. The model consists of (1) talking with the prospect, hoping to build rapport, (2) offering to send the prospect . . . stuff, (3) hoping your stuff is better than the other agents', and (4) praying that you eventually get an appointment.

Talking with the Objective of Building Rapport

The objective of a desperate agent is to secure a lead. A Champion Agent's focus is not securing the lead, but securing the appointment. The lead has limited value; the appointment has significant value.

Sending the Prospect . . . Stuff

The average agent wants a phone number and e-mail address so he or she can send the prospect stuff. There is no substitute for the call. I recently began working with a dynamic young couple in the Atlanta area. They are effective Internet marketers. They had about 300 leads for whom they had phone numbers. These 300 leads were getting property match information based on their preferences as homes came on the market. They produced a couple of deals a month from this Internet strategy.

When I began to work with them, I asked them why they hadn't called all 300 of these people that they were working with. They said, "We get a few deals a month from this. Why bother?" I told them to call all 300 in the next week. They made 79 calls and reached 39 people at home. Of those 39 they talked to, they set up 16 face-to-face presentations. That is a 41 percent close ratio. They conducted 11 face-to-face buyer interviews and committed 7 to a buyer's agency contract. That is a 64 percent close ratio. They had already sold two homes, and expected to sell several more in the following few weeks. They ended up selling six homes in the next 30 days out of their 7 clients, 11 appointments, and 39 leads. However, they also found out after contacting the 40 people, they couldn't reach the first week, that every one of them had already bought or sold with another agent.

Hoping Your Stuff Is Better

Unless you can prove and clearly show that your marketing materials, philosophy, sales strategies, and track record are superior, it will be rare to convert a buyer via properties that you e-mail to them based on a profile. If you secured them through an ad call, sign call, open house, or the Internet, you must assume that other agents have all the information you do. If you manage to convince them to share their e-mail address, you must assume that five other agents have it as well. Whoever meets them face-to-face wins.

Praying That You Get the Appointment

There was a huge difference in results when my couple from Atlanta went after the business by scheduling appointments. They stopped waiting for prospects to call when they were interested in a home. They went after the prospects other agents knew about, but were waiting to hear from—just as they used to.

When I say appointment, I am not talking about an appointment to show property. I am talking about an appointment to conduct a buyer interview; to determine the desire, need, ability, and authority of the prospect; to assess the odds of you servicing this client and earning a commission.

Coach's Tip: *A Champion Agent knows that the primary objective of a sales call, either inbound or outbound, is an appointment. The truth is that Champion Agents have more appointments than other agents, and they make more money because of it. They are more fundamentally sound in their philosophy, skills, and focus. They know the objective is a greater number of appointments.*

Risk Losing the Sale

If you need the deal more than the client needs you . . . you have lost. It's hard to take the risk, create a little tension, and close assertively if you need the deal to cover your mortgage or other bills. To be effective and successful in sales, you have to be willing to risk losing the prospect or client. This willingness is first in the form of asking for an appointment to meet. It is followed with the conviction that you ask prospects to work with you using the service system that you have laid out for them. You are the expert, so why not use your system for service? (It's hard to guarantee successful results if you use someone else's system or approach to home purchasing, especially the buyer's.)

Champion Rule: *"When you need it more than the prospect, you lose control."*

Be an Agent in Command

Champion Agents are in command of the prospect, the client, the service they provide, and how they provide it. They are also in command of their time and knowledge. Most other agents are *on demand.* They are at the beck and call of the prospect, client, other agent, or other people in the transaction (lender, inspector, appraiser, etc.). The need for the deal can cause an agent to lose all control.

> **Coach's Tip:** *Be willing and able to walk away from a prospect if he or she does not follow your procedures in doing business. As an agent trying to reach the Champion Agent level, you need to act as though you are a Champion now.*

Get the Appointment on the First Call

A Champion's approach is to convince a buyer, on the first call, that an appointment with you has specific, valuable benefits. Because your client will understand the marketplace better, he or she will be able to select a better home, make better decisions for the family, and engage in a smoother, less stressful transaction.

Receive a higher level of service. Your client will receive more professional service because of working with you. Currently, according to the National Association of Realtors, over 52 percent of licensed agents have been in the business less than 36 months. Most agents in real estate today have seen only one type of market. What if we are experiencing a change in the market? The odds are that, based on the number of agents and experience, expertise, and knowledge of those other agents, they will most likely select someone who is not properly prepared to represent their interest.

Gain a negotiating advantage. Through your understanding of the marketplace, the inventory, and current emerging market trends you can link your knowledge with a clear understanding of the goals, objectives, and expectations. You will position yourself to be a more effective advocate and negotiator on the client's behalf.

Secure a better lender for a smoother transaction. Too often, agents allow the buyer too much latitude in lender selection. While you don't want to be accused of steering a client, you do want to ensure a high level of service with minimum risk to the client. A Champion Agent guides a client to a preferred lender relationship. This creates better service, a more timely closing, fewer surprises, and a lower stress level for the client and agent.

If the wrong lender is involved, you put the long-term referral relationship you are trying to establish at risk. There is nothing you can do or say to extract yourself from the negative feelings and emotions created in a client when the lender blows it. This is true even if you have nothing to do with the problems the lender causes in the transaction.

Save money in both the short and long run.   By meeting with you face-to-face, you can help your client secure a better home in a stronger-appreciating area with the amenities required and for the specific amount of available money. A home that doubles as an investment will be better than others they might have selected without the meeting.

Receive the representation they deserve.   In the end, it's about understanding the type of representation your clients want. It's about understanding their expectations, so you can achieve a high level of customer satisfaction. In return, your clients are willing to talk about you to others who are buying and selling.

Use Strong Dialogue

Using strong dialogue to convert the prospect to a face-to-face appointment is your objective. You must be able to deliver scripts that clearly explain the benefits of coming to your office for a buyer consultation.

I have included here scripts aligned with the six benefits that prospects will receive from an appointment with you.

1. Having helped _____ number of families in my career and more than _____ in just the last year, my clients have found that by meeting with me they have a better knowledge of the current marketplace and greater opportunity to live in the right property for them and their family."

2. "In order for me to provide you with the highest level of service and representation, we simply need to meet. Would _____ or _____ be better for you?"

3. "I have been able to acquire properties for my clients at _____ percent of the asking price when the market average is _____ percent. This saves my clients, like yourself, thousands of dollars. You end up buying a home for less money with less money out of your pocket. For me to be able to save you thousands like my other clients, we need to spend a few moments together. Would _____ or _____ be better for you?"

4. "Over the years in this business, I have seen many occasions when a loan originator didn't deliver what was promised. The worst

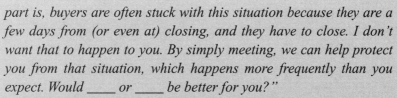

part is, buyers are often stuck with this situation because they are a few days from (or even at) closing, and they have to close. I don't want that to happen to you. By simply meeting, we can help protect you from that situation, which happens more frequently than you expect. Would _____ or _____ be better for you?"

5. "In order for you to maximize your initial equity position and minimize your up-front investment in a new property, we need to meet. Would _____ or _____ be better for you?"

6. "Every buyer has an expectation of service from a real estate agent. Few of them receive it. Based on a recent survey, only 13 percent of consumers went back and used a previous agent. That clearly demonstrates the odds of receiving poor service are better than the odds of receiving the representation you really deserve. To ensure that doesn't happen to you, we simply need to meet. Would _____ or _____ be better for you?"

Realize that most of the people will resist making an appointment. They will throw out objections to meeting with you. Again, you must be prepared for them. Mastering dialogue and delivery in this area can significantly increase the odds of securing an appointment. Here are some sample dialogues.

1. Them: "I really can't come into the office [it's too far, I'm too busy, I work long hours, I don't drive, etc.]. Can't you just pick me up and show me houses [or fax me printouts, drop off copies of listings, etc.]. I'll tell you what I'm looking for over the phone."

You: "You know, if it were all about the number of bedrooms, baths, and price, you'd buy the first home you looked at, right? I've really found that it will save you much time and frustration if we spend a little time together up front. It really is a shame that you can't come into the office, because I've found that by showing you how I search on the MLS, it helps you know the marketplace and your options with greater clarity. It gives you knowledge to make the best decision for you. I understand your dilemma. Would there be a time, either late this week or early next week, when we might meet at my office?"

2. Them: "There is just no way, with my schedule that I will be able to meet with you!"

You: "I understand your busy schedule. To really do the best job for you and your family, we really need to meet for a short time. When would be the earliest you could do that?"

Or, here's an alternative response.

You: "I understand your busy schedule. Looking at property takes time as well. Will you have enough time to devote to that to ensure we select the right home for you and your family?"

Or, here's a third possibility.

You: "I understand your busy schedule. Again, what is your time frame to be moved into your next home?"

There are two areas of persistence. The first is the willingness to continue to call them for days, weeks, and even months until they are ready to move forward in a purchase. Most agents quit long before they call a few times. Be persistent with prospects during your lead follow-up process. The second and most important area of persistence that only Champion Agents possess is continuing to ask for the appointment on the initial call, even in the face of a negative response from the prospect. Only a Champion Agent would ask for an appointment multiple times on the same call.

Champion Rule: *Ask for the appointment more than once.*

Most salespeople quit long before the sale is made or even before the appointment is booked. Salespeople quit when they receive the first no or first rejection.

When Salespeople Quit

44%   First time the prospect says no
22%   Second time the prospect says no
14%   Third time the prospect says no
12%   Fourth time the prospect says no

Amazingly, 92 percent of salespeople quit before they acquire the appointment or the order from the customer. Only 8 percent of salespeople will ask more than four times. And yet 60 percent of all sales made or appointments set occur after the prospect has said no *four times*. The net result is that 8 percent of salespeople control 60 percent of the business . . . just for asking. Persistence will create the payoff.

The most frequent first contact with a prospect is experienced over the phone. Agents who are contacted directly via sign call, ad call, or even floor time are likely to be working or focused on something else when the opportunity to interact with a prospect arrives. Don't lose sight of the objective of that prospect encounter. It's to set a face-to-face appointment. That is the primary objective in prospecting. The fallback position is a phone appointment for a specific day and time in the future. The concern and hesitation on the prospect's part can increase the longer we manipulate to keep them on the phone. This is especially true if prospects feel there is a verbal judo match going on between you and them. Their mind begins to think that you are asking questions because you are trying to make a quick sale, that you are just trying to acquire information to use against them in the future. The more they feel this way, the greater the resistance you will encounter from them.

Once you secure the appointment, you have been granted permission by the prospect to ask qualifying and service expectation questions. Most trainers in real estate will teach you to ask a litany of questions prior to booking an appointment. These questions will, however, raise the resistance on the part of the prospect. The best approach is to secure the appointment and then ask the questions. Unfortunately, you can't always select the best approach. We often have to ask a few questions to keep the dialogue flowing long enough to ask for the appointment a second, third, fourth, or even fifth time.

Qualifying the Buyer

Having a solid set of qualifying questions is essential when prospecting over the phone, and taking notes directly on the questionnaire page for each prospect is paramount. Record their responses accurately. Remember, however, the true objective isn't to have all the questions answered but to secure an appointment. I can never say that enough. A sample questionnaire follows.

Qualifying Questions

Hi, this is _____ with _____. My desire for each of my clients is to provide them with outstanding service and counsel. For me to achieve that, I need a few minutes of your time to understand your goals and objectives for your family.

1. Where are you hoping to move to?
2. How soon are you hoping to be there?
3. If you could design the ideal moving situation for your family, what would it look like?
4. Time frame?
5. Why are you moving at this time?
6. _____ please tell me what is wrong with your present home.
7. What is right about your present home?
8. May I ask, how long have you been looking?
9. Describe to me the home you are looking for.

_____ Bedrooms _____ Square feet

_____ Bathrooms _____ Style of home

Type/style:
Why? _____

How important? _____

Specific features:
Why? _____

How important? _____

Location/area
Why? _____

How important? _____

Price range expected?
Why? _____

How important? _____

Yard _____

Landscape _____

Condition of property _____

Neighborhood _____

10. Have you met with a lender yet?
11. Have you seen anything you really like?
12. Do you own, or are you renting?
13. Do you need to sell before you purchase?
14. Is your home currently on the market?
15. Are you currently committed to another agent?
16. What are the best days for us to meet and see the property?
17. Would this _____ or next _____ be better for you?
18. What can I do to make it easier for you to get the kind of real estate information you are looking for?
19. Tell me the process you typically use to make decisions like this.
20. What price range are you considering?
21. What is the most important service you want from a Realtor like myself?
22. Besides that, what's next? [Go three deep.]
23. So, if I provide _____ and _____ and _____, we would have a basis for doing business together?

_____ I really believe we can help you achieve your list of goals. To really do the job for you we need to meet. Would _____ or _____ be better for you?

I look forward to our meeting at _____. Our office address is _____.

The objective of qualifying can be segmented into four categories.

1. *Separate qualified and nonqualified prospects.* The faster we can separate qualified from nonqualified, the more resources we save for other prospects. We must design our qualifying process with the objective of quickly separating these two groups.

2. *Eliminate or refer nonqualified prospects.* Being able to remove or disengage non-qualified prospects frees you up to work with or find better-qualified prospects. As you reach the Champion level in skills, ability, and mindset, you open the possibility of referring prospects. Maybe these prospects don't meet your standard for clients, but they might meet another agent's. Those other agents might be willing to work with lower-quality,

longer-time-frame, or lower-motivation prospects. Don't automatically throw away a lead if it doesn't meet your personal standard. Start by referring this business to people in your office. Then, if you feel this is happening frequently (I would define frequently as around four to six times a month, depending on the convertibility of the leads), you might need to consider starting to build a team.

3. *Trade commitments with qualified prospects.* In the risk and reward arena of real estate sales, the exchange of commitments is the cornerstone of compensation. We set up that exchange of commitments at the qualifying stage. This is especially true with a buyer. Sellers have been educated that they must be exclusive to a real estate agent, but there are still many buyers who don't feel the need or haven't been shown the benefits of an exclusive relationship with an agent to represent their needs and interests. Through qualifying, we need to determine their willingness to exchange commitments or exclusivity for our service.

4. *Provide counsel to qualified, committed prospects.* On the last of these four steps, we begin to enter the servicing part of our relationship with the prospect, who has now turned into a client.

Our fear of prospecting can shape our decision to work lower-grade leads. Because we have leads, we excuse ourselves from prospecting for the day, week, or longer. We focus so much on a lead (or a few of them) that, when they don't pan out, we put ourselves in dire straights quickly. We end up wasting our time on people with a low return. The time we invest is really the opportunity cost of the real estate business. In evaluating the buyer opportunities, we find that a typical buyer will, on average, take three to four times more investment of our time than a seller.

I often ask audiences when I try to drive this point home, "If you have a $300,000 seller and a $300,000 buyer, which do you make more money from?" The shout from the audience is always the same: "*The seller!*" I usually ask them again, and a few start to get it. The truth is the commission dollars are the same. The difference is in the time you must invest to earn the income. The variable is the time in the analysis.

The quickest way, when working with buyers, to determine their qualifications and motivation isn't by asking them all of the qualifying questions. The quickest way to determine their motivation is to ask for an appointment. The last place on earth a low-motivation buyer wants to be is in front of a salesperson. If you don't want to buy a car, do you go to a car dealership and talk with a salesperson? For most of us, that's the last thing we'd do.

Characteristics of a Qualified Prospect

A Champion Agent only works with highly qualified prospects.

Strong Motivation

Motivation is simply the desire to do something. The stronger the desire on the part of the buyer, the easier it will be for you to satisfy or even exceed their expectations. The stronger the motivation, the lower the expectations they will have for a property or your service. Low-motivation prospects are willing to look for extended periods of time until they find the perfect home. In essence, they are looking for something that doesn't exist in many cases.

Financial Capacity

We can find people who have a desire or high motivation to live in a much nicer home. That certainly needs to be balanced against financial capacity: the availability of a down payment, decent credit score, steady employment, and sufficient income. Most people want more than they can afford. Champion Agents find out before they invest time on prospects what their true financial capacity is.

If you show property before you know clearly their financial capacity, you run the risk of disappointing your clients. Buyers end up seeing homes they want but can't afford, causing them to become frustrated with the properties, themselves, and you. This is a sure way to lose clients.

Authority to Take Action

Far too frequently, low-producing agents find out late in the game that parents, friends, aunts, or uncles will have an influence on the decision. This can easily cause a blockage to the sale. The other party, often a parent, will come in after the home is selected and talk the buyers out of the home they want. Knowing who will have influence on the decision is critical.

Realistic Expectations, Willingness to Compromise

Qualifying the buyer and the buyer interview have so much value in this area. We are in a compromise business. Buyers must be willing to have realistic expectations of their desires and budget. They have to be able to forgo things that might be luxury items in their budget. They might not be able to afford that third garage space based on their budget. They might have to forgo it because the area in which they really want to live is older and very few of the homes have three-car garages. If the house doesn't have a three-car garage but has room to add one, is in the right location, and has all of the other features your client is looking for, would that be okay?

Willingness to Understand the Marketplace and Competition

This has been a difficult area in the past. Buyers have not liked the bidding war in real estate. They have felt taken advantage of by the sellers. In some cases, they lost a few houses or had to pay 5, 10, or even 20 percent above asking to acquire a home.

For prospects to become clients, they must understand the marketplace, whatever it currently is. In the end, the market is the market! All Realtors and buyers can do is respond to the market. One thing agents should always know is the percentage of list price to sales price for the homes in the price range their client is trying to purchase.

Commitment to Work with You Exclusively

My position on exclusive commitment is that clients should sign a buyer agency agreement. The buyer agency agreement is becoming more commonplace in our industry. There was even an article by Kelly Spors on the increase in frequency and acceptance of buyer agency contracts in the December 2, 2004, edition of the *Wall Street Journal.*

In the article, Spors shared with consumers that buyer agency is increasing in use nationally. She cited a recent survey by NAR that 64 percent of buyers using agents used buyer's representation in 2004. That is a 17 percent increase from 2001, when it was 47 percent, which means that almost two-thirds of people using a Realtor to purchase a home are using an exclusive buyer agent relationship.

Coach's Tip: *Get a copy of the* **Wall Street Journal** *article. It would be valuable in your portfolio of tools. It could be shown to buyers to prove that the norm in the industry is buyer agency and exclusive right to represent. That 64 percent clearly backs up your desire to have clients sign an exclusive right to represent agreement.*

The exclusive relationship, at its core, is about a trade of commitments. We are committed to providing a certain level of service, skill, expertise, and time to ensure clients achieve their goals. The clients, in turn, must trade exclusivity and assurance of compensation for the services rendered. Anything short of full trade of commitments is damaging to both parties.

I know of many agents who have a strong enough presentation and presence to get away without a signed buyer agency contract, but I don't recommend that. They will get burned every once in a while for lack of a contract. Why take the risk?

Dealing with Buyer Misconceptions

Buyers have a number of misconceptions when using the services of a real estate agent. There is confusion on the part of consumers about why they should use the services of an agent. What advantages do they gain from using an agent? What are the benefits of exclusivity to one agent?

Champion Agents are aware of these misconceptions. They have developed the knowledge to deal with them appropriately. Every buyer believes one or more of these misconceptions. A Champion is prepared to respond.

I Don't Need an Agent

Too many buyers are faced with the advent of information available on the Internet. They acquire all the information they need, and they think that they can search for and select a property every bit as well as an agent could.

Those consumers are correct; they do have access to the same information as agents in today's world. Properties listed in the MLS can be searched by any person who has an Internet connection. For years, that access to MLS properties was our advantage to mandate consumer use of our services. The Internet has caused an increasing group of people to secure the information about homes on their own. However, I believe the access to information is one of the least valuable services that we provide.

Analyze and interpret the marketplace.   We must analyze the marketplace as well as clients' needs. What provides the most complete home, based on their requirements of the features they want against the budgetary constraints of monthly payments and down payment to secure the home? How competitive is the marketplace for good properties, and what's the probability that your clients can secure one, given the competition for homes, the level of buyers they are, and their expectations? All of these are factors and services a Champion Agent would provide.

Establish realistic expectations.   In counseling clients, we are exposing to them the odds of the marketplace. We help them establish a realistic expectation for securing a property, and what type of property it will be, based on their financial capacity. We should counsel them about what they can expect at each stage of the home buying process. The ultimate goal is no surprises for the client. Surprises are for birthdays, not for real estate transactions.

Protect the client.   Through a properly executed contract, we can establish security and safety for our clients. With the addition of disclosure, inspections, specific timelines, and performance deadlines, Champion Agents know how to explain to a prospect the need for their services strictly from the standpoint of client security. They will always be safer with a skilled agent representing their interests each step of the way.

When you hear a prospect say, "I really don't need an agent" or "I don't need an agent; I can find what I need on the Internet myself," the correct response is one of isolation. Your goal is to try to find out why.

> *"I'm curious. Why do you feel that way?"*

Or, alternatively,

> *"Is the reason you don't need an agent based on a previous poor experience with another agent?"*

I always approach defending my value through the easy pathway first. If that doesn't work, I move on to more complex and sophisticated benefits and reasons. Always start reeducation with what I call the "why not" technique. The "why not" technique clearly asks prospects, why *not* use an agent?

> *"Wouldn't it make sense to use someone else's energy, someone else's expert guidance, someone else's time to find and acquire what you really want? If it costs you nothing as the buyer, why not?"*

You could further explain, if you still encounter resistance, that the seller is paying the fee for your service. Whether they have an agent or not, clients have already committed to a fixed fee. How often can they receive professional representation without the cost of it coming out of their pocket . . . in other words, why not?

I Don't Need to Work Exclusively with an Agent

Too many prospects want to keep all of their options open. The only way you will ever really know if you are working with people like that is to ask them for exclusivity: ask them to sign a buyer agency agreement or exclusive right to represent agreement.

Champion Agents have a no-exception rule to buyer agency contracts. They would rather lose a prospect now than someone they thought was a client later on. With a prospect, you have invested a small amount of time; with a client, you usually have substantially more invested.

We must educate prospects that the best agents work exclusively. If they are working with a few agents, then those agents must be marginal. You could even appeal to their sense of fair play. How would they feel if they invested time in helping someone, only to find out later that all of their effort was wasted and they wouldn't be paid for doing their job? Would that be fair?

> *"The best agents work exclusively. Attorneys represent only one party at a time in a particular case. To achieve that level of counsel, one has to be exclusive. Doesn't that make sense? Is that the level of service you want?"*

You can also explain to buyers that they will receive a lot of duplicate information. They will possibly see the same house through a few different agents. There will be wasted time for them because of this repetitive and duplicate information.

> *"By working with many agents, you will receive duplicates of the information, wasting your time, energy, and effort and raising your frustration level. While you are looking at the home on Primrose for the third time, the home that is really right for you on Marigold has just sold. I am sure that would frustrate you, wouldn't it? Is that something you would like to avoid?"*

This is one of the best tie-ins to be able to convince them that the only way they will receive the best service is through the exclusive representation relationship, that, ultimately, this is the only way you will provide your extensive service benefits.

> *"The very best skilled agents, those who offer the greatest benefits to you, work exclusively only. They work with fewer people, who are more committed, so they can invest more time in them. This raises the service level the clients receive, reduces the risk in the transaction, and raises security for their clients. In the end, this can easily mean the difference between securing the right home for you and your family over the other buyers who want it. It could also increase your negotiating power because, by being exclusive, I have more information and am better able to position you on the house to your benefit. The best agents work only exclusively, and I am one of the best. Do you see how this approach benefits you?"*

I Don't Need to Be Financially Prequalified

People who say, "Trust me, I have the money" or "Trust me, I have the means to secure the financing" are usually the ones who don't or can't. A Champion Agent doesn't leave to chance a prospect's ability to perform.

Convincing prospects that it's in their best interest to meet with a lender is a skill. Completing their paperwork with a lender and achieving preapproval puts them in a strong negotiating position. The truth is, just as the buyer is trying to select the best house, the seller is trying to select the best buyer. One factor is certainly sales probability when selecting a buyer. Equally important is the ability of that buyer to perform. The more we can convince the buyer to minimize that risk by preapproval, the stronger our position and the stronger the buyer's position in negotiating.

You have to sell this as a benefit to the buyers. Two key benefits to your service are enhanced by prequalification.

Writing the purchase agreement to correctly and clearly express clients' intentions and represent their interests. It would be almost impossible to counsel them on their many options and suggest what the best ones might be based on your experience without a clear picture of their finances. Any agent would be providing a lower-quality service than clients would expect because of the lack of financial disclosure.

> *"In order to write a purchase agreement correctly, you must express your intentions and needs clearly on the financial components. What type of loan do you need? Does the seller need to contribute closing costs? Are we trying to achieve 80 percent loan to value (LTV) so you avoid mortgage insurance premiums (MIP)?"*

Or, alternatively,

> *"If you are stretching your monthly payments, you may need a two-to-one buy down to lower the payments initially. Is this a long-term home, so you can secure long-term financing? Or do we need to look at a shorter-term fixed loan at a lower rate since you will be moving in five years, which can save you ½ point on the interest."*

Submitting the purchase agreement in a manner that will represent clients' interests in the most favorable position.   You should be able to demonstrate to the sellers and the listing agent that you have the best buyer in terms of financial capacity and closing ability of the loan. The listing agent wants to know whether buyers can perform. Can they do what they are proposing to the seller? Good listing agents will protect sellers from the most significant risk of the transaction . . . falling out. The transaction that falls apart just days before the scheduled closing is the worst-case scenario for sellers. It is worse than if the home had never had an offer.

We have to be able to convince buyers that financial preapproval or prequalifying is one of the most important factors in positioning themselves well. If they don't, and they want to buy a high-demand home in a superior location or because it has a very competitive price, they will probably lose out to a buyer who is better prepared and carries less risk.

> *"My objective is to convince other agents and sellers that you are the best buyer available in the marketplace, to position you so favorably that they don't want to take the risk of having you purchase another home. This will help us exert a little control in the transaction, giving you a better position and more potential options."*

If I Look Long Enough, I'll Find the Perfect Home

This misconception has two parts. The first is assuming that the "perfect home" really exists. In reality, there is no such thing as the perfect home. The other is time-related: "If I hold out longer, a better property will come on the market."

Most buyers think they fall into the exception rather than the rule. They believe they will be the lucky one to get the perfect home at a discount. Most people in this category think there is a perfect home and that they will find it. We must educate them that there is no perfect home, that if they can get 80 percent of what they want in a home, they have done well. No one ever acquires 100 percent of their wants when purchasing a home. There are always things people change to make the house they bought a home.

A Champion Salesperson works to differentiate *wants* from *needs*. What must a client really have without question? Why does the client want that particular feature in a home, and how important is that feature?

> *"On a scale of 1 to 10 (with 10 meaning you absolutely can't buy a home without it), where does _____ fall in as a needed feature of the home?"*

Or, alternatively,

> *"Is that something you absolutely need in the home or something you are hoping to have in the home?"*

We need to be skilled at helping clients lower the bar on their home choice in line with reality. We certainly want clients to acquire a home that they will enjoy. We also want them to be realistic about what they can expect and afford, based on today's market conditions.

> *"Bob and Mary, I have discovered after helping _____ families like yours that there is no perfect home. I have had clients build from the ground up what they thought would be perfect, only to discover when they moved in that there were quite a few things they would change. Do you see how that would happen? Because of this truth, I am going to have a conversation about the requirements you have for a home in terms of absolute needs versus features you would like to have in the home. Doesn't that make sense?"*

I Will Never Write a Full-Price Offer

Consumers have been taught by someone like their parents or Uncle Ned never to offer full price, that you are a fool if you offer full price. Negotiating has a place in real estate sales, but if the property is a good value, why risk the acquisition of it for a few thousand dollars?

At times, based on the inventory and frenzy of the marketplace, you might have to offer more than the asking price to secure the property. When we counsel clients, we have to be able to convey the true cost of the difference between their projected low offer and the full-price offer.

Too many buyers see the lower offer as a huge savings to them rather than what it is. For a well-priced home in a competitive marketplace of good homes, buyers may save at best between 2 and 3 percent of the sales price of the home. That 2 to 3 percent is really just additional money they end up borrowing. For example, if they managed to save 3 percent on a $200,000 home, that would equate to $6,000. The real cost when borrowed at a reasonable interest rate would be $35 a month, or $1.13 per day. That is probably the best that they can do when competing for a high-demand home in a good marketplace.

When you factor in the tax savings and inflation, the effective rate of costs drops well below a dollar a day. If a client really loves a home, isn't it worth another dollar a day to make sure they end up with it?

A Champion Agent can explain the value of a full-price offer.

"Is it worth the risk?"

Or,

"Are you willing to lose the right home over $1.13 a day?"

Or,

"My experience with _____ number of clients is that they don't miss the money, but they do miss the home if they don't end up buying it."

If you allow this type of thinking on the part of your clients, then you might be faced with the house they didn't get. Once they fall short on a home, they will compare every other home to that one. Every house you show them will be compared to the home they lost. The one they lost will develop mythical proportions. They won't settle for anything less than the home they could have acquired. To be blunt, they didn't acquire it because you didn't convince them to offer full price.

We Can Always Start Low and Come Up Later

This is the cousin of "never offer full price." You will often hear them together. The view is that sellers always counteroffer. They want to sell their home, so they will negotiate back and forth on paper.

Early in my career, I was working with a car dealership sales manager from Southern California who had moved to Portland. He wanted to make low offers and negotiate everything. When he saw he was not going to get anywhere on the price after a few rounds, he started in on the furniture and personal property. Fortunately, I was smart enough to put the two parties in the same office in separate conference rooms. I was also, fortunately, working with a good listing agent. We must have created almost 10 counteroffers in an hour of back-and-forth negotiating. It was early in my career, and I hadn't prepared my buyer for how the seller would react to his haggling mentality (acquired in selling cars). The seller was becoming insulted and upset. This was especially true when the seller bottom-lined the price, and my buyer started in on his possessions. As I said, it was my first year in the business. I didn't have the control of the client I would today.

Most buyers don't understand that sellers can be very emotional about their homes. They can easily be insulted by a low offer and become defensive and illogical. They often counteroffer at a higher price than they really want just because the initial offer was insulting. We must ensure the buyer understands the seller's options and what may be at stake with a low offer.

Combat misconceptions in the low-offer area by explaining what can happen to the seller. Take the time to educate buyers about the risk that they are taking when they push the seller into one of the four categories previously mentioned. Then, lead in with the key questions to ask buyers when they might attempt a low offer.

Question 1: What will it take to be the seller's best buyer?   Sellers want the best buyer for their home in terms of sales price or net proceeds. They also want a low-hassle, easy-care, emotionally connected buyer. For some sellers, being able to identify with the buyer has value to them. While most sellers want the highest price they can get from the sale of their home, a large group would rather identify with the buyer. This can be especially true for people who have lived a long time in the same home and raised their family there. Just as the buyer wants the best home and best seller, the seller wants the best buyer available.

Question 2: What will it take to avoid offending the seller?   If you offend the seller with your initial offer, you have a long uphill battle ahead. The probability of being paid for your effort now and the probability of the buyers purchasing the home they want is reflected in this question. We must be cognizant of offending the seller and try to avoid it if possible.

A Good Property Will Wait for Me to Act

We must educate buyers that the speed at which they make decisions matters. The best-priced, best-quality properties won't wait for them to act. A good listing can't be kept secret from other agents in the marketplace who are trying to make a sale. People will find out about it and try to sell it. When the marketplace has limited inventory, it is easy to build urgency. Champion Salespeople can also build urgency to take action in a more neutral marketplace, where not all of the listings sell, or do not sell quickly. They have the mindset and skill to be able to build urgency in a prospect. Champions build urgency through the value of the property, the length of time and hard work expended to find the property, market inventory levels, and how closely the property aligns with the needs, wants, and desires of the buyer. All of these lead to the client taking competitive action sooner. We don't know exactly when the property will sell. Educating the purchaser on the need to take immediate action on a good or even great property enables strong revenue growth. The best properties sell fast.

Good properties sell fast . . . great properties sell overnight.   Too many buyers need to move more quickly and take more decisive competitive action. In any marketplace, the best priced inventory will be gone in a matter of days or a few weeks. The challenge is that, even at three weeks, we don't know when the home will sell. When your buyer finds something through you that you know will be sold quickly, don't forget to drive the point home . . . this home won't last.

If you wait, you may lose it.   The best properties won't wait for people to make decisions.

The toughest sale I ever had to make was to someone I knew who made decisions slowly. I also knew that I was in heavy competition for this piece of development land. I knew it wouldn't last more than 24 hours on the market, and it didn't. Fortunately, I convinced my buyer to pull the trigger. From the sale of that land, development lots, spec houses, and presales, I made in excess of $300,000 in a 24-month period—just from that one deal. I had to convince the buyer that if he waited, he would lose it. There were at least five other buyers who wanted this piece of land and were in the process of making offers. They lost out on over $650,000 that my client made in profit in less than 18 months on an investment of about $500,000. If your clients wait, they could lose.

Coach's Tip: *Deal with these seven misconceptions up front, in the early stages of qualifying or during the presentation. Don't wait until you are writing an offer. You will be doing it at a time when clients may feel you care only about yourself and your commission check rather than about their needs, wants, and desires. They may question whether you really have their best interests in mind.*

If you sleep on it . . . you may not sleep in it. Buyers need to know that even overnight consideration for the best properties is a significant risk. We need to ask them, "How will you feel if you lose it?" and "What's your disappointment value?" The disappointment value is what it is worth to them not to be disappointed in the morning when they find out it's gone. What's it worth to avoid that feeling?

16

Buyer Counseling Interview

My belief has always been that Champion Agents work predominantly with sellers. However, they must acquire the skills to work with buyer leads first so they can select only the cream-of-the-crop prospects. That enables them to create a high profit, even from a buyer. Many Champion Agents, as they transition their business to include buyer's agents, don't have a system to ensure conversion and commitment of those leads.

Champion Agents have the ability to communicate their professional services and value to prospects in a manner that creates a strategic advantage over their competition. They clearly know why someone should use their representation services. They are able to concisely articulate the specific services their clients will receive. Moreover, Champion Agents know the services specific to them that their competitors don't provide, and they know how to use those competitive points of difference to their decisive advantage.

Build Your Value with the Buyer

There are nine specific ways to build your value to a buyer and separate your services from the competition. If you employ them effectively, they will provide you with a tremendous advantage over your competition. Non-Champion performers attempt to sell based on access to information and rapport. Champion Agents sell their services based on skill, knowledge, benefits to the clients, and statistical proof or empirical evidence of success. (They don't leave their income to chance.)

Nine categories of professional service and value
1. Identifying and defining your specific services
2. Identifying and defining your points of difference

3. Illustrating specific client benefits
4. Identifying and defining the value of your service and benefits
5. Educating the client on the sequence of the buying process and events in chronological order
6. Demonstrating value through specific examples and stories of success
7. Sharing your performance record, including testimonials
8. Pledging your loyalty and performance
9. Guaranteeing your activities and their results

Presentation Process

The buyer consultation is centered on a planned presentation process. This process follows the nine categories of value of service. Champion Agents softly lead the clients into questioning by foreshadowing the next few steps. Here are a few scripts that will lead easily into your questions.

> *"My experience has been that, if we spend more time on the front end by clearly understanding your needs, it will take less time in a car. I surely don't want to waste your time by showing you homes that you won't like."*

Or,

> *"My job is to uncover and understand your needs, to educate you on the market (what is currently available and what you can get for your money), and to negotiate in your interest and help arrange financing if necessary. Your job is to buy the house!"*

Or,

> *"Do you have any questions?"*

Or,

> *[At this point, pull the interview questions out of the file.]* *"Now, may I ask you some questions? Do you mind if I take some notes?"*

Agent's role in the real estate transaction process. The initial section in Champion Agents' buyer interviews is to define their role in the process. The average consumer knows very little about the role of real estate agents, other than they drive people around and find homes for them. The fundamental role, when representing buyers, is to help them select and acquire their next home. This includes evaluating the marketplace. You must blend this with their desires and wants and factor in the financial parameters, with the overall goal of selecting the best property for them and their family.

Either of the following scripts, if you practice and perfect their use, can set the stage that you are a different kind of real estate agent than they have ever met before.

> *"My job is to help you evaluate the marketplace, evaluate the opportunities and values in the marketplace, and make the best selection for you and your family. Then I can help you acquire the home that meets your family and financial needs in a manner that reduces the stress and anxiety associated with a new home."*

Or,

> *"My focus is the creation of lifelong clients. My role is to provide a service to people who place a high value on integrity, high ethical standards, and successful results. My job is to provide objective counsel and professional, knowledgeable representation in the real estate field. A properly selected piece of real estate can be a building block for their family unit and their financial present and future. Assisting them in achieving their goals and dreams for themselves and their family is my fundamental role."*

The sooner you can position yourself as different, the more willing they are to consider working with you. Your job is to better educate consumers about your role and function. They know that agents' roles have changed because they have been reading about the change in the newspaper a few times a month for the past four to five years. Now, all the information is available on the Web; they think that their need for agents (especially full-fee agents) is a thing of the past. The better you can define your role and function and convey it quickly and early in the relationship, the higher the probability of your earning a fee from a satisfied client.

Buyer Interview Agenda

The buyer interview, buyer consultation, or buyer counseling section (whichever term you want to use to describe your meeting with a buyer face-to-face in your office to secure an "exclusive right to represent" contract before you show property), for most agents, is less structured and planned than a listing presentation. Most agents completely wing it in this critical meeting that will set the tone for the working relationship with the buyer.

If you had a simple agenda for the meeting that you handed to the buyer previous to beginning your discussion, it would enable you to conduct the meeting and convert and commit the buyer to your service more quickly

Sample Agenda

1. My role in helping my client
2. My specific services and benefits
3. Current and emerging market conditions
4. Your financing options
    a. The value of preapproval
    b. Earnest money deposit
    c. Life of a loan
5. Discussion of your wants and needs in your next home
    a. Preferred style
    b. Preferred features
    c. Preferred location
    d. Price and payment penalties
6. Selection assistance services
7. Representing you to the seller
8. Professional negotiation as your agent
9. Communication and closing coordination
10. Servicing you after the sale for life
11. Exchange of commitments

After establishing your role with the prospect, then move into the discussion of your services (provided you have already asked them sufficient questions to qualify their desire, needs, ability, and authority to proceed with a purchase). An option before you define your services and benefits is to take a refresher trip down the qualifying trail to confirm your understanding of their expectations.

Core Messages of Your Service

Three messages need to be conveyed in the "My services" section. These need to be the first things discussed with a buyer; however, most agents never discuss these concepts, which are directly linked to building the value of your services and obtaining exclusivity of your services in return.

1. All real estate agents are not the same.
2. It really matters who represents your interests.
3. My market knowledge is superior to that of other agents.

All real estate agents are not the same.   One of the primary messages used by inferior agents and discount agents is that we are all the same, that there is essentially no difference between Champion Agents and other agents. You need to convey that each agent operates an independent business and applies different techniques to arrive at the purchase of a home. One may employ a Kia-level strategy of service, amenities, and experience, while another uses a Mercedes-level strategy of service, amenities, and experience. You want to create a clear distinction between what you do and what other agents do. Using an analogy outside of real estate to illustrate service and quality differentials is highly effective. I have found that car comparisons are easy to use because car companies have spent billions over the years branding their products and establishing the fact that all cars and car dealerships are not the same. Our job, at this stage, is to show and demonstrate the differences between us and their preconceived feelings and beliefs that real estate agents are all the same.

> *"There is a tremendous difference in the agents you can work with. Each agent operates independently and approaches business in a different way. There are differences in knowledge, skills, strategy, attitude, experience, communication, negotiating style, and ultimately, results. I spend time with you up front to clearly understand your objectives and needs to ensure a successful relationship. Does that make sense?"*

It really does matter who represents your interests. In this section, you are building the value of your service and moving it away from agents who merely look up properties to show and open doors. Champion Agents know those are the least valuable parts of their service. Any agent can plunk a few keys on a computer and get an MLS key.

There is a story about a senior executive who was having problems with his computer. He called in a technology expert to fix his problem. The technology expert looked at the computer diagnostically for a few minutes. He then reached into his briefcase for a small hammer; he tapped on the computer three times, and it was fixed. He then handed a bill to the senior executive for $500, who said, "I won't pay this; you were here only five minutes. That's outrageous! I want you to itemize this bill." The technology expert then itemized the bill. It read: "Two dollars for tapping on the computer and $498 for knowing where to tap!" You are trying to tell the buyer is that it's easy to get a hammer and start hitting the computer, but difficult to know where to hit.

The buyer needs to know that you are one of the few agents in the marketplace who knows where to tap. Convey to buyers that their choice of an agent to represent their interests in securing a house can affect the following:

- The home they select
- The long-term appreciation of the home
- Their financial position years down the road
- Their ability to avoid legal pitfalls
- How the offer is presented
- The financing they receive
- The stress they experience through the transaction
- The timeliness of the closing
- The communication during and after the transaction
- The price they pay for a home

Listing all of these factors that an agent influences makes it easy to demonstrate the importance of choosing the right agent to represent their interests in their purchase. Besides factors that affect them financially and emotionally, there are security issues as well. These factors can have negative consequences that can extend well into the next decade for them. Selecting the wrong agent now can affect the next few houses down the lines, as well as long-term financial security for them and their family.

> *"Do you see an agent's influence and the effect on your home purchase if the agent isn't the right one?*

Or,

> *Doesn't it make sense when I say that it fundamentally matters whom you select to represent your interests?"*

Your market knowledge is superior to that of other agents.   Because many of the previously listed factors are intertwined with market knowledge, the home they select, appreciation, long-term financial position, how the offer is presented, stress, and the price they pay are all connected to market knowledge. You have to prove that your market knowledge is top notch. Market knowledge comprises two core areas.

Analysis and evaluation of supply and demand in the marketplace.   Understanding supply and demand enables you to have a solid discussion with clients about how the market can change quickly. If a lot of houses sell quickly in the next 30 days with limited new inventory coming on the market, the selection will be lower, and their bargaining power will also be reduced. Few agents really understand the effects of the law of supply and demand on the marketplace. Yet this age-old law dictates a lot of what happens in the marketplace.

Champion Agents track active inventory of predetermined price points. They track the number of homes sold monthly at those price points as well. Additionally, they monitor the list price to sales price ratios and days on the market. Finally, true Champions will calculate the absorption rate, or month's worth of available inventory. This figure can be easily calculated by dividing monthly sales into the current inventory numbers. This will give you a clear, quantifiable measure of the competitiveness of the marketplace buyers will encounter. It will also convey the breadth of selection they can expect to encounter in the marketplace. If your marketplace has six months' worth of inventory, they can expect a good selection of homes. If it has only one month, the volume of choices is diminished.

By completing this type of analysis either quarterly or monthly, you receive a tremendous snapshot of how competitive the marketplace is currently and how competitive you will need to be. The reason I use the word *snapshot* is because the analysis is for one moment in time. You have to explain to a client that clear distinction. Too often, people feel that your analysis, whether for a buyer's or a seller's CMA, should be valid forever. It's just a snapshot of a moment in time.

> *"Do you see why my clients can make better decisions?*

Or,

> *Is it clear how this creates an advantage for my exclusive clients?*

Or,

> *Is this the type of service you are looking for?"*

Transaction process knowledge.   This allows the buyers to experience less stress and anxiety. Most purchasers experience, at best, what I describe as controlled chaos. The transaction and clients are being thrust into emergency deadlines because the lender, the attorney, another agent, or even the buyer or seller don't perform in a timely manner and we find out later than we should.

> *"My clients experience a well-timed, structured process that leads to our end objective of a smooth closing. Having helped _____ people in my career, and more than _____ in the past year, you can rest assured that we will complete each step of the process in a timely fashion, with excellence, and will communicate all activities throughout the transaction."*

Financial Options and Qualifications

The next segment in your buyer consultation needs to focus on the five specific areas of the financial picture. Don't let a prospect get away with the response, "Don't worry. I have that handled." Whenever someone said that to me, I began to worry more than usual. It was a clear sign, in most cases, that the person didn't have it handled. The five specific areas to discuss are types of financing, where to obtain it, the difference between prequalifying and preapproval, earnest money deposit, and access to funds.

Types of Financing

Express to the client the vast array of financing options they should evaluate. The product line for home mortgages has changed dramatically since 1990, when I became a real estate agent. I believe there have been more changes in the past five years than there were in the previous 10 or even 20 years.

With the birth of adjustable rate mortgages (ARMs), hybrid loans, interest-only loans, two-to-one buy downs, 5-, 10-, 15-, 20-, 30-, and now 40-year fixed loans, the options for the consumer have never been greater. The need for agents to have enough knowledge about the loan options to provide some level of counsel is more important today than in the past. The loan your clients ultimately select could have a bearing on when they see you again for your services to represent their interest in another purchase.

Many studies have shown that consumers are moving away from long-term, fixed products to more flexible loans with lower initial interest rates that will ratchet up. In some studies and areas, over 40 percent of new loans are interest-only, low-money-down loans. By knowing and studying interest rates in your marketplace and by knowing your clients' basic loan information (i.e., whether they have a hybrid, five-year fixed, or ARM loan), you will be able to be there at the right time when they personally need your services in the future.

Where to Obtain Financing

I believe this is an area in which agents fail to exert enough influence. Agents and brokers are too scared of Real Estate Settlement Procedures Act (RESPA) laws and of being accused of "steering" the client. Where the habit of agents giving out three names of lenders got started I will never know. However, this approach is not the Champion Agent's approach and is a recipe for disaster. I believe this philosophy reduces referrals, opens the door to future competition, increases stress for the clients, and reduces service quality. I am convinced that any one of these is a valid reason to help your clients select the best solution for them in the short and long runs. Numerous benefits accrue when they work with your number one mortgage person or mortgage partner.

Use your mortgage partner. The service is always better at your favorite restaurant or the restaurant you frequent regularly. You get that extra special level of service. The same will be true of your clients who use your mortgage partner. Too often, early in my career, when clients brought their mortgage with them, it didn't turn out the way they had hoped.

Lenders didn't do what they said they would in terms of rate, points, fees, or timing. The stress level on the client's part went through the roof, especially right before closing. Often, I was drawn into fighting battles for them because they couldn't.

That type of situation is bad enough, but it's worse when it costs you future referrals, and it will, even if you had nothing to do with selecting the lender. If a certain level of service is not met and exceeded by everyone involved in the transaction, you share in the blame, even if you are not the cause of it. You will be forever linked (until the next transaction, if there is a next transaction) to all the people in this transaction. This position of limited control in exceeding expectations will affect your long-term referrals and referability.

> **Coach's Tip:** *One of the first rules of generating referrals is to be referable. If you don't do a good job, don't expect referrals. The amount and quality of your referrals will also be influenced by others who provide real estate service.*

Champion Agents are masters at evaluating time invested against the return on investment. They are focused on leveraging themselves to create more income. Your clients will receive better service and a high priority when working with your mortgage partner, and you won't be caught in the fire drill where everyone has to move heaven and earth to close the transaction.

Remember, your income is essentially fixed when you decide to work with a client.

> **Champion Rule:** *If the lender is not your mortgage partner, you will work harder . . . guaranteed.*

Usually, people who are looking to buy a $400,000 home don't change their minds and decide to buy a $750,000 home instead. The money you will earn has been determined as a relationship between sales price and commission percentage. The remaining questions are how soon and how much effort in time it will take, because your fees are basically set based on sale price. The variables that kill productivity and profit are the time and energy you have to invest to earn the commission. Those expenditures of resources are the only variables that are left. You increase your odds of a smooth transaction while investing the minimum time on your part by using your well-selected mortgage partner.

Threat of third-party lenders.   There is a significant threat in our industry from third-party lenders. Besides exposure to poor service, another real threat is loss of future business due to competition for the client. These third-party lenders, especially many of those that are Internet-based (some even have local offices), come with huge television ad budgets and are trying to reposition real estate agents in the transactions. They are working diligently to move us out of the hub of the transaction and move themselves in to it.

They are trying to establish their relationship with your clients for current and future lending and real estate services. Once they get a foothold, they offer large inducements or incentives for your clients to use them or their affiliates to sell their home or buy another one in the future.

If your client uses them for a loan, your client will be bombarded after closing with offers of inducement for years to come. In the worst case, you lose the client's future business. At best, they will have a negative impact on your future earnings and commission rate.

Prequalifying versus Preapproval

The goal in this section of your interview process is to get prospective buyers to understand the importance and value of preapproval. You need to sell the benefit of this approach. In an inventory-short marketplace, you won't get a home without preapproval. There won't be an option for a buyer. In a more neutral marketplace, buyers can be less prepared and sloppy if we let them. The value of preapproval centers around three benefits: (1) negotiating, (2) stress, and (3) security. These three, when linked, can save money, time, and unpleasantness for clients in acquiring their next home. You can help your clients achieve a stronger negotiating position with the seller.

Preapproval reduces the stress in the weeks from the offer to approval of the loan once the appraisal is completed. Buyers know that they have the loan, so all parties can start packing once acceptance is complete. It also increases the security because there are no surprises. When preapproval is granted in writing, it allows the client to avoid surprises of changing interest rates or increases in points or fees at closing; all these items affect the purchaser's security.

Earnest Money Deposit and Access to Funds

Too many agents don't counsel their clients about earnest money before they make an offer, so clients don't understand the power, position, and attention that strong earnest

> **Coach's Tip:** *Lenders have increased the use of this strategy as a result of the Do-Not-Call Registry. The lenders have figured out that after closing, a real estate agent is limited regarding phone contact unless you receive written permission to call. Without written permission, you can call past clients for only 18 months after the sale. The 18 months is significant because of exclusions in the law. The law states that contact is allowed for 18 months after the last sale, last payment, or last delivery. Lenders can use the last-payment provision for, in some cases, 30 years if the mortgage goes full term. (The last payment for most of us is thirty days previously.) This usurping of your client relationships is a growing threat that can be dealt with only by directing your clients to your preferred mortgage relationship and maintaining solid service and communication after the sale.*

money commands. Significant earnest money demonstrates to the seller the serious nature of the buyer. The purchaser will be putting this amount of money into the house and more. Champion Agents want their clients to be noticed as high-demand buyers. What is typical earnest money in your marketplace as a percentage of the sales price? If it is low (e.g., $5,000 on a $500,000 home), be sure to counsel your client to raise the amount.

You must know where this earnest money is coming from and how accessible it is. Too often, buyers "think" they have it, are "saving for it," "expect to get an inheritance" or some other big windfall, and it fails to come through. Dealing with this up front can save you embarrassment later on when things are delayed because clients couldn't get earnest money or were taking longer to acquire it than expected.

Quantify Your Total Value

When you look at your total value and the process of representing buyers' interests, the service of a professional real estate agent carries a high level of value. If you can quantify the value the client receives, you can sell your services more effectively and easily. At Real Estate Champions, we have charted the value of the services that buyers receive from most real estate agents. Figure 16.1 shows this information as a percentage of sales price.

Buyer Services	Value as a Percentage of Sales Price
Process knowledge / counsel	½ %
Market knowledge	½ %
Need assessment	½ %
Selection assistance	½ %
Correct contract writing	1 %
Presenting favorably	1–2 %
Negotiation / representation	1–2 %
Financing assistance	1 %
Closing processing	1 %
Follow-up communication	?
Total	7–9 %

©2006 Real Estate Champions, Inc.

Figure 16.1 The Value of a Champion Agent's Services

> *"You will easily receive 7 to 9 percent of the sales price in valuable services from me. The best part is that you receive all this, and it costs you really nothing. Isn't that great?"*

Or,

> *The seller actually pays the fee through the transaction costs. All the services that you receive from me are covered through the transaction. So you get someone with knowledge, assessment skill, selection assistance, proper contract preparation, presenting and negotiating skills, financial counsel, management and orchestration abilities, and after-sale service for free! The only thing I ask in exchange is your commitment, which we will talk about in a few minutes. Okay? Does this sound like the kind of service you are looking for? Does what we have gone over thus far make sense? Do you have any questions?"*

While most agents' conversations center on the home the client wants to buy, the Champion Agent doesn't talk about that subject until this stage of the presentation or later. Once enough value and differential for you and your services have been established, you have two options: continue down the agenda to completion or work to close the client immediately on the buyer's agency contract by moving to the exchange-of-commitment section of your presentation.

Home Selection and Budgetary Considerations

Your job, as a Champion Agent, is to help your clients uncover their desires and needs for their next home and guide them to achieve that goal based on market conditions, financial capacity, investment influences, and short- and long-term value. You might use a script like the following to open this discussion with your prospect.

> *"One of my primary jobs is helping you select the home that best suits your needs and budgetary considerations. I will counsel you on*

> *different options and features with each home. We will also discuss school districts, resale value, potential features that are functionally obsolete that could affect the future value of the home, area and neighborhood value trends, and anything else that would affect your short- or long-term enjoyment and equity in the home you are considering."*

Desires based on preference.   You need to clearly understand their desires and needs based on preferred style, preferred features, preferred location, price range, and payment parameters. These are all core areas of probing and discussion for a Champion Agent. The key word is *preferred.* One of the skills, after you secure a client to represent, is to manage the expectations. You need to know what your clients want, but the marketplace will ultimately determine what they can purchase. The style of home, features they desire, and location categories are pretty straightforward for a skillful agent. Most people will easily tell you what they want in these areas. They have been thinking, dreaming, and planning for weeks, months, and years. If you leave this discussion of style, features, and location at a surface level, you put your ability to manage expectations at risk. Just knowing what they want isn't enough. You have to first know *why* they want it.

Why do they want a certain style of home? Why do they want a three-bedroom or four-bedroom home or a pool in the backyard? Why do they want a certain size lot or certain school district? It is paramount to know why. You gain the perspective of how they think. It also gives you a view of the reasoning and motivation behind their decisions.

Coach's Tip: *Dig deep to find out why particular features are wanted. If you don't, you are merely finding out about bedrooms, baths, square footage, location, and neighborhoods. That level of service will not induce your clients to refer prospects your way.*

Features based on importance.   Another question to ask after each answer about style, features, and location is, "How important is it?" The style, features, and location are a collection of wants, needs, and dreams. What happens if you become fixated on the dream items and fail to fulfill the needs in a home? If we don't know how important the pool is, or that fourth bedroom or three-car garage, we have no way to guide them through the marketplace challenges. A Champion knows how important the pool is to a client. Does the home have to have an existing pool? Can it have room in the yard to add one later? Is this a "10" in terms of *have to,* or is it a "5"? "If I find you a home that has everything else you want and need without a pool, how strongly would you consider the home?"

Discussing a Monthly Payment

The part that is most challenging in the financial area is determining a comfortable or acceptable monthly payment. The trends of the 1970s and 1980s have led to a high percentage of your prospects having car loans and credit card debt. The average American has in excess of $8,500 in consumer credit card debt. Less than 40 percent of people who have credit cards pay them off monthly. Car loans and credit cards make discussion of monthly payments significant at this stage of the counseling interview.

Proper Contract Preparation

One of the benefits Champion Agents provide to their clients is security. While they provide security in many forms, certainly proper contract preparation is essential for the security of the client. By understanding your clients' timing, financial position, inspection needs, personal property desires, repair requirements, and a host of other factors, you are better able to express their intentions and protect their interests.

Too frequently, I have seen poorly constructed agreements that leave clients vulnerable to broad interpretation of ambiguous language. Educating your prospect on your value in this area creates an understanding that there is risk if they don't use your services. There is risk in a poorly constructed agreement: legal risk before and after the transaction, financial risk of undiscovered issues that affect value and appreciation, emotional risk of sleepless nights and general emotional distress. The following script can easily point out the difference between you and other agents.

> *"Bob and Mary, how an agreement is constructed determines the outcome of a transaction. For most people, this home purchase represents their largest investment, their biggest purchase in life, their longest obligation of debt—so how all these issues mesh in a purchase and sale agreement can affect you for years into the future. You have my guarantee that I will balance all these issues and craft a purchase and sale agreement that reflects your true intentions and protects you from the pitfalls of a real estate transaction."*

Presenting Your Offer to the Seller

While most of the real estate world has gone to faxing offers to the selling agent, there are times when presenting an offer face-to-face is advisable. At minimum, Champion Agents present the case that their buyer is the best buyer available in the marketplace. In heavy competition for a high-demand home, Champion Agents will get the client to write a letter to the seller, maybe including pictures of the family. Get strong loan commitment from the lender. Champion Agents will do everything in their power to swing the pendulum in their client's favor.

> *"The skill of presenting you favorably to the seller and other agents can mean the difference between you owning the home or another buyer owning the home. We need to be the seller's best buyer to be selected."*

Or,

> *"Presenting yourself favorably can set the tone as we negotiate the final terms and conditions of the purchase and sale agreement. The stronger we position you through financial capacity, human connection, and buyer commitment, the more the negotiating process can swing in your favor."*

Professional Negotiation

Too often, buyers view negotiation as you working on the seller for a price reduction. They often have the "I win, you lose" mentality. Their first thought or inclination on negotiation is price-related—that a good negotiator will get the home for less. That is not necessarily true in all cases. The market has influence on the buyer's ability to negotiate. The motivation of the seller also influences the negotiation. The demand level of the property will also influence negotiation. Being able to convey all these factors to the buyer is critical.

"Negotiating can take many hours. The marketplace, quality of the property, price of the property, demand for the property, and motivation of the seller all are factors in negotiation. They all influence the negotiating process in each transaction. I will evaluate each of these factors, and we will discuss them at the time we decide to make an offer. These can be fixed depending on the marketplace, and the quality and price of the property take primary position. Other times, negotiating the terms (meaning price, possession, and seller repairs) is more important than other parts of the agreement. You can be assured that, when we work together through negotiation, we will evaluate and execute on all of these areas. Do you see how there are more factors than just the price?"

Selecting the Right Financing Vehicle

I believe that Champion Agents provide more counsel and direction in this area than do other agents. I believe they are more willing than other agents to take the risk in the relationship to ensure their clients' satisfaction. It boils down to a philosophy of playing to win with a delighted client, or just going for a paycheck. You can make a lot of money, for example, finishing in the top 20 regularly in golf tournaments on the PGA tour. There are a lot of people who can make a lot of money doing that. There are few players, however, who are willing to take the risk to win the tournament. The one who wins gets the recognition, emotional lift, renewed confidence . . . and the money. Those in the top 20 get the money. Which one are you playing for?

Thirty years ago, there were not even one-tenth the options we have today. Because of my knowledge and experience in serving people just like you, I will be another person, to help you evaluate the options that are best for you. I view your real estate investment as more than a place to live. It is also a building block to your financial present and future. That can help you to reach your goals and dreams in life for you and your family. Isn't that what you are looking for in an agent?"

Closing Coordination and Communication

This area of the presentation offers multiple questioning and closing positions to see how things are going.

> *"How frequently would you like me to communicate with you?"*

Or,

> *"How best would you like me to communicate with you?"*

A word of caution: just because e-mail is easy doesn't mean it's best for your client. I am personally a telephone person. I don't really like e-mail as much. "Call me and give me the update." There are, especially in the younger generations, people who really prefer e-mail to the phone. Check with your client on their preferred method of communication.

> *"There are many steps to closing a transaction. We have to deal with many people in the process: Other agents, brokers, sellers, lenders, underwriters, inspectors, appraisers, construction repairmen, title insurance administrators, escrow agents, attorneys. There are many people who need orchestration and communication. There are also the pounds of paper that follow every transaction that we manage. We provide a comprehensive approach to managing and directing all these people and activities on your behalf, all the while communicating our efforts in the stage we currently are in and informing you of what is coming next. That way, you will know at all times how the transaction is progressing. We communicate with our clients at least weekly about our progress. Is that frequent enough, or do you want to be contacted more frequently?"*

Follow-up after the Sale

You want to set the stage so your service and connection doesn't end when the sale is closed, so clients can call you about anything they might need. The Nordstrom positioning, as an elite customer-focused service provider, is key at this juncture. The reason most people don't go back to do business with real estate agents is lack of follow-up after the sale. Convey the different service models you employ.

> *"Though I receive my compensation with the completion of the sale, my job has just begun. My desire is to create clients for life. You can be assured that you won't have to go through this process again to find an agent to represent your interests. After the closing, we will provide you keys and access to your new home. We will also check back with you right after your move to make sure any problems that present themselves are resolved quickly. We typically call our clients a few times in that 30 days to make sure the condition of the property is as we expected, that there are no surprises. We will then continue to be a resource for you on your growing equity position, market-place trends, tax assessment, and equitability against your home's value. And, if you have friends and relatives who need the same type of help you are in need of now, we would be delighted with your referral to help them, as well. The real benefit is that there is no risk in working with me. I am willing to do as much work after the sale as I do before it to ensure your satisfaction."*

17

Buyer Exchange of Commitments

The exchange of commitment section of your presentation is the most important section. The future steps you are able to take hinge on how you deliver the exchange of commitments and the responses you receive in this section.

After you conduct this discussion with your prospects, either they will become clients or they will be deemed nonqualified to work with you. Either of these outcomes must be acceptable. Non-Champion agents are far too attached to getting the client. It would be impossible and foolish to assume you can close everyone to an exclusive relationship, nor would you want to.

Prospects could be qualified in every way in terms of motivation and financial capacity. They could have the proper desire, need, ability, and authority, but lack the willingness to enter into an exclusive representation relationship. They are unwilling to exchange commitments with you. That would deem them unqualified to work with a Champion Agent.

Benefits of Exclusive Relationship

To be an effective relationship for the agent and the buyer, each must exchange mutual commitment of loyalty. Champion Agents commit themselves to a high service standard. That service standard is communicated clearly to the prospect buyer. The only way a prospect can receive that high level of service is to work on an exclusive basis, forgoing all other previous, potential, and possible relationships with other agents. You are, in effect, entering into a covenant relationship with a client. You need to explain the scope of that commitment-based relationship. Prospects need to clearly understand both the expectations that you have of their conduct and the benefits of exclusivity.

I Don't Work with Everybody

The public's perception is that real estate agents will work with anyone, that they are just hoping to sell a house, so consumers feel free to use them and abuse them. Because the perceived value of our services is low, customers don't feel the need to work exclusively, and most agents won't ask for that level of commitment.

Your potential buyer needs to understand and accept that you operate an exclusive practice, that you can't and don't work with anyone and everyone who walks in the door, calls you, or is referred to you. If you really don't work with everybody, then it shouldn't matter, even if someone comes via referral. If people are nonqualified, they are nonqualified.

You must convey the message that you select the clients you want to work with. It's the only way you are able to deliver such a high level of service and have such high satisfaction numbers. Demonstrate to them that the only way they will receive all of the services they want is through exclusivity. You won't be able to provide those without this exclusive focus. The benefit to them is it doesn't cost more to receive all of these benefits and high service level. The only way you can follow through on all of the services and commitments you make to them is to work with a small group of clients rather than

> *"Bob and Susan, I want you to know that I don't work with everyone who calls or even with everyone I meet with. To be able to provide the services I do, and that you indicated you want, I have to choose my clients. The big benefit for my clients in this approach allows me a greater amount of time to invest in my clients' total satisfaction. My clients end up securing the best homes in the marketplace at the best values in the marketplace. In the end, by working this way, my clients save time, frustration, even money, and especially stress because I am able to give them the attention they deserve. Based on our discussion so far, do you see the benefit in that?"*

a large group. In the end, you have to explain that, because you work with this smaller group, you need to ensure that they are committed to working with you and buying a home through you.

I Work on a Contingency Fee Basis

I am a firm believer that Champion Agents educate their clients on how their compensation works. I believe far too many agents are unable to talk about this subject. It's almost as bad as trying to talk with our kids about sex. We need to recognize that the elephant in the room is our commission and deal with it accordingly. There are still people in the world who think we are paid in some format other than the completed transaction. They don't realize we are paid similarly to personal injury attorneys, who are compensated *only* when the case is won. You would be surprised at how many people in today's world still don't understand that fact. That's our fault, plain and simple.

The vast majority of the people in the world don't work on a contingency fee basis. They don't really know what that is. They also can't imagine working that way. Often, if you show them the risk you are taking, they will help you minimize that risk by committing to work with you.

Another option to further demonstrate the risk you incur, as an agent, is to show them what is really generated from a sale. This is a great technique for both the buyer and the seller. Most people, again, think that all the money you receive is pure profit. They see the gross number and don't have any concept of the costs you pay to run your business.

Champion Calculation

Where the commission goes:

- 6% × \$200,000 = \$12,000
- Co-op agent − 50% = \$6,000
- Total commission earned = \$6,000
- Broker split 70/30 = \$1,800
- Net commission earned = \$4,200
- Cost per transaction = \$1,200
- Net profit = \$3,000
- Self-employment taxes 15.2% = \$456.00
- State (9%) and federal (30%) taxes = \$992.00
- Real dollars earned = \$1,552

"Bob and Susan, I want you to understand that I work on a contingency fee basis. That means that this meeting and all the services I will provide to you will be in the hope and expectation that I will be paid at closing in the future. It's a risk, as an agent, I am willing to take with the right clients. I have had situations where I did a tremendous amount of work, and yet the transaction didn't close, so all that work, time, effort, energy, counsel, and advice went out the window as unpaid."

Coach's Tip: *Use this technique to combat the notion that you are paid too much, that you aren't worth what you charge, that getting a rebate or inducement from a less skilled agent is beneficial to the buyer.*

The last technique is to make you human, like them. Demonstrate that you have bills just like they do; you have mortgage payments and car payments; you have to pay for braces for the kids and save for college educations, too, just like they do. Using this technique takes the focus off the commission and places it on your service and your family, similar to their own family. The more they can identify with you, the more likely they are to connect and commit to you.

"Just like you, I have a mortgage payment and other bills. I owe it to my family and two children to ensure I work in a manner that serves my clients well in addition to ensuring my compensation. The benefit to you is that I will do an outstanding job for you so I receive payment at the conclusion of your home purchase."

I Carefully Select My Clients

This segment dovetails with the contingency fee section. Now that you have established your compensation structure, it's natural to talk about how you must carefully select your clients to ensure compensation. Again, you owe this to your family to protect your financial present and future. It's almost as though you are in the process of carefully selecting a job each time you work with a new prospect. There are too many jobs where the client resembles Enron, and bankruptcy is right around the corner.

You can also share with prospects that your desire is to exceed their expectations. In order to achieve that goal, you have to select the right clients. Not everyone will allow you to exceed expectations, because they have unrealistic expectations—of the market, their own financial capacity, your role—and they lack commitment. There are a number of factors that, blended together, could add up to a tremendous client relationship, which is what you are looking for.

> *"Because of the contingency fee basis of compensation, I also must be selective in whom I work with as clients. I need to be confident I can meet and exceed client objectives. I need to make sure potential clients want to exchange their commitment of working together exclusively for the vast array of services I offer to my exclusive clients."*

I Can Succeed in Today's Marketplace

Your job is to demonstrate the level of work and commitment that is necessary in today's market for clients to reach their goals. The level of work can increase or decrease based on the marketplace. You must be able to give them an accurate picture of the challenges you will face together in the marketplace.

You can use market data to express the level of work. You can use testimonials, stories about clients, or survey results that demonstrate the lengths to which you are willing to travel for your clients. Let them know that your intent is to go to work right away, that in fact you are already working on their behalf right now. You will begin by focusing on their goals, objectives, and the opportunities in the marketplace that align with their goals and objectives in life.

> *"I am sure you'll agree that providing all the services we talked about takes hard work, correct? We also agreed that these are the services you are looking for, right?"*

I Believe That I Can Help You

Having conviction and belief is one of the secrets of Champion Agents. Champion Agents will clearly express their belief in their service and value to prospects. They will act on that belief by telling clients that they can help them better than other agents in the marketplace.

The simple approach to this is to do a summation close by just summing up the key points and key services that they want from you and feel are important. Then, once you have confirmed those, simply plug those into a strong conviction statement that you can help them achieve what they want.

> *"Bob and Mary, you indicated that the three main services you want from me are weekly phone communication, monthly market trend reports, and help with a mortgage originator, is that correct? There isn't a doubt in my mind I can fulfill these desires of yours better than anyone else you could select to work with. Shall we start working together now?"*

This statement of belief, linked with a strong close, is the turning point of the presentation. The level of confidence and conviction that you exude right here will cause them either to commit to you easily or to struggle against you. The first stop toward moving them to your way of thinking and doing business is *your belief* level. They won't believe if you don't.

It Matters Who Represents Your Interests

I realize this is repetitious from earlier in the buyer consultation; however, the prospect needs to be clearly reminded of the pitfalls of working with any old agent or even a bad agent. Too many consumers think they can negotiate for themselves better than a professional agent who truly represents their interests. They think, why not work with the listing agent and work to reduce the fees? You need to put that thought out of their head. You need to demonstrate clearly that it matters who represents their interests.

Exchange of Commitments

You have now arrived at the moment of truth. You need to say, "I'll commit to you if you commit to me." This is the big close moment. It really should be easy by this time if you have done a good job up until this point.

When executing a great presentation, it should be benefits-based. It should clearly explain what's in it for them. It should have trial closes throughout the presentation to build momentum to the close. It should be delivered with enthusiasm, conviction, confidence, and assertiveness.

This part of the presentation should be assertive. Most agents approach this crossroad and wimp out. If you followed the Champion process I have laid out for you thus far, you have earned the right to secure an exclusive right-to-represent contract.

> *"Bob and Susan, I will commit to providing you every single service we talked about that you agreed you wanted. All I ask and require is that you commit to working exclusively with me. Can you do that?"*

Ask your closing question; then be quiet.   The key, once you have asked the question, is to be quiet, to not utter a single word. Let tension build if you must, but don't say anything. A Champion Agent asks a great closing question and waits for the response.

The difference between *great* and *good* is very small. It's the last inch or two that separates great from good. It could be the smallest detail that is overlooked by most people, but, to the person who wants to achieve greatness, it is never overlooked.

One of the key concepts between good and great in the presentation is silence. It's the silence after a direct question. Too many salespeople fear the dead space in a conversation and think they have to fill it up. That need to fill the void will keep you from greatness in sales. The void of silence causes our client or prospect to think. At this moment, the sale is made.

If you step into the pause, you invalidate, or soften, the last question. You are at the moment of truth. You will find out valuable information about your client or prospect at that moment. The power of silence is deafening. Make sure to use it to your advantage. Becoming a Champion Agent requires attention to the little things.

Coach's Tip: *Arthur Rubinstein, the world-famous pianist, was once asked, "How do you handle the notes on the page as well as you do?" He responded, "I handle the notes no better than many others, but the pauses . . . ah! That is where the art resides." Your sale process needs to be like a great piece of music. It causes a reaction and emotion from your client or prospect. The real artistry is in the pauses. Rubinstein would let the note resonate throughout the hall. Let your question resonate in the conference room, the living room . . . wherever you are making your presentation.*

Add a condition *only if* it's necessary.

If, after pausing, waiting, waiting, and then waiting some more, you still can't get a commitment, you have to move in another direction. I am a firm believer of getting a buyer client to sign an exclusive right-to-represent agreement without conditions. However, if you can't get it without conditions, put the condition in the contract.

The main argument people use not to sign an exclusive right to represent is that they don't want to be tied up. They play the what-if game in their head. What if he doesn't perform? What if I decide not to buy now? What if friends call me about their house? What if I find a property for sale by the owners? They come up with all kinds of examples, but the probability of that happening is about zilch. If they insist, however, then include the condition that allows them to cancel the agreement.

> *"I will commit to you the service we have talked about if you commit to buy exclusively through me. You can cancel our agreement at any time, if you tell me first, if you call me personally or meet me personally. Does that meet your approval?"*

This script and technique lowers their risk substantially (in their minds). In truth, there is no risk to them at all. In addition, there is little risk for you if you do your job right. When agents find out someone they had spent a lot of time with bought from another agent, when do they find out and from whom? Usually, you find out just before or after it closes. You also find out from another party: your lender, their lender, or another agent. You rarely find out from the buyer. The buyer usually doesn't have the guts to call you and say, "I found a for-sale-by-owner house . . . found another house . . . bought it through the listing agent . . . you were doing a poor job." They just go away and hide, hoping that you never find out.

Dialogue for explaining exclusive agency agreement

> *"This form is our contract (agreement of loyalty) that spells out the details of our working together. It is dated today and ends 90 days from today. If needed, we can always add an extension.*
>
> *I have some specific duties to you that are spelled out in this agreement: First, I will use my professional knowledge and tools to find a house that meets your needs. Second, I will guide you through the offer process. And third, I will be representing your interests throughout this process and negotiating in your behalf.*
>
> *There are also some specific duties that you have: You will be working exclusively [circle and emphasize this] with me through the term of this agreement. It also states that you will supply me with necessary financial information I will need to negotiate an acceptable offer. Thank you, by the way, for supplying me with the preliminary information in advance. It also outlines here that if you see ads,*

signs, open houses, for sale by owners, and new construction, you will need to contact me first. Let me just say that I get so many calls from people already working with other Realtors who say they don't want to waste their Realtors' time, but they just need a quick price or location. I want you to know that you are hiring me to do a job, and you will never be wasting my time to give me a call to ask questions; that is what I'm ultimately paid to do.

Now, I do receive compensation, and this part outlines how I am paid. I will be collecting a fee of _____ up front when I write the offer, and then I'm paid 3 percent of the sales price when you have secured a house to buy. This also has a broker protection clause for two months after the expiration of this agreement for any house I've shown you.

Although my fee is earned when you've found a property, that fee is deferred until settlement. In most cases, the 3 percent fee is by the seller through the Multiple Listing Service. This paragraph authorizes that. Please acknowledge here. If we run into a situation where that would not be the case, I'll let you know before I even show you the property.

This entire agreement may be terminated by either of us with mutual consent in writing.

Most of the rest of this has already been explained to you in the other form. However, I do want to point out that I may have other buyer clients I'm working with who may be looking for homes similar to what you want in a house.

So that is basically it . . . please acknowledge here."

Handshake is better than nothing . . . almost. Your other option is to look them straight in the eye and say, "Let's shake on our agreement." A handshake commitment is better than nothing, but it falls far short of the written document of exclusive agency. I recently surveyed a group of 30 agents I was working with in our Performance Accountability Coaching II Program. These agents were getting only verbal commitments rather than written commitments. On average, they were losing two clients or transactions a year that they thought were committed to them. The average commission check was $15,000, so their loss was $30,000 per agent. They were all from the same company, so the loss to the company was $900,000 in commissions per year!

According to NAR, in 2004, over 64 percent of the transactions involved exclusive buyer's agency relationship with the buyer. I believe 64 percent is a significant number of people who accept and operate via exclusive right-to-represent agreements.

Recap Exclusive Relationship

At its core, the exclusive relationship is centered on three fundamental statements:

- You will use me if I find you what you want . . . right?
- You will use me if you find what you want . . . correct?
- You will use me if another agent finds you what you want . . . right?

Without an affirmative response to those three fundamental questions, you should put Roy Rogers on the CD player and sing "Happy Trails." If you get a pause, a stall, or a balk, you could go back and explain the value page again and reemphasize the value you bring to the transaction—demonstrating each service and why it's worth it.

Coach's Tip: *If you follow this process and you still can't get the prospect to commit exclusively to working with you, determine them unqualified and move on to your next prospect!*

In the end, your final argument could be, *why not?* Why not use someone else's time, experience, knowledge, expertise, and gas to find the right home. It costs the buyer nothing, because the seller pays for it.

PART IV

BUILDING A CHAMPION AGENT'S BUSINESS

18

Time Management Is Life Management

How you use your time determines the quality of your life. It determines how successful you are in business and how effective you are in your business and personal life. Time management is the most challenging skill to master in life. Most people don't control time . . . time controls them. This is especially true with the high-distraction, high-interception business of real estate sales. We spend our whole lives trying to acquire the skill to use our time to create the greatest return.

Time management is really self-management. It's the management of yourself—to invest your time in the highest-reward activities, the activities and pursuits in life that create the greatest rewards in satisfaction, relationships, connections, and equity return.

> *"You can't manage time; you can only manage yourself."*
> *—Peter Drucker*

Time is truly your most valuable asset, but you do not know how much of it you possess. Each day, we invest 86,400 seconds. The time of tomorrow is not guaranteed.

> *"Unlike other resources, time cannot be bought or sold,*
> *borrowed or stolen, stocked up or saved, manufactured,*

> *reproduced, or modified. All we can do is make use of it,*
> *and whether we use it or not, it nevertheless slips away."*
> —*Jean-Louis Serran-Selseiben*

Real Estate Agent's Time

There are three categories that every waking work hour will fit into. The percentage of time you allot to each of these three categories of time will determine your income and net profit. Champion Performers in real estate sales quickly learn which actions account for the great majority of the results they achieve. They save their time for the activities that present the highest return on investment, with the intention of improving the consistency and intensity on those high-value activities.

Direct Income-Producing Activities (DIPA)

I describe the activities that account for the majority of results in the real estate area, as direct income-producing activities (DIPA). The DIPA allotment and investment separates the Champion Performers from the middle of the pack or even good producers. The activities that qualify as DIPA are things you do that have a direct connection to your production and revenue creation.

- Prospecting
- Lead follow-up
- Listing presentations
- Buyer interview presentations
- Showing property to qualified buyers
- Writing and negotiating contracts

I have watched countless agents take a firm grip on the wheel of these DIPA activities and have seen explosive results in income. I have watched agents add $100, $200, even $300 an hour to their value in less than six months through focus and adherence to increasing their DIPA hours each day.

Typical agents invest less than 20 percent of their hours in DIPA. This low percentage relates to their income fluctuations. An agent must spend a minimum of 15 hours a week in direct income-producing activities. It means most agents need to spend that 15 hours a week in prospecting and lead follow-up if they want growth. If you do that, you will guarantee your success. If you fail to do that, your success will be questionable.

Champion Agents go beyond the 15 hours a week. They are far beyond the 20, 30, even 40 percent level. A Champion Agent client named Kim Heddinger, who works for Windermere in Eugene, Oregon, has increased her income by more than $200,000 a year for the past two years. The reason for this is that she focuses 80 percent of her time each week on DIPA. That's the highest percentage of any agent I have ever heard of in the real estate industry. She guarantees her growth, net profit, and quality of life because she doesn't let anything reduce her 80 percent number each week. She is truly a Champion Agent.

My opinion is that the other categories competing for your time, the indirect income-producing activities (IIPA) and the production-supporting activities (PSA), are far less valuable. They are also the worst part of the job as a real estate agent. These are areas that generate all the stress, emotion, frustration, and problems. If you spend too much time in these areas, you get burned out, chewed up, and spat out. Why would you want to spend time investing more than is absolutely the minimum amount in them?

Indirect Income-Producing Activities (IIPA)

Indirect income-producing activities are the tasks you do to help create income that cannot be directly linked to revenue, as DIPA can. It's the marketing pieces you create for your farm or some other direct mail strategy. It's the e-mail you send to a buyer who hits your Web site. It's the ads you create for newspapers, magazines, or online sources. It's all the things you do to try to generate leads or opportunities that are more difficult to convert and track. They cannot be as easily linked to revenue.

Production-Supporting Activities (PSA)

Production-supporting activities comprise all the tasks you must do to service clients and prospects: creating in-home flyers; faxing, copying, filing, and letter writing; all the phone calls made to lenders, other agents, inspectors, appraisers, and repair people. It's anything that supports the production you created. I realize that PSA stuff must be done. When you prospect and do lead follow-up effectively, you create PSA work to be completed. It's the cycle of sales. The question is, "Are you spending the minimum time possible doing the PSA work?"

One way to minimize the revenue lost during the time you spend doing PSA is to do this work in low-value time. We all have a time during the day when we have more energy, intensity, and focus; when we are the most productive toward our goals. That time must be reserved for DIPA—and DIPA only. You can ill afford to let IIPA, or even worse, PSA, slip into those slots. My time of focus and intensity is highest in the morning. I need to protect that time from 7:00 a.m., when I begin my workday, to about 11:30 a.m., when my mind starts to focus on lunch and loses a little of its edge for DIPA. Production-supporting activities don't produce revenue, so you can't let them take over your days. If you do, you won't get back to revenue-producing pursuits. Too many agents take whole chunks of days, even weeks, working on their deal. Yes, I said deal—as in one!

Champion Rule: *Don't attack the time management problem out of order.*

Being successful at selling is about determining the steps you need to take to be successful and putting those steps in the right order. If you think success is a one-step process, think again! In real estate sales, you can take the right steps but in the wrong order, and you will not achieve the result you want. The steps and the order must both be correct for change to occur with efficiency. In time management, most salespeople start trying to change without taking proper evaluation.

We have been taught to plan our work and then work our plan. That approach sounds reasonable, but it leads to failure without taking more particular steps before you plan your work. Most of us start with planning our work or our tasks. You have a few phone calls to return—you list those. You need to make these marketing pieces or put a sign or lockbox up at your new listing today.

The truly productive Champion Agents start at the opposite end from where most people begin. They start by working to determine where their time actually goes. They don't begin by planning—they begin by exploring where their resource of time goes. Once they know where their time goes, then they work at managing the time to increase the amount of time devoted to DIPA.

They focus on lowering the PSA that they do in their business, and then they work to increase and compartmentalize their discretionary time in the largest amounts possible. These blocks of discretionary time are grouped together, so the Champion Agent achieves the greatest value from his or her time invested in personal enjoyment. This three-step process consists of the following: (1) record your time; (2) manage your time; and (3) consolidate your time.

The Activity Tracking Tool

Use Figure 18.1 to track how you use your time by the half hour. We ask our clients to track their time by indicating the activity and determining whether it's DIPA, IIPA, or PSA. We usually find that, for the first few times, they spend around 10 to 20 percent doing DIPA

Name: _____ Date: _____

6:00–6:30	_____	DIPA	IIPA	PSA
6:30–7:00	_____	DIPA	IIPA	PSA
7:00–7:30	_____	DIPA	IIPA	PSA
7:30–8:00	_____	DIPA	IIPA	PSA
8:00–8:30	_____	DIPA	IIPA	PSA
8:30–9:00	_____	DIPA	IIPA	PSA
9:00–9:30	_____	DIPA	IIPA	PSA
9:30–10:00	_____	DIPA	IIPA	PSA
10:00–10:30	_____	DIPA	IIPA	PSA
10:30–11:00	_____	DIPA	IIPA	PSA
11:00–11:30	_____	DIPA	IIPA	PSA
11:30–12:00	_____	DIPA	IIPA	PSA
12:00–12:30	_____	DIPA	IIPA	PSA
12:30–1:00	_____	DIPA	IIPA	PSA
1:00–1:30	_____	DIPA	IIPA	PSA
1:30–2:00	_____	DIPA	IIPA	PSA
2:00–2:30	_____	DIPA	IIPA	PSA
2:30–3:00	_____	DIPA	IIPA	PSA
3:00–3:30	_____	DIPA	IIPA	PSA
3:30–4:00	_____	DIPA	IIPA	PSA
4:00–4:30	_____	DIPA	IIPA	PSA
4:30–5:00	_____	DIPA	IIPA	PSA
5:00–5:30	_____	DIPA	IIPA	PSA
5:30–6:00	_____	DIPA	IIPA	PSA
6:00–6:30	_____	DIPA	IIPA	PSA
6:30–7:00	_____	DIPA	IIPA	PSA
7:00–7:30	_____	DIPA	IIPA	PSA
7:30–8:00	_____	DIPA	IIPA	PSA
8:00–8:30	_____	DIPA	IIPA	PSA
8:30–9:00	_____	DIPA	IIPA	PSA

DIPA payoff hours _____

IIPA payoff hours _____

PSA payoff hours _____

Total hours _____

©2006 Real Estate Champions, Inc.

Figure 18.1 Activity Tracking by the Half Hour

Champion Example

An agent makes $100,000 a year. He is a typical agent, spending two hours or less each day in DIPA. (I have asked thousands of agents to honestly look at their time allocation of DIPA, and it always comes out to two hours or less daily . . . when they are honest about it.) He will work 250 days this year to make that $100,000. He is worth, in effect, $400 a day, or $50 an hour—a respectable wage to most. He works an eight-hour day to produce that $400.

However, here is where the real breakdown begins. He works two hours a day in DIPA and six hours in PSA and IIPA. A person who does the PSA work that an assistant does is paid about $15 an hour. He works six hours a day at $15 an hour, for a total of $90. That means his two hours of DIPA is worth $310, or $155 an hour. This person has a choice each and every moment of the day to earn $15—or 10 times that amount ($155 an hour). Which would you choose? Adding an hour of DIPA to each workday would roughly increase his income by $155 a day. Multiply that by the 250 days he works each year, and that equals an extra $38,750 a year. Shifting one hour a day from PSA to DIPA for a year is worth at least $50,000.

work, about 65 to 70 percent in PSA work, and the remainder in IIPA work. (That's when they are being honest with themselves.)

As you invest more time in DIPA, your value per hour, or hourly rate, increases. It increases because your skills and discipline increase. Your listing inventory and buyer leads increase. Everything that a Champion Agent wants to have happen in business happens when he or she increases the amount of time invested in DIPA. Our example of an hourly rate of $155 would increase to somewhere in the neighborhood of $200 to $225 in a few months by adding one hour per day to the DIPA investment. Not only does this agent make $155 for the extra hour of DIPA work, he also makes a bonus of $45 to $70 an hour for all three of his DIPA hours. That would move the annual increase from $38,750 to $91,250. Now we are talking about a Champion-level pay increase! These types of results have been accomplished by thousands of agents we have coached about this simple change in time philosophy, discipline, and daily execution.

The Champion Agent's Time Block

The vast majority of agents have heard of time blocking as a form of improving their efficiency in their business. I believe the goal for time blocking is to increase the amount of

	MONDAY	TUESDAY	WEDNESDAY	THURSDAY	FRIDAY	SATURDAY	SUNDAY
6a.m.							
6:15							
6:30							
6:45							
7:00							
7:15							
7:30							
7:45							
8:00							
8:15							
8:30							
8:45							
9:00							
9:15							
9:30							
9:45							
10:00							
10:15							
10:30							
10:45							
11:00							
11:15							

Figure 18.2 Real Estate Champions Time Blocking Schedule

	MONDAY	TUESDAY	WEDNESDAY	THURSDAY	FRIDAY	SATURDAY	SUNDAY
11:30							
11:15							
12p.m.							
12:15							
12:30							
12:45							
1:00							
1:15							
1:30							
1:45							
2:00							
2:15							
2:30							
2:45							
3:00							
3:15							
3:30							
3:45							
4:00							
4:15							
4:30							

Figure 18.2 Real Estate Champions Time Blocking Schedule (*Continued*)

	MONDAY	TUESDAY	WEDNESDAY	THURSDAY	FRIDAY	SATURDAY	SUNDAY
5:00							
5:15							
5:30							
5:45							
6:00							
6:15							
6:30							
6:45							
7:00							
7:15							
7:30							
7:45							
8:00							
8:15							
8:30							
8:45							
9:00							
9:15							
9:30							
9:45							
10:00							

Figure 18.2 Real Estate Champions Time Blocking Schedule (*Continued*)

time you are investing in DIPA. The problem is that few agents have really mastered the use of time blocking.

There is a direct correlation between your income growth and better investment of your time. A Champion Agent is a Champion *time manager*. To be successful at time blocking, you must start with a good tool. If you are going to be a Champion Agent, the time block tool must break time into 15-minute increments. (See Figure 18.2.) Because the value of time is high for a Champion Agent, 15 minutes can mean a lot of lost revenue and production. If a loss occurs only a handful of times a day, it can add up to hundreds of dollars.

Most agents have never mastered time blocking because they repeat common mistakes when creating and executing their time block. Beyond prioritization, you need to think about your time with the right mindset. You need to attack the issue of time management from the right perspective.

Mistake 1: Not Creating a Time Block Schedule with the Right Mindset

You tend to create a schedule from the "squeeze it in" mindset. You are trying to fit everything into our schedule. You must approach the problem of time management in the proper order.

For years, we have used the following story, "Big Rocks," in our coaching. I do not know the origin of the story, other than that Stephen Covey used it in his book *First Things First*. (An associate of his heard it at a seminar, so Covey did not cite the origin, either.)

───────────

One day an expert in time management was speaking to a group of business students and, to drive home a point, used an illustration those students will never forget. As this man stood in front of the group of high-powered overachievers, he said, "Okay, time for a quiz." He pulled out a one-gallon, wide-mouthed Mason jar and set it on a table in front of him. Then he produced about a dozen fist-sized rocks and carefully placed them, one at a time, into the jar. When the jar was filled to the top, and no more rocks would fit inside, he asked, "Is this jar full?" Everyone in the class said, "Yes." He said, "Really?"

He reached under the table and pulled out a bucket of gravel. He dumped some gravel in and shook the jar, causing pieces of gravel to work themselves down into the spaces between the big rocks. He asked the group once more, "Is the jar full?" By this time the class was on to him. "Probably not," one of them answered. "Good!" he replied.

He reached under the table and brought out a bucket of sand. He started dumping the sand in, and it went into all the spaces left between the rocks and the gravel. Once more, he asked the question, "Is the jar full?" "No!" the class shouted. Once again, he said, "Good!"

Then he grabbed a pitcher of water and began to pour it in until the jar was filled to the brim. He looked up at the class and asked, "What is the point of this illustration?" One eager beaver raised his hand and said, "The point is, no matter how full your schedule is, if you try really hard, you can always fit some more things into it!" "No," the speaker replied, "that's not the point. The truth this illustration teaches is: If you don't put the big rocks in first, you'll never get them in at all."

Time Blocking Order

You need to put the big rocks of your life in first to make a time block schedule run correctly. That means you need to establish a time block for each day of the week that goes through the evening. Insert your personal life first, since that's clearly a big rock.

Block in Your Personal Life First

Do this before you put in your business activities. Put in your workout time, prayer time, quiet time, family time, kids' athletic events and practices, personal learning time—anything that happens either daily or weekly. I have a client who blocks specific time for dinner every night to ensure he is home for every evening meal with his family.

Blocking time allows you to tell prospects that you already have a previous appointment. They don't have to know the appointment is dinner with your family. They merely need to know you are booked. You build value for your services through scarcity. Scarcity can be increased by adhering to a solid time-blocked schedule that includes your personal life at the forefront.

Take a designated day off. I personally believe two is better, but most agents go through withdrawal just having one. Agents are too available. We want to be there for our clients. What the heck does that mean? Even God took the seventh day off. He had a lot tougher task in creating the world than we do.

A day off means no real estate calls, faxes, ad calls, sign calls, or cell phones. Focus 100 percent on family, relaxing, and recharging. If you take one call, it becomes a business day. NAR did a study a few years ago, and well over 60 percent of the families that responded said, "The Realtor in the family works too much, and we can't count on them to be there when they say they will be or to take a day off when they say they will." Ouch!!

Take most evenings off.   Set the boundaries so you don't have to work every evening. For a Champion Agent to work more than two evenings per week is unnecessary. I personally worked only on Tuesday evenings. I was willing to take my last appointment at 8:15, which put me home by 9:30 p.m., but I was not gone any other evening. Move your prospects into your work evening and into your preferred time slots by asking, for example, "Would 5:15 or 6:15 be better for you on Tuesday evening?"

Block your other personal time.   If you plan to work out each morning, like I do, schedule it. Block in your personal development time to read, study, and grow. If you need prayer or meditation, block that in as well. Whatever your daily routine, it needs to be planned for. Many agents feel that if they put in all their personal time and time off, there won't be enough time for business production. If you really count the hours left after sleeping is removed, you still have more than 70 hours of possible work time per week. That's more than you should be working anyway. Once you have your personal life blocked, you need to move to your work life.

Block Your Direct Income-Producing Activities

For most people, mornings are the best time for the DIPA of prospecting and lead follow-up. I would suggest 90 minutes of prospecting and 60 minutes of lead follow-up daily. I am sure some of you reading this are saying, "But Dirk, more people are home in the evening." I won't argue that point; that is probably correct. I will argue, however, that most agents won't prospect in the evening because they are too tired. It doesn't matter if the contact-to-dial ratio would be better if you won't do it or don't do it. Few agents have the personal discipline to make the calls with regularity after a long, tough day. I was not one of them, but I could make calls on Tuesday, when I didn't have appointments.

Schedule time for appointments.   My typical listing presentation was no more than 45 minutes. I could schedule my appointments in one-hour increments because I needed 15 minutes of drive time between appointments. My schedule was set to conduct appointments at 3:15, 4:15, and 5:15 Monday through Thursday. On Tuesday evenings, I also had 6:15, 7:15, and 8:15 appointment slots. If I didn't have Tuesday evening appointments, I would use that time to prospect or to follow up on leads to secure more appointments.

Because I operated with specific appointment times, I wasn't asking what time would be best for them. I was closing on them for a specific time to meet. There is a big difference between these two approaches and their effectiveness. Offering alternative choices is an effective technique: "Sue, would Monday or Tuesday at 4:15 be better for you?" If the reply was, "I don't get home until 4:30 usually. Can we do it then?" I would move her to a 5:15 p.m. appointment. You want to keep your slotting and not deviate. (A doctor has predetermined slots for patients. Your business is really no different.)

Schedule return phone call times. We need to have designated times to return calls. There should be one in the late morning, after your prospecting and lead follow-up is completed. If you return calls before finishing prospecting or lead follow-up, you run the risk of not getting to them that day. Nothing in real estate is so urgent it can't wait an hour or two to be handled.

Schedule Ongoing Production-Supporting Activities

All administrative tasks need time to be completed. I often see new clients' initial time block schedules that have zero administration time in them. That's not realistic, even if you have a large team of assistants. You will always have administrative time.

You might also block a regular time to meet over the phone with your primary lender, title company, or closing attorney to receive status updates. It saves the half-dozen phone calls that usually go back and forth each week. You can update all your in-process transactions in one 15-minute call. This call should be the same time and day each week. (The recipients, just like you, should not schedule anything during that slot.)

Schedule time for staff. If you have staff, you must monitor and train them. This should be done through daily meetings that are short, informative, and question-focused. These meetings keep the team going in the right direction. The weekly meetings are strategy, tactics, and training meetings. Most agents fail to have any type of ongoing dialogue and training for their staff.

Schedule for emergencies each day. The use of flextime is essential if you really want to stay on your time block schedule. Create 30 minutes of flextime for every two to three hours of productive time per day. If you can use the flextime to handle the emergencies and get back on task, you will be highly effective with your time.

Mistake 2: Making Each Day Different

If you can create a schedule of similarity, you raise the probability of success. If you allow your days to fluctuate (i.e., times for prospecting, conducting administration, etc.), you will fail to maintain your schedule. Each day must be very similar—with one exception. The day you conduct office meetings and property tours will tend to deviate from the other days. That should be the only significant exception. Build a schedule in which your work-days are carbon copies of each other.

Mistake 3: Being Too Available

You can get sucked into the interruption game when there is too much access or availability. The key to success is focus. You can't focus if everyone and anyone can break into your schedule. You must limit your availability to predesignated times. For example, I would almost exclusively negotiate contracts in the afternoon from 1:30 to 2:30. If an offer came in overnight, my assistant would set up a time for me to present the contract to my seller between 1:30 and 2:30 that afternoon. She would fax or courier the documents to the seller less than 30 minutes before our appointment. The reason it was less than 30 minutes before the meeting—I didn't want them to call me all morning to ask questions or become frustrated with me because the offer was lower than they wanted. A Champion will minimize distractions by being booked.

Mistake 4: Allowing Distractions

We are the most interrupted professionals in the world. We need clients to have access in a controlled way. Prospects need to be able to get ahold of us easily. We can't allow the phone, e-mail, other agents, clients, and other things to become distractions from us fulfilling our objectives. When you need to focus, turn off your cell phone, e-mail browser, office phone, and shut your office door—anything that could cause you to misdirect your time block.

Mistake 5: Failing to Operate on an Appointment-Only Basis

Through time blocking, you can drive prospects into your appointment slots. That's exactly what your doctor, attorney, or accountant does. Why not you? Too many agents don't operate through appointments, so they meet with clients on the client's schedule, not on their schedule. Giving people total access means we don't control our time. It also sends a clear message to others that we are not busy. Ben Franklin said, "If you want something done right, ask a busy man to do it."

Four Quadrants of a Real Estate Agent's Time

I read a good book about eight years ago that is now out of print. It was written by Roger Merrill, who was one of Stephen Covey's right-hand guys. The book he wrote was called *Connections: Quadrant II Time Management.* He used a quadrant concept to describe our use of time. (See Figure 18.3.)

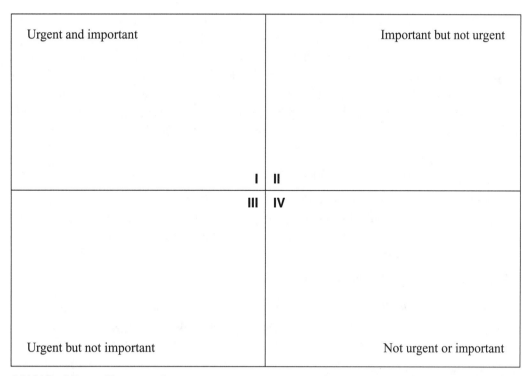

Figure 18.3 The Four Quadrants of a Real Estate Agent's Time

These four quadrants encompass every possible use and activity of time. We can easily end up in a quadrant during the day that produces little value for us and our business.

Quadrant I: Urgent and Important

This is the *emergency quadrant.* Real estate agents spend too much time in this quadrant. We are working to get the transaction closed at the last minute, getting a flyer made for a property, or writing an ad. Our stress level, blood pressure, and frustration go up the more time we spend in this quadrant. This is what I call the *burnout* quadrant. If you are spending large amounts of time here, you will burn out . . . guaranteed.

Quadrant II: Important but Not Urgent

This is the *quadrant of revenue.* This is the quadrant of success and effectiveness. When an agent is spending large amounts of time in this quadrant, his or her income rises dramatically, and quality of life follows. Your family time, workout time, and spiritual time are all located in this quadrant. If you skip a day, it's easy to justify. It's easy to put it off because there isn't the same urgency or immediate pressure as in Quadrant I.

Your business growth activities are located in Quadrant II. Your prospecting and lead follow-up activities are here waiting for you each day. This quadrant is the one *you* control. It is self-directed. The challenge is that all the other quadrants are frequently externally directed. People in your life, clients, prospects, family, and friends drive you out of this quadrant to the other three quadrants. Quadrant II contains the seeds to high income and quality of life. The more time you spend in this quadrant, the more money you make—the greater the feeling of success and personal accomplishment, the better your quality of life.

Quadrant III: Urgent, but Not Important

This quadrant is directed by others. I call this the *quadrant of delusion.* We fool ourselves into thinking that these urgent needs are helping us achieve a successful business. This quadrant and the activities in it don't contribute to the important goals of life.

Quadrant IV: Not Urgent or Important

This is clearly the *quadrant of waste.* There is usually a lot of wasted time in most people's days. We can be led by others into this quadrant. The coffee-and-doughnut bunch in the office can lead us here. Low-motivation prospects who want a little time are in this quadrant. They say, "I am not ready, but if you could send me some information, that would be great" . . . waste!

Coach's Tip: *Your job is to direct your business and time to increase the use of Quadrant II, to not allow people to push you into other categories because they view something as urgent when it's not. Real estate agents are most commonly redirected to Quadrants I and III. Don't let the outside focus cause you to spend more time in those quadrants than is absolutely necessary.*

Handling the Land Mines of Wasted Time

There are numerous challenges to and land mines in the time management equation. Entrepreneurial small businesses face a large number of these challenges. As a real estate agent, you are the owner of an entrepreneurial small business. This business type tends to put us on the front lines, with multiple job descriptions at once, trying to drive strategic objectives in sales, marketing, management, leadership, customer service, accounting, administration, and research and development all at the same time. The probability for land mines that can blow up and wreck your day, hour, or even half hour of production is lurking around every phone call, e-mail, fax, cell phone call, and meeting. My goal in this section is to give you tools, strategies, and implementation techniques to help you achieve the highest return on investment for your time.

The Constant Stream of Interruptions

In our profession, we delight in the inbound sales inquiry calls. We all live for the potential seller or buyer who calls to ask about a property or, better yet, about our services. The problem for most agents is that there are never enough of those calls and too many problem calls. We can compound these interruptions with the use of cell phones, pagers, and access to our home phone numbers.

Money calls.   One tactic is to use your cell phone for lead-generation calls, or what I call *money calls.* You might have to reeducate your clients (those you have listed, sold, or are securing a home for) to call the office line. It will help you reduce the number of cell phone calls. The more you can direct only the "money" calls to the cell phone, the easier it will be to control and convert those calls. If you can divert non-revenue-producing calls to the office, you will then know that when the cell phone rings you should answer it. (Another technique is to simply turn off your cell phone and operate only through voice mail for much of the day.)

Create a short list.   That's a list of people your assistant knows to put through to you right away when they call. You want about half a dozen people on your short list. For me, it's my wife, my attorney, my father. All other people must leave a message or book an appointment as soon as I am free. Remember, there is rarely anything in real estate sales that can't wait an hour.

Procrastination—the Silent Killer

Procrastination is caused by thinking that you have more time to complete a task than you really do. It also signifies a lack of urgency on your part. There is a difference between procrastination and prioritization. *Prioritization* is the skill of a Champion. A Champion puts off the things that don't matter as much and uses time to do high-value activities. *Procrastination* is putting off everything that is challenging and difficult. The challenging and difficult items are usually the most important and valuable items. How you execute your priorities has a dramatic effect on your income and results. Distinguish your *objectives* from your *priorities.* Too many agents view these terms as synonymous. Objectives are really the results you are aiming for in your business. Priorities are the individual steps sequentially ordered to accomplish the objective.

Too many workdays blocked.   Procrastination can be caused by having too many workdays blocked. In your mind, you think, "I can always do that later." It allows you to do the activities a few days later, even though today would be best. We can really fake ourselves out by not having set workdays. (The old adage that work expands into the time allotted is true.)

Unclear vision, objectives, and priorities.   Procrastination is caused by a lack of clarity in goals and a lack of connecting the goals to important activities that link with the goals. The key question: "Is what I am doing right now bringing me closer to or further away from the goals I have set?"

Procrastination can happen because of a lack of clarity in your vision and what you do. Why are you in real estate sales? What are your objectives in gross commission income for the year? What percentage of your business is devoted to the listing side versus the buyer-controlled side? How many listings do you need to take yearly, quarterly, monthly, and weekly to reach your goals? How many buyer-side sales do you need to make in the same time frame? What's your conversion ratio of leads? How many leads do you need to generate and how many appointments do you need to make to reach your income goal? Every agent who wants to achieve the Champion level must have clear objectives and a clear vision of what needs to happen next to accomplish specific objectives.

Champion Rule:	*We have too much to do and not enough time.*

Most people who are Champion Performers are running at 100 percent of capacity all the time, and more stuff is added to their plate daily. As we get better and more successful, our opportunities and responsibilities increase.

I am blessed with more opportunities and responsibilities today than when I sold real estate. I have more now than when I founded Real Estate Champions almost 10 years ago, and 10 years from now, there will be even more. With greater success comes greater responsibility and greater opportunities. You also experience greater problems. As you expand your business, the problems and challenges increase in number and difficulty. The good news is that with larger problems comes more money. We are problem solvers in the real estate business. Your value as an agent increases when the markets shift and problems increase.

Time management myth.   More successful salespeople have fewer distractions. Because of their production and the opportunities they are constantly creating, they experience more interruptions, distractions, and challenges on a daily, weekly, and monthly basis. They are, however, better than others at handling these demands. They have the ability to solve the challenges much faster. They let the negative things that happen to all of us affect them mentally for shorter periods of time. If you are a Champion Agent, like many of my clients who earn $500 an hour or more, which means each 15-minute block of time is worth $125, you can't let too many of those 15-minute blocks slip away during the day. Because Champion Agents control all of their 15-minute time blocks well throughout their day, it raises their value per hour. You could say it's one of the main reasons they earn $500-plus an hour. If you control your attitude and control your time, you will dramatically increase your earnings.

Champion Rule: *We will never get caught up.*

Something's Always Not Completed

For Champion Agents, there is no hope of ever getting caught up. Why would you want to? It means you are not getting new opportunities, challenges, clients, and prospects to sell to. It means your business has stagnated or receded. Champion Performers will go home each workday with something undone or not completed. You could stay in the office past midnight each day and would still not have everything completed. You must get over the "clean up and get everything done" syndrome. The question isn't, "Did you get everything done?" The question is, "Did you get the most important things done?" The ability to develop a system to select and execute the high-value tasks enables you to align your priorities with your objectives.

Establish Daily Priorities

Establishing your daily priorities will help you make each day a "10." I created a tool few years ago that truly enables you to get the maximum value from your time. It is our Real Estate Champions Daily Priorities Tool. (See Figure 18.4.)

Step 1. *List the activities that need to be done for the day.* As you list activities in the right-hand boxes in Figure 18.4, brainstorm to get your thoughts down on paper. Just focus on what needs to be done . . . all of it. Do not let your mind think about the importance or order of completion. If you do, that will stop your brainstorming process.

Step 2. *Categorize the activities that need to be done.* Most agents, once they create a list of activities, number them or create an order. The Champion Agent categorizes them to determine the level of importance. Assign each activity a category of A, B, C, D, or E:
   A   Something that has a serious consequence if you don't complete it today
   B   Something that has a mild consequence if you don't complete it today
   C   Something that has essentially no consequence if it is not completed today

Priorities		Category	Activities
A-1		1.	
A-2		2.	
A-3		3.	
A-4		4.	
A-5		5.	
		6.	
B-1		7.	
B-2		8.	
B-3		9.	
B-4		10.	
B-5		11.	
		12.	
C-1		13.	
C-2		14.	
C-3		15.	
C-4		16.	
C-5		17.	
		18.	
D-1		19.	
D-2		20.	
D-3		21.	
D-4		22.	
D-5		23.	
		24.	
E-1		25.	
E-2			
E-3			
E-4			
E-5			

Figure 18.4 Real Estate Champions Daily Priorities Tool

D   Something that can be delegated to another person on your team or an affiliate

E   Something that should be eliminated because it is unnecessary

Step 3. *Prioritize the categories.* Select the A category activities and determine which one is most important. Continue to number in order of importance and write them in the squares on the left-hand side.

My belief is that, each and every day for the remainder of your sales career, A-1 and A-2 are already spoken for. A-1 is always prospecting and A-2 is always lead follow-up. You are really starting at A-3 each day. I believe the most significant penalty or consequence comes from not prospecting and doing lead follow-up daily. The reason you don't think there is a penalty for that is that it doesn't show up today. It appears in 90 days when you fail to prioritize those activities higher on the scale and fail to do them first. It is usually easy to place something else in the A-1 or A-2 slot. Usually, the Quadrant I activities or emergencies will try to crowd out the prospecting and lead follow-up. The most important activities in the A category are the Quadrant II activities. They are the activities that, if not done, carry a significant penalty. You just can't see it today.

Proceed down through the Bs, Cs, Ds, and Es. (If you want to earn what a Champion Agent earns, don't waste your time on Ds and Es.)

For me, during my sales career (and even today), the most important question is, "Did I finish my As?" If I did, I had a great day. There were times that, when I really looked at my priorities for the day, the only As were prospecting and lead follow-up. After my prospecting and lead follow-up was finished, I would give myself a choice of rewards on those days: go home or head to the golf course early!

Time management is a problem that will never go away for any of us. I view time management as a muscle that needs to be trained and worked in order to strengthen the skill. It is a series of systems or skills that we all need to acquire. I have shared with you a number of techniques and tools that can really take your time management skills to the highest level. Take time in the next 24 hours to select the tools that will help you the most. Decide on the order in which you need to implement them. Make the commitment to start using them tomorrow.

19

Building Your
Ideal Business

Champion Agents have a custom approach to their business. They evaluate the market trends and their skills, abilities, opportunities, knowledge, organization, and systems to create a comprehensive plan of action to execute to their success.

Four Core Plans

There are four fundamental plans that any agent needs to construct to increase the production and quality of life. It doesn't matter where you are on the success continuum, you must construct and execute these four core plans. Your level of success at any given point in your career directly relates to where you are in the construction of these plans. If you are a new agent, you have a lot of work ahead. If you are inconsistent in your production and income, you might have a rough outline but few details. If you are consistent in your earnings, you likely have filled in a few of the details, but the big growth for you will come when you complete the construction. If you are already a Champion Agent, you are in the fine-tuning stage. You must be vigilant in your focus to execute and tweak your four core plans.

Time Management Plan

If you are challenged in managing time, as most agents are, you might want to turn to Chapter 18, "Time Management Is Life Management." In it, I take you through the steps to increase your productivity and the profitability of your time investment. Time management is always ranked as one of the top three problems in surveys we conduct with agents, brokers, and real estate companies. I am asked to speak on time management more than on any other topic. The implementation of a solid time management plan alone will increase your revenue by well over 30 percent in the next year if you are a new or inconsistent agent.

Business Management Plan

A business management plan is essential to determine the results of your efforts. What does the financial scoreboard say about your business? Too many agents run businesses that are only marginally profitable. That's bad enough. The worst part is that they don't even know it. They don't have a system of checks and balances to monitor the business results. As you expand your business and include more people, marketing, and advertising, you must be able to monitor the physical and financial results of your team's efforts. You must have clear standards and practices to evaluate performance and results.

Personal Management Plan

A personal management system is probably the hardest plan to work on. This one takes dead aim at you. Are you investing in your largest business asset . . . *you?* Are you holding yourself accountable enough for the things you need to do? Are you able to look at yourself and your performance with a discerning eye?

Champion Rule: *Champion Agents are honest with themselves about where they fall short.*

I am not saying that Champions are in a constant state of self-criticism. They just have the willingness to be able to see their shortcomings and work to change them. If they feel they are not as strong on the listing presentation as they should be, they admit it and work to improve it. The people who are Champion Performers are the most honest with themselves. They are able to ask themselves this series of questions on a regular basis to create urgency and change.

1. What are my strengths?
2. What are my weaknesses?
3. What new behaviors do I need to embrace to achieve a higher level of success?
4. What key abilities do I need to possess to unlock my true potential?
5. Why am I not taking the action I need to take?

These are all the questions Champions will ask themselves, at least quarterly, to see how they are progressing. The goal in life is progression . . . moving forward. Earl Nightingale defined success as "the progressive realization of a worthy goal or worthy ideal." Your progressive journey to the Champion level of income, quality of life, business, and family is definitely worthy. It's worthy of the investment of time and energy.

I want to share with you my favorite question for Champion Agents. It's focused on improvement, but also on the fact that there are priorities. The question is, "What's the one thing that, if you mastered it right now, would make the biggest difference in your life?" Now *that* is a Champion question for a Champion Agent. It focuses on your most significant barrier to greater success. You have to look at what creates the biggest return and declare your willingness to change. This question makes you recognize that you *could* change. However, you might select a less valuable area in which to change. This lower-priority area will produce a diminished result.

Champion Rule: *A Champion focuses on removing the limiting step . . . now!*

Through years of coaching top-performing agents, I have come to realize how powerful it can be to remove the limiting step. Each of us is faced with a bottleneck. It's a choke point right in front of us that we need to remove. Until you remove the limiting step or choke point, your improvement and change will be minimal. You will make strides of improvement, but they won't be explosive, exponential, or vast. Major breakthroughs in business and life come from the removal of your limiting step.

_____

A few years ago, I was working with a successful agent in Champaign, Illinois. He was the top agent in the marketplace. The challenge was that his profitability could have been a lot better. He was a veteran agent who worked mainly by referral for over 20 years. We traced his problem to overexpenditure in marketing, advertising, and personal time invested in each listing. We didn't stop there, because that wasn't the limiting step. We traced it back to the fact that his days-on-the-market average for properties was much higher than the local real estate board's. This longer marketing time increased his expenses. It also influenced his average list price to sale price. On average, he had to do 2.35 price reductions on the 123 homes he listed each year before they sold.

His limiting step was the price counseling segment of his listing presentation. The sellers talked him into asking more for their homes, even though he was the number one agent in the market, worked for the number one company, had over 20 years of experience, and did mostly referral business. Mastering that one area in the next few weeks dramatically changed his business and life. He netted over $5,000 a month more, cut his days on the market by 50 percent, and increased his list price to sale price ratio by 7 percent in just a few months. He also enjoyed the business more because he was spending less time getting price reductions, and he had happier clients because they were not set up for failure.

═══════════════

Activity Management Plan

An activity management plan is a plan whereby each day's activities are monitored, counted, measured, and the results compared. There is clearly a cause-and-effect relationship between activity and results. The question is, what are the ratios of connection? What can you expect the return to be?

═══════════════

Recently, I was working with a client in Detroit. Because the local economy has been affected by the floundering automobile industry, the market has toughened substantially. By reviewing my client's activity management plan, we determined that the number of leads he was generating through his marketing efforts and prospecting efforts had dropped. In the previous three months, his leads per thousand mail pieces had declined by 33 percent. His conversion ratio on those leads had dropped another 18 percent. Not only was he getting fewer leads overall, but the lead quality and conversion rate had also declined. His telephone prospecting leads had not dropped as much, but nonetheless showed a 21 percent drop in lead generation and an 11 percent drop in conversion.

We concluded that he needed to double the amount of contacts he was making in the mail and telephone lead-generation areas to make up for the marketplace change. I can tell you, he wasn't excited about having to do it, but he could clearly understand why he needed to do it. That's the value of a good activity management system.

═══════════════

Figure 19.1 is a tracking sheet for your business. If you use it, this form will enable you to monitor the activities for yourself and other agents who work for you. (The need for an activity management system increases dramatically as you expand your business to include other agents.)

> **Champion Rule:** *When performance is measured, performance improves.*

If you want to become a Champion Agent, you need to measure your performance. You need to count, track, and calculate your daily, weekly, monthly, and quarterly numbers for contacts, leads, appointments, listings, and sales. The sheer act of measuring raises the awareness and improves the results you achieve.

> **Champion Rule:** *When performance is measured* and reported, *performance improves faster!*

Champions want to move beyond the awareness level of improvement. By reporting your performance to your broker, your spouse, another agent, or your coach, you increase the speed of change. You increase the speed of your income and earnings. You must have a way to report your performance and efforts to someone who will help you or hold you accountable for what you need to do.

This is certainly a role that we, at Real Estate Champions, know well, since we are one of the longest-running, most established coaching companies in the real estate industry. The vast majority of Champion Performers have coaches, or at least mentors, at one time or another. I firmly believe that agents trying to achieve Champion-level performance need to consider a coach.

> **Coach's Tip:** *Before you make a decision on a coach, whether internal (i.e., a coach inside your real estate company) or external (i.e., an outside coaching company), go to our Web site at www.RealEstateChampions.com to really understand what coaching is and isn't. There are many imposters who sell basic training or marketing programs dressed up as coaching.*

DISC Assessment

Now that you know you need these four core systems, you need to understand how to build your ideal business by using them. For the past almost 10 years, we have been mon-

Date _____   Name _____

T-Chart

Daily Disciplines	Contacts		Leads	Appts	Activity		Personal Growth
	Face-to-Face	Phone					
Past Clients/ Sphere					Total contacts		Personal Development
					Number of hours prospecting		Quiet time/prayer
Expireds					Leads generated		Workout
					Listing appts set		Review life plan
FSBO					Listing appts gone on		Review business plan
					Listings taken		Coach staff
Calling around listings and sales					Listings canceled or expired		
					Listings (I turned down)		Time in
Door knocking					Listings (I didn't get)		Time out
					Price reductions		Total hours
Cold calling					Listings sold		
Current lead follow-up							
					Buyer appts set		
Goals					Buyer interviews		
Totals					Buyer contracts		
					Qualified showings		
					Offers written		
					Buyer sales		
					Escrow fallout		
					Listings closed		
					Buyers closed		
					Commission paid out		

REAL ESTATE Champions

Direct Income Producing	Indirect Income Producing

RATE YOUR DAY (0–10)
Why I rated it this way: _____

_____
_____
_____
_____
_____
_____
_____
_____
_____
_____

Number of Hours: _____
Percentage of Time: _____ %

"The daily disciplines lead to success. Don't neglect to do them today."
—*Dirk Zeller*

©2006 *Real Estate Champions, Inc.*

Figure 19.1 Daily Activity Record and Evaluation

itoring, tracking, developing, and coaching people to high success levels by studying their behavioral styles. Through our extensive research, I can tell you, based on your behavioral style, exactly what problems and challenges you will have in your business. I can also tell you the sources that you should use to generate leads and opportunities. Aligning your behavioral style with these sources to find out how you should prospect and market dramatically increases your results. It also enables you to build a business that is sustainable.

Anyone can browbeat you into prospecting for a short period of time. Short-term behavior modification can improve your income for a short period. The problem is that all of us will cease to do what is not aligned with our own behavioral style at some point in the future. It is inevitable that you will quit doing the things that made you successful if those activities are not behaviorally aligned. Being able to build a business that is complementary to your personal behavioral style solves this problem for good.

Our revolutionary research has transformed the use of DISC analysis when working with salespeople. DISC is the universal language of observable human behavior. DISC doesn't measure your intelligence, values, skills, experiences, education, or training. It measures how you act or react in your behavior. Your behavior, how you act, is an integral part of who you are. It determines how you will respond. The developer of the DISC language was Dr. William Marston. He published his landmark findings in his book, *The Emotions of Normal People,* in 1928. Understanding who you are enables us to increase your sales effectiveness dramatically.

DISC Behavioral Profile

D Dominance (D factor): How you *handle problems* and challenges.
- High Ds have a tendency to be very active and aggressive in gaining results. They will go directly at a problem with little or no fear.
- Low Ds have a tendency to go at a problem with a calculated, organized, well-thought-out approach to gaining results.

I Influencing (I factor): How you *handle people* and influence others, how you interact with other people.
- High Is have a tendency to have high contact ability; they are outgoing, social, very verbally persuasive.
- Low Is have a tendency to be more sincere and reserved. They enter situations and relationships with a more cautious approach. They are fact- and information-oriented yet very skeptical.

S Steadiness (S factor): How you *handle change* and pace yourself, how you handle a steady pace and work environment.

- High Ss have a tendency to prefer a more structured, predictable environment, having the boundaries clearly defined. They prefer a secure situation.
- Low Ss have a tendency to prefer an unstructured, undefined environment with a great deal of freedom to operate.

C Compliant (C factor): How you *handle rules* and procedures set by others.

- High Cs have a tendency to follow rules set by others and are very aware of the effects of not complying with rules and procedures.
- Low Cs have a tendency to do it "my way," establishing their own rules.

I will give you the nuts and bolts of how to build your business through a customized and comfortable approach. In using the word *comfortable,* I must preface it by saying it's impossible to build a business without doing some things you don't like to do. It is possible, though, to build a business in which you don't have to hold a gun to your head every morning to make yourself prospect. Certain types of prospecting align better with different behavioral styles of individuals.

You can guess what behavioral style you are by evaluating the descriptors in the preceding pages. However, I caution you: that is a less than accurate way to accomplish something as important as understanding your behavioral style. We offer a free basic version of the DISC assessment on our Web site at www.RealEstateChampions.com/DISC. This will enable you to better use the material in this chapter.

Coach's Tip: *I suggest making an investment in yourself by securing a complete diagnostic DISC Behavioral Style Assessment, which gives you over 24 pages of information about yourself.* **This comprehensive report will enable you to use this chapter at the highest level. You can access such a report via our Web site at www.RealEstateChampions.com/DISC.**

Because people are an amalgam of each of these styles, all four factors will influence your behavior. A low score in S, for example, will influence how you operate or how you deal with pace and change in your business, work environment, and the marketplace. You might have two high scores. For example, I score high in Dominance and also in Influencing. Both of those factors shape my behavioral style. While my most controlling or shaping factor is the high D, I also have to be aware of the opportunities and challenges that my high I score creates. (In this book, I focus only on the four major behavioral styles.)

The High Dominant

These people need to be direct and in control. They are constantly looking for the next challenge and will become bored if they don't get one. They are very direct and to the point, with their ultimate goal being the result they want. High Dominants are risk takers. They have the capacity to be working on numerous projects at once. They are very pressure- and deadline-oriented. (See Figure 19.2.)

For a high Dominant, results are the name of the game. They want a specific result quickly. They are change agents in any organization. They should be focused on building a

D—Dominance	
Descriptors: • Adventuresome • Competitive • Daring • Decisive • Direct • Innovative • Persistent • Problem solver • Results-oriented • Self-starter	**At best:** • High ego strength • Gets things done quickly • Seeks change • Wants to win • Wants direct answers • Can move/act fast **At worst:** • Egotistical—resists criticism • Never slows down • Changes without planning • Fear losing—being taken advantage of • Impatient listener • Sometimes moves too fast
Ideal environment: • Freedom from controls, supervision, and details • An innovative and future-oriented environment • Forum to express ideas and viewpoints • Nonroutine work • Work with challenge and opportunity	**Tendency under stress:** • Demanding • Nervy • Aggressive • Egotistical

©2006 Real Estate Champions, Inc.

Figure 19.2 Dominance Behavior Style

high-intensity, results-driven business. One of their mottos would be, "Don't ask how I got here, just whether I did it." It's not about the process, but the result. Their prospecting should be centered on high impact with high return. They have a high-tolerance threshold for rejection. They are willing to run through a burning building if that's what it takes to achieve the result of success.

Highly competitive. The higher the dominant score, the more they enjoy the competition of the business. If you are a high Dominant, you have to put yourself in competition with other agents regularly, or boredom will set in. The best prospectors of FSBOs and expireds come from this behavioral category. They revel in the competition, and the time span or sales cycle is short from initial contact to appointment with prospects in FSBOs or expireds. Expireds are really the perfect fit for the high Dominant because of their short sale cycle, results-oriented sale, competitive environment, and potentially challenging clients. It's really a match made in heaven.

I had a high Dominant client in the Dallas market for a number of years. When we started working together, she would do the listing presentation, and one of her assistants would go out and get the paperwork signed the next day. I told her she was not giving herself the feeling of winning—that rush of getting the contract signed. She also was ending up with overpriced listings because her assistant was not as strong in holding the price as she had been the night before. We changed her structure so she signed her listings the night of the appointment. She called me a week later and said, "I love my job again. You were right . . . I need the win."

Little patience. Everything on the listing side must point to securing the listing at the appointment. The Dominant will get bored, follow up poorly after the presentation, and feel less of an emotional rush by not getting the listing when in front of the seller. Dominants need to focus on the "now" in business. There is no patience to cultivate long-term leads. Time is of the essence for them.

Challenges for the Dominant. Detailed tasks, systems, and organization will challenge them. Their lead follow-up system will be inadequate. They will need a team to organize them, but the management and, especially, delegation will be challenging. They tend to be seagull managers—they fly in, poop on everyone, and fly away. Their most preferred method to success is by becoming a workaholic. They are willing to pay the price for success, but so can the family. The balance of family and business can lead to disaster for these people. Referrals, too, are a challenge. They are so focused on the next deal, it's hard for them to stop long enough to get the most out of the current relationship. Referrals take time to build and cultivate, and they don't have (or aren't willing to invest) the time.

Solutions for their success.   If they center new lead generation in highly competitive, high-return areas of business and develop a structured plan for work time and family time, their success is guaranteed in most cases. The question is, what price will they pay to achieve it? They need a written, well-scripted process for referrals, because it is more difficult for them to ask for and generate them. There must be identified places in the relationship and spots in the presentations where referrals are asked for. These types can't wing the referral process, because they just won't do it.

The High Influencer

These people are the most optimistic lot of people around. Due to this optimism, they trust people quickly in a relationship, often even before trust is earned. They love to talk to and interact with others. They have a need to be liked and accepted. That desire to be liked can drive their decisions. They will do almost anything for public recognition. These people are also highly emotional and use emotion to sell. (See Figure 19.3.)

Very social, the life of the party.   A high Influencer behavioral style creates a lot of opportunities in how one might run a business. Because they are so relational, if they can prospect through personal relationships, they can generate significant business while enjoying themselves. These people are the life of the party in social settings.

Client events and parties are a very effective prospecting technique for them. Such activities allow these types to get in front of the crowd. They will be the center of attention for the entire events. These people are also effective in community service events, networking clubs, and organizations. Their personal visits to past clients and sphere are highly effective.

Gets bored easily.   These people need a large variety of lead sources or prospecting sources or they will become bored. The business has to be fun. If the business ceases to be fun, the high Influencer will move on. Because of the ease of distraction, a daily goal of personal contacts is a must. The high Influencer has the attention span of a flashbulb, so there must be structure in addition to variety.

Challenges for the high influencer.   The challenges for these people are focus and structure. They are not the best time managers. They must be on a time schedule, but it needs to be looser than with other behavioral styles. The natural tendency is for the high Influencer to talk a lot but rarely ask questions. Having a scripted process with questions as the mainstay will dramatically improve their performance. The Influencer can also get burned out by prospects. They have never met a person from whom they weren't absolutely sure they

I—Influence	
Descriptors: • Charming • Confident • Convincing • Enthusiastic • Inspiring • Optimistic • Persuasive • Popular • Sociable • Trusting	**At best:** • People-oriented • Open—willing to share feelings • Doesn't need to be neat • Wants to be liked • Optimistic • Verbal **At worst:** • Has difficulty staying focused • Can talk too much about themselves • Can be very disorganized • Fears not being liked/easily led • Pollyanna—out of touch • Verbose
Ideal environment: • High degree of people contacts • Freedom from control and detail • Freedom of movement • Forum for ideas to be heard • Democratic supervisor with whom to associate	**Tendency under stress:** • Self-promoting • Overly optimistic • Gabby • Unrealistic

©2006 Real Estate Champions, Inc.

Figure 19.3 Influence Behavior Style

had a commission check coming. Because of their desire to be liked and their optimism, they usually fail to test the motivation, desire, need, ability, and authority of the client because they don't want to risk offending them.

Solutions for their success.   These include a specific qualifying process for buyers and sellers (including scripts, dialogues, qualifying questions, and categorization rules). These need to be created and adhered to as much as possible. An Influencer needs clearly defined leads and probabilities of conversion so they can move on to clients that are real. These people's greatest gift is their ability to communicate and connect with people easily. They are simply amazing at this natural trait. The key for them is putting themselves in those situations more frequently and with a little bit more structure.

The High Steady

The high Steady behavioral style exactly mirrors the word *steady*. These people are stable and predictable. You might even call them plodders. They are like the Energizer Bunny. They keep going and going and going. They want to help and serve people. They have a high level of loyalty to others. They want stability and security—two words not generally associated with full-commission sales businesses. Their focus is to sell via long-term relationships. They are not change agents; in fact, they prefer the status quo. These people finish what they start and do it in a patient, relaxed way.

Our research indicates that these people take a longer amount of time to establish their business. Once established, however, they can be very successful over the long haul, especially when aligning their behavioral style with their business model. (See Figure 19.4.)

S—Steady	
Descriptors: • Amiable • Friendly • Good listener • Patient • Relaxed • Sincere • Stable • Team player • Understanding	**At best:** • Loyal—predictable • Family- and group-oriented • Very well organized • Creates stability—safety • Makes changes carefully **At worst:** • Holds on too long/can be stuck • Martyr/takes on others' problems • Sometimes lacks creativity • Afraid to take risks • Procrastinates—paralysis
Ideal environment: • Stable and predictable environment • Environment that allows time to change • Long-term work relationships • Little conflict between people • Freedom from restrictive rules	**Tendency under stress:** • Nondemonstrative • Unconcerned • Hesitant • Inflexible

©2006 Real Estate Champions, Inc.

Figure 19.4 Steady Behavior Style

Effective in converting leads.   The high Steady types should build their business in less confrontational or competition-oriented areas. Putting them in an office to make countless cold calls to strangers is a method of lead generation that produces limited results for them. They are more effective in converting leads than in producing leads. They will work a lead patiently over an extended period of time. The natural lead generators for these people are their current clients, past clients, and sphere. They are comfortable enough to call these people on a consistent basis as long as they are servicing them or helping them. Phone calls and mailing pieces are paramount to helping their current clients, past clients, and sphere.

> **Coach's Tip:** *Some of the more passive approaches to lead generation also work well with high Steadies. Open houses, leads and networking groups, and farming will work well for them. The interactive voice response system is a wonderful way for a Steady to build warm leads to serve. Using an IVR system for their listings (e.g., www.callcapturesuccess.com) can produce a few hundred leads a month. These people are terrific lead nurturers.*

Challenges for the high Steady. Challenges for the high Steady types are centered on their lack of confrontational skills. The biggest of these are competitive listing situations, pricing property, and price reductions. Being able to tell sellers they are over-priced is a challenge for Steadies. They don't want confrontation, and pricing property and price reductions hold the seeds of confrontation with clients . . . ouch!

Another challenge is getting in front of enough people to generate leads. Since their focus is more on lead follow-up and servicing, they have a lower lead pool, but higher conversion rates of those leads. Getting more leads and getting rid of the low-quality ones faster needs to happen. Coupled with their desire to serve everyone to an extreme, that can at times create a danger point. They will fall on the swords for their clients and prospects. Improving their ability to say no and to select better clients who act more quickly and demand less time can produce a large jump in income.

Even though service for their clients and prospects is at an extremely high level, they will have challenges asking for referrals directly. They don't want to bother anyone, so they don't ask. Until they can connect the referral prospecting call with serving, they are challenged to make the call.

Solutions for their success.   These include needing a specific pricing process that they adhere to before they see the home. They need to know the list price and "big-money sale price," or BMSP, which is the price at which they are so convinced the house would sell that they would bet big money—the house, the farm, or the kids—on it. The list price and BMSP can't be too far off. The list price is the price that they absolutely will not go above in taking the listing. High Steadies also need a specific process for price reductions to ensure sale of the home. They must have a step-by-step approach, using scripted letters and calls, to get the home down to the right price before six weeks go by.

A scripted referral process that enables them to ask for referrals on the phone is important. They should have a process that engages and enables them to improve the quality of the referral, gain additional information about the referral, and even get the referrer to call or make the initial introduction. If the high Steady types get referrals, it's usually a name and phone number. They don't want to bother people. When I say referral process and dialogue, it's far more encompassing than a throwaway line like, "Oh, by the way . . ."

The High Compliant

The Compliant behavioral style is the most challenging for success in real estate sales. They are naturally introverted, so their ability to be comfortable around people is diminished.

Systems-oriented.　　They have never met a system they didn't like, but they have never met a system that didn't need improvement, either. These people are by-the-book types. It can make them too rigid at times (e.g., when the client or prospect does a 180-degree turn and now wants a condo instead of a single-family home). Their attention to detail is at the highest level. They will ask precise questions to clarify the data. For many, a 95 percent probability is too low and much too risky. They will invest large amounts of time to remove that last 5 percent. Since their desire to be right is so high, their willingness to take risk is very low. They want to follow the rules. (See Figure 19.5.)

Challenges for the high Compliant.　　The sales aspect of the business is the hardest for these people. They provide thorough information and data; they service completely with minute detail. Our research has determined that having Compliants build their business through business channels is very effective. The relationship part of the business creates their challenges. If they are secure and operate in a more business-oriented environment, they will be more effective.

Compliants invest too much time in systems and procedures before they ever pick up the phone to make a call or see someone. This flaw drives most of them out of the sales aspect of the business. This perfectionism creates a lower volume of leads. They don't see enough people to secure the leads necessary to succeed.

Solutions for their success.　　Carving out niche markets where analysis is valued and where they can create unique winning situations for their clients is effective. Business niches, REO properties, even family law attorneys or investment buyers and sellers are very

C—Compliance	
Descriptors: • Accurate • Analytical • Conscientious • Courteous • Diplomatic • Fact finder • High standards • Mature • Patient • Precise	**At best:** • Follows rules/expectations • Watches people carefully • Motivated to be accurate • Value work • Asks careful, thoughtful questions **At worst:** • Perfectionist/never satisfied • Overly sensitive • Nitpicky/efficient—not effective • Fears criticism of work • Self-questioning
Ideal environment: • Where critical thinking is needed • Technical work or specialized area • Close relationship with small group • Familiar work environment • Private office or work area	**Tendency under stress:** • Pessimistic • Picky • Fussy • Overly critical

©2006 Real Estate Champions, Inc.

Figure 19.5 Compliance Behavior Style

profitable areas for Compliants. These niches want data for information. The decisions by these buyers and sellers are made on the numbers and return on investment rather than on the emotion of a typical home buyer or seller. Investors are one of the best niches for Compliant types.

Building strategic alliances with other professionals who are consultants creates another avenue of sales. Working with professionals such as attorneys, loan officers, and financial planners can really be developed into a consistent stream of income. The best connection can be accountants. Accountants usually have behavioral styles aligned with those of Compliants.

The past-client sphere area is also effective. The comfort level of getting all warm and fuzzy with their past clients and sphere will be much less than for an Influencer or a Steady. Their current clients should really be worked, because Compliants provide high-quality detail and service, but some of that is forgotten by clients after closing.

Compliants need to script out their sales presentations—from ad calls to sign calls to listing presentations to buyer interviews. It won't be comfortable in the beginning . . . nothing ever is. The investment of time to practice and perfect this necessary skill could enable Compliants to succeed in this business.

Greatest Strength: Greatest Weakness

There are problems and challenges building your business no matter which behavioral styles you possess. The truth is, for most of us, our greatest strength can also be our greatest weakness, as I have demonstrated through the description of the challenges, solutions, and business-building tactics for each behavioral style. I want to caution you again, most of us have at least two styles with high scores that blend together to form our behavioral style.

Coach's Tip: *These insights are guidelines and action plans from years of research, testing, and validation working with real agents just like you. I have given you the "Cliffs Notes" version of building your ideal business. If you are interested in exploring a more complete, fun, and results-oriented approach to this subject, contact us at Real Estate Champions (877-732-4676) for further information.*

20

A Peek Behind the Curtain

Being able to build a Champion's business takes focus, skill, and determination. It takes the desire to move, change, test, adjust—and then to change again. One of the ingredients that most agents fail to execute is the ability to regularly pause. The ability to pause, evaluate, ponder, meditate, and clarify at regular intervals will move you from being a good businessperson to being a Champion. The pause helps you learn, and to invest what you have learned, into your future success.

Pause at the end of each day to reflect on what went right. If you had to rate the day on a scale of 1 to 10, how would you rate it? Why did you rate it there? What could have been improved on? What are you most proud of for the day? What are the priorities for tomorrow? I typically spend 30 minutes at the end of the day reviewing the day and learning from it. Too often, we continue on, without pausing, pondering, and evaluating, so we make the same or similar mistakes repeatedly.

Weekly Evaluation

At the end of the week, take an hour to pause. A week is a pretty good chronicle of time that has gone by. Evaluate the prospecting numbers, leads generated, and appointments booked. What did you learn this week? What would you change? How should next week be approached? Which priorities didn't get accomplished that need to be moved to next week? How's your energy level and reserve? How's your attitude at the end of the week? If you have staff, evaluate their performance as well.

Monthly Evaluation

Pause at the end of the month for two hours. Invest those two hours in your future wealth, growth, and happiness. Besides the previous questions for the daily and weekly evaluations, review the leads in your database. Did you miss calling anyone? Is there someone you should call earlier than scheduled? Too often, agents call someone they have as a lead just after they have made a decision to commit to someone else, or they have bought and sold using someone else. By taking a few minutes to review the leads monthly, you will catch oversights that could cost you thousands of dollars.

At the end of the month, review your prospecting leads, appointments, and overall numbers for your business. You also want to review the numbers on your market trends report. We must already know where the marketplace is heading in real time, rather than reaction time.

Quarterly Evaluation

The break at the end of the quarter should be a half day, to give you the opportunity to repeat all the steps I have given you thus far on a larger, deeper, and more focused time frame. When you get to the quarterly evaluation, I really believe that it needs to be conducted off-site. This time is of paramount importance and needs your full attention without the distractions that occur in your office. If you feel you need to be in the office because of the availability of your data to analyze, then come in four hours before your normal day would begin, or stay in the evening and evaluate. Again, evaluating the marketplace for the quarter is an integral part of the quarterly pause.

Six-Month Evaluation

The pause at six months should be approximately a full day. Six months is a significant amount of time. I know agents who have been way behind initially, but caught up to their goal in the past six months by making the right adjustments. I know others who were way ahead of their goal, but who didn't take the time to review and weren't paying attention. They missed the mark on their one-year objectives.

Annual Evaluation

The pause at the end of the year should be from three days to a week. I personally prefer a week. The final week of the year has developed into my favorite week of the year. It is the time

I hit the rewind button for the whole year and replay the tape. I immerse myself in questions and evaluation to guarantee the mistakes remain in the past and the victories flow into the future. I check my business plan, business vision and values, systems, lead-generation sources, and conversions. I check my mental state and commitment level to my goals for the next year.

> **Coach's Tip:** *This week isn't to build a business plan for the next year. In fact, if you are doing that in this week, you are too late. Your business plan for the new year needs to be constructed no later than the end of October of the preceding year.*

Three Areas of Your Business

Any successful businessperson over a span of years has focused on building three areas of their business simultaneously: growth, working *in* the business, and working *on* the business.

Growth

Growth is the part that brings in the revenue of the business. The more time invested—daily, weekly, monthly—the greater the resulting income. The vast majority of agents spend too little time on growth. Growth is the DIPA activities that I have talked about throughout this book. Growth is the critical part of the business. Without growth, a business will fail.

I know a lot of agents who earn large amounts of money, are highly skilled at growth, but poorly skilled in administration and business planning. I know very few Champion Agents who are not highly skilled at growth. You can have huge deficiencies in administration and even customer service (I don't recommend it) but still win the income game through growth. You can't be deficient in growth and win. Growth is the engine that powers the train; you must first pay attention to growth. Your prospecting should comprise 65 percent of the time you invest in growth daily. If you don't prospect, the other growth areas won't happen.

In the Business

Working *in* the business is the administration or production of supporting activities. These need to be done, but not at the expense of growth. This area focuses on you being an employee, working in your business, doing functions any employee would do. Your goal through the segment of working in your business is producing results for your delighted clients. You are trying to turn clients into evangelists so they generate referrals. Transition to that level of customer satisfaction comes from working in the business. If you create good systems, processes, checklists, and have highly trained staff, you can reduce the time you invest in this area.

On the Business

This is the segment most agents neglect until they want to retire and then find out they have nothing to sell. In *The E-Myth,* Michael Gerber talks about the myth of an entrepreneur. He describes how most entrepreneurs have really bought a well-paying job and don't really own a business. Most Realtors clearly fit into the category of entrepreneur. We also clearly fit into buying a well-paying job.

When you work *on* your business, it really shapes your long-term success and growth. Your long-term financial wealth is contained in working on your business segment. Your ability to earn a profit and to increase the profit is key. Remember, sales is a margins game. The more time you invest to plan, strategize, evaluate, and implement new tactics and strategies, the more you evaluate the market, your time, your numbers, your return on investment, and your business. Becoming the owner of your real estate business happens only through diligently working on your business. Instead of being a highly compensated employee who pays the bills, why not become the one who orchestrates the growth of the company? Be the one who has something to sell when you want to transition or retire.

Working on your business is critical to helping you move to the next level of production: to decrease time worked without reducing income or to find where to cut expenses by 10 percent. Working on your business will help you create economies of scale in administration and new ways to produce growth and income in your business. You need one hour per day to work *on* the business. For every minute you plan, you will save 10 minutes in implementation.

What do you think your business would look like in 90 days, or even six months, if you were to implement the following daily routine?

Growth	3 hours
Administration	1 to 2 hours
Business	1 hour

By following the review patterns or pausing at the end of a day, week, month, quarter, six months, and year, you automatically increase the time you work on your business. Another technique is to schedule a block of additional planning and execution time at the end of each week. Most of our clients have 90 minutes of weekly planning time, during which they work to improve their business. If you work to employ these techniques, you will transform the results of your business in a few short months.

Champion Agent's Key Numbers

Most agents don't have a quick test to see how they are doing in their business. They don't have a series of numbers to use that show them the health and prosperity of their business. You must realize and accept that sales is a margins game: the investment of resources, time, and capital against an expected return in money and satisfaction. We need a vehicle to test the margins easily and effectively. Seven key numbers in a Champion's practice can serve as a personal measuring device.

Hourly Rate

You calculated this earlier. It's the amount of money you generate with every hour that you invest in your real estate sales business. Multiply the hours you work in a day by the number of days you work in a week by the weeks you work in a year. You will arrive at a total number of hours worked—between 1,500 to 4,000 hours. (Hint: 4,000 hours is a bad number, but I have seen it.) Divide gross commission income you earn by the total hours. This is your hourly rate or hourly value. Be sure to use gross commission income, before expenses or company split. In business terms, gross commission income is equivalent to gross sales or gross revenue. Use the gross number because you create that level of income for your business.

Average Commission Check

In order to write an effective business plan and create sales projections, you must know your average commission check or average earnings per sale. If you want to test your sales margins or revenue versus expenses on a per-transaction basis, you need to understand your average commission check. If you ask any good restaurant owner the average amount spent per person on a meal, he or she will be able to tell you. The casinos in Las Vegas know what the average person spends in Vegas at the gaming tables. Take your gross commission income and divide it by the number of units you close. (If you represent both the buyer and the seller in a transaction, be sure to count that as two transactions.)

Average Sales Price

The average sales price will tell you the part of the marketplace that generates most of your business. It will demonstrate where you are currently more effective investing the bulk of your time or where you are investing most of your marketing dollars. As an example, if your average commission is low, you work most often in the entry level or lower middle of the price point. Determine your average sales price by taking your gross sales volume (counting sales volume twice if you represent the buyer and seller) and dividing that by the number of transactions you do.

By knowing your average sales price, you can consciously move it higher or lower, depending on the market conditions and the return on investment you desire. This number illustrates how effective you are in proving your value to a client. When you divide your average sales price by your average commission check, you will learn what you charge (on average) for your services. It's a fast and easy way to know how well you are at defending your fee structure. If the average percentage is lower than you want, take corrective action. (Many agents find out that they are giving away their fee in most transactions.)

Cost per Transaction

This is a primary number in an agent's practice, and over 98 percent of all agents haven't any idea what the number is. The average cost per transaction will tell how successful you are as a business owner and how much net profit you should expect. To calculate, your number, first total the costs of your business (cell phone, marketing, advertising, signs, gas, car, insurance for car, business, even health insurance (it's a deductible expense), your assistant's compensation, anything that is a legitimate business expense). Divide your total expenses by the units you do. This gives you your cost per transaction. Your cost per transaction will go down as your units increase. (Sit down with any McDonald's franchise owner in the world and he or she will be able to tell you what it costs to make a Big Mac. These people know down to the penny.)

Marketing Cost per Transaction

Check to make sure that this number isn't too high. You can't spend more than a couple hundred dollars exposing a low-end property and still turn a reasonable profit. Determine what you spend in marketing and advertising and divide by the number of units you close. (A listing agent will have a larger number here than an agent who works predominantly with buyers.)

Time Invested per Transaction

How much time do you invest (on average) on every transaction? I believe a real estate agent wears two hats. One hat is "lead salesperson," which accounts for the hourly rate you should be paid. It's what you are worth per hour. You are also "CEO" or owner of the company. That person deserves a profit for the work. The profit is what is left over after everything is paid, including your hourly rate. You will live and spend your hourly rate. It's in essence the wage you earn. The creation of wealth and financial independence comes from the profit you generate.

Champion Example

Average commission check	$3,900.00
Average cost per transaction	$1,184.00
Revenue after expenses	$2,716.00
Time invested per transaction	$ 975.00
Net profit	$1,741.00

I have just shown you an actual breakdown of my numbers when I was selling real estate. The average commission check was lower than today due to lower sales prices. My time invested, on average, was three hours per transaction—prospecting, lead follow-up, qualifying, preparation for the appointment, conducting the listing presentation, signing the documents, negotiating the contract, and managing the closing. I am sure that three hours to some seems small. Remember, I had a couple of people who helped me reduce my time invested in the PSA activities that most agents spend 80 percent of their day on. I made $325 an hour, so the time invested per transaction was $975. If I were selling today, at today's prevailing sales prices, my hourly rate would be triple what it was then because my sales prices would be triple. I would make close to $1,000 per hour.

Net Profit Goal per Transaction

I believe you must have a goal of what you will net (on average) for every transaction. You can't afford to leave this net profit to chance. My goal was $1,500. It would be higher today because of the average sales price increase. If I couldn't net $1,500 from a transaction, I referred the opportunity to another agent. Maybe the clients wanted to overprice the home, which would increase my marketing costs per transaction, days on the market, and my time invested in talking with them week after week about lowering the price. All those factors would drive down my net dramatically.

Or perhaps I have high-maintenance clients. They want overkill on reporting, calls, and customer service. These expectations are outlandish. This again could increase my time invested per transaction, reducing my net profit. I am only going to make about $1,500 net dollars in profit. I have to determine whether my three hours of time invested could create a higher net profit somewhere else. By referring the prospect, I know that I can generate a 25 percent referral fee of $975 with only 10 to 20 minutes of my time invested and limited other expenses. With high-demand, challenging, and/or problem clients, I am better off to refer rather than represent.

Financial Management: The Achilles' Heel

One of the major problems for most businesses is controlling the finances and cash flow. A real estate agent's practice is no different. How you categorize, budget, and structure your business financially will determine your profit, savings, and taxes. Following is a step-by-step process for setting up your books.

Step 1. *Establish a separate checking account for your business. Do not commingle personal and business funds.* You need to create an arm's-length separation between yourself and your company. Use one credit card for business expenses only. That will save you time in sorting out the bill at month's end. The business then pays one credit card statement that goes to your office. Your personal credit card is mailed to your home. If you put a lot of your expenses on that designated business credit card, you will be able to write fewer checks and have easier accounting. You will also be able to float expenses and potentially earn airline miles or reward points.

Every commission check goes into the business account. You are paid out of the business account as an expense. Determine a monthly salary to draw out of the account and learn to live on it.

Step 2. *Incorporate as a company or private corporation.* Consult your accountant and tax attorney, but there are reasons I believe you want to incorporate. It reduces your liability if something happens while doing business. Even a well-constructed S corporation has a corporate shield or corporate veil. That means your personal assets are not exposed in the event you are sued.

There are currently significant tax benefits as well. You will be able to draw a salary from the corporation, just as if the money was paid to you directly. You will have to pay the employer and employee side of the taxes, since you are the registered holder of the corporation. You pay that now, anyway. You will pay 15.2 percent in payroll tax for the employee and employer, along with your federal tax withholding or estimates for that income.

The good news is you can take a substantial amount of income as a stock dividend rather than as salary or a bonus. That stock dividend will be taxed at capital gains rates without FICA, medical or Medicare expenses, employer or employee taxes. You will owe tax, but only at the prevailing capital gains rate, which is currently 15 percent, rather than at the tax rate (up to 33 percent) that you could be charged if you took the money as salary or bonus income. This is a big savings, and it is scheduled to go away after 2010, so take advantage of it now. Again, consult your tax advisor and attorney to receive their interpretation of the federal and state laws.

Profit and Loss Statement

Most agents either don't produce a profit and loss statement (P&L) or they produce one that is so detailed and categorized that you have to be the CFO of a Fortune 500 company to understand it. You don't need a 20-page P&L. You need something that breaks down categories effectively so you can see where the money is being spent.

The Revenue Side

Keep the revenue side to commissions, referral fees, and transaction fees if you charge them. You might take it one more level and put each one of these areas into revenue from buyers or revenue from sellers. That is the extent of what you need.

The Expense Side

On the expense side, you can segment and categorize down to the gnat's eyebrow. The major categories you need to track are your car expenses, telephone expenses, marketing, and advertising. These all relate to your expenses and net profit. If you have recurring charges in marketing (e.g., listings in a homes-marketing magazine each month), you might want to establish a subcategory under marketing for that item.

Personal development.   Don't forget personal development. One of the best investments you can make is in your training, education, and coaching. The cost of a university degree is more than $50,000 at a public university for a four-year degree. Yet most agents spend far too little on books, CDs, DVDs, teleseminars, Web-based training, seminars, and coaching. I spent 10 percent of my annual income on my education. It ensured that each year my business improved over the previous year. (In many of those years, my income actually doubled!)

Quicken or QuickBooks

Using an electronic program like Quicken or QuickBooks will help you to easily manage your books. Keeping up with the bills each week or every other week will ensure you don't end up with a shoebox full of receipts at the end of the quarter, or worse yet, at the end of the year, trying to determine your tax liability. Running a P&L becomes easy with an electronic program. It takes only a few keystrokes and you are finished. You need to run a P&L monthly at a minimum. It's one of the best techniques to control your money and cash flow.

Think and Control Your Way to Profit

While I have been coaching, teaching, and observing many agents over the years, I have noticed that few agents share success stories about how profitable their business is. They often relate success stories about sales volume, units sold, plaques, awards, and recognition—but not about profitability. They become caught up in the company recognition system and for years lose all sight of the true function of a business. The true function is to turn a profit, but the thought of selling one more house to pay for this new service or that new marketing idea seems to be the pervasive way of thinking. This mental philosophy leads agents down the slippery slope of financial destruction. This philosophical flaw does not happen overnight, or even in a few months, or sometimes not in a few years. Nevertheless, it will surely reach you eventually, just as eating high-fat foods and not exercising regularly leads to arteriosclerosis.

Examine Your ROI

In order to keep your business directed toward turning a profit, you must examine return on investment. You want to evaluate all expenditures based on the return you will receive from the dollars you spent. Most companies are not looking for a one-for-one type of exchange. In other words, they do not want to spend a dollar to make a dollar. You must not be satisfied with this type of exchange either. In a one-for-one exchange, you lose money. Let me repeat—in a one-for-one exchange *you lose money.* It does not matter what the exchange— you will lose. The reason is that you have not factored in all your costs.

Agents have a tendency to see the ad they ran on Sunday as the cost of the ad, $75 or $100. They do not view the *true cost* of that ad. By *true cost* I mean all the components of the cost. They have the cost of the ad, let's say $100. They have the time and energy to produce the ad. Their assistant writes it or they do it, but they still have to review the ad. No matter how big or small the task, they need to block a minimum of five minutes.

I will give you an example from my own experience. Suppose it took 15 minutes for my assistant to write the ad. She was paid $15 per hour, which is $3.75. I had to review it and make corrections, which took five minutes. Since I made approximately $325 per hour when I was selling real estate, that cost was $30. Then she had to correct the ad, reprint, and send the ad to the newspaper, which took another 15 minutes, or $3.75 more. I could also factor in office equipment, computers, paper, and list goes on and on. Those costs, in some cases, can be significant. In this example I will not factor those into the overall costs. In this example, I had already invested $137.50.

When Sunday rolled around, I had received 10 calls on this ad. That was before I had buyer's agents and I worked weekends. Each call took me away from what I was doing when I answered the call: my family, open houses, or buyers. You get the idea. The Sunday calls took 50 minutes of my time, or $290. I had invested $427.50 so far in this ad.

If I set one appointment to show the property—that is another hour invested. I had to drive to and from the appointment and show the home. In addition I had to spend extra time on the phone to qualify and confirm the appointment before I met the prospects. I also called my lender (or theirs) to make sure they could qualify for a loan before I invested my time. I had invested at least another hour into this client, so there is another $350. I have now paid $777.50 for the cost of one ad and one showing. I realize that I would receive a good return on my investment if I sold the home to these people. But if I have to go through 10 ads and 10 showings and then finally have to accept a co-op sale, unless I am getting a very high commission dollar, there is no profit. I have earned wages, but no profit.

Here is the painful part, as if the preceding scenario isn't bad enough. In most states in this nation, in order to pay the state income tax plus the federal tax, you need to make close to $1.50 to take home a dollar. When you spend a dollar, you have to bring in $1.50 in revenue to actually get that dollar back. In the case of the ad, even if we do not factor in my time at all, I have paid $100 to the newspaper and $7.50 in staff expenses. I also had payroll taxes, FICA, and workmen's comp. I had sunk $107.50 in hard costs into the ad. I need $161.25 in actual dollars of revenue to cover the ad and the taxes I would pay for parting with my money.

Large, successful companies think this way: they focus on return of time and dollars invested. Maintaining this focus is how they get to be large and successful. They did not get there by accident. They thought their way to that place of prominence. If you wish to be equally successfully, you must do the same.

Track Your Dollars

You must run profit and loss statements monthly. You need to be able to track your expenditures and your revenues at all times. Casinos in Las Vegas do profit and loss statements hourly. Because millions of dollars are changing hands, they need to know exactly where they are and how they are doing that frequently. You do not need that kind of detail, but you do need to know where you are at any given time, income versus expenses.

The only way to adjust your expenses downward is to know what they are. If you do not know them and track them, how can you adjust them? You can adjust them via the slash or crisis system, but you will have yo-yo income and yo-yo staff. You have to reduce expenses methodically, according to a plan.

I have looked at many agents' profit and loss statements and found that most agents could trim at least 15 percent from their expenses without affecting revenue. How would you like a 15 percent raise without putting forth any more effort? Start tracking your expenses. Make a goal to cut 5 to 10 percent in every category. Look at every expenditure carefully. Do you really need it? Remember it is your money; do not be so free with it.

ROI on Training

The last area is return on investment in training and education. This is your best area of expenditure. There is a direct correlation in the dollars you spend here and an increase in your income. You need to allocate dollars for yourself and your staff in training and education. Many companies have huge training and research and development departments. *Research and development* is a fancy name for education. You probably do not have the resources of IBM to gather new knowledge. You do, however, have the ability to spend 10 percent of your income on books, tapes, seminars, workshops, and coaches. (You are not really spending the money; you are investing the money in yourself.) There is no better place to invest that money for tremendous long-term growth. You will not get a better return, even in a bull market in stocks.

You can change your life and start achieving profitability. Profitability does not happen overnight, but the decision to strive for it does. You must decide whether you want profits or just wages. No one will give you profits; you have to search diligently for them. They are there in every business and every person. You just have to work to find them.

Controlling Your Income

Being able to control the income is really where agents get into trouble. Too many agents' paychecks come irregularly. Champion Agents' income comes consistently. It enables them to control it better, save more, and invest more to create wealth. It is not what you make, it's what you keep. I have met too many agents who make $300,000, $500,000, even a million dollars a year and yet are broke. Part of their problem is their expenses. The other part is in their personal and business system of controlling the income. I will share with you a simple plan to help you control your income and become wealthy.

First, follow all the strategies I have shared with you thus far. If you don't implement them, the next bunch will not be as effective.

Your business checking account is merely a holding tank. Don't keep large amounts of money in there. When a commission check is received, put it all in the business checking account. Set up a business savings account and deposit 10 percent of your gross commission in there. That is your rainy-day fund, dividend fund, and source for the future. You can build up a lot of funds by this method. At the same time, set up a tax savings account. Deposit 20 percent of every check to the tax savings account. This method guarantees you have the funds available when quarterly taxes are due.

Income

Commission
  Buyers
  Sellers
    Total commission

Interest

Referral fees
  Buyers
  Sellers
    Total referral fees

Transaction fees
  Buyers
  Sellers
    Total transaction fees

Uncategorized

Total income

Expenses

Advertising
  Newspaper
  Magazines
  Advertising—other
    Total advertising

Automobile
  Gas
  Insurance
  Loan
  Service
  Automobile—other
    Total automobile

Bank service charges

Buyer's agents
  Commission
  Office fees
    Total buyer's agents

Computer
  Lease
  Services
  Software
    Total computer

Contract labor

Contributions

Copier
  Repair
    Total copier

Credit line

Dividends

Dry cleaning

Dues and subscriptions

Education

Entertainment

Finance charges

Gifts

Insurance
  Health
  Liability
    Total insurance

Licenses and permits

Marketing
  IVR systems
  Signs, stickers
  Web site
  Pay-per-click ads
  Marketing—other
    Total marketing

Miscellaneous

Office
  Equipment
  Supplies
  Office—other
    Total office

Office fees
  Monthly
  Transactions
  Forms
  Rent
    Total office fees

Office utilities
  Garbage
  Gas and electric

Utilities—other
    Total office utilities

Payroll
  Individual employees listed
  Paycheck fee
  Payroll taxes
  Payroll—other
    Total payroll

Petty cash

Phone
  Cellular
  Long distance
  Pager
  Phone service
    Total phone

Postage and delivery

Printing and reproduction

Professional fees
  Accounting
  Legal fees
  Professional fees—other
    Total professional fees

Reimbursement

Repairs
  Equipment repairs
    Total repairs

Repay loans

Retirement—Keogh/SEP IRA
  Money purchase pension plan
    Total retirement—Keogh

MLS service charge

Taxes

Travel

Uncategorized

Void

Total expenses

Net ordinary income

Net income

Figure 20.1 Profit and Loss Categories

Create one last account for your investment savings account and deposit 10 percent in that account. This account can be built to fund your retirement account, 401(k), SIMPLE IRA—whatever vehicle you use. I am a firm believer that, as a business owner, you need to take advantage of these tax-free investment opportunities. You can save the money to buy property. The more you can segment or even hide money from yourself, the greater the chance you can prevent wants from becoming needs. When the money comes in bunches, wants can easily become needs. If you are unable to put 10 percent in each of these savings accounts, start with 5 percent, 2 percent or even 1 percent. It's the *habit* that you are trying to establish. The habit will lead you to wealth.

Collect a significant monthly personal compensation from the business in salary and dividend that you can segment. You want to pay yourself enough to cover your personal expenses while at the same time saving and investing in your future. I have used the 70/10/10/10 way of managing my money for years. It's a simple approach; I don't have to budget extensively, and it works. The 70 percent is what my family lives on. Joan and I can spend it any way we like. We usually have long discussions about that in our home. We give 10 percent of our income to charity, which for us is our tithe to our church.

We save 10 percent in a general savings account for emergencies, property taxes, family fun, and large purchases like a new car. I am not a believer in debt, whether for cars or credit cards. My philosophy is to accept debt only on appreciating assets like real estate or possibly business-related. Because we have been doing that for so many years, we rarely pull money out of savings for anything. It's just another area to create wealth. We then save 10 percent for investment. This can be real estate investment or after-tax investment in stocks, bonds, CDs or any other source we choose.

When I started this system well over 15 years ago, I was not able to do 70/10/10/10. Too much month left after the money ran out. Much of our money went to pay off debt. I wanted to do 70/10/10/10, but couldn't, so I started with 95/1/2/2. That quickly became 90/3/3/4. Within 24 months, I was able to do 70/10/10/10, and my life has never been the same.

The real skill of a Champion is to control the resources and money to create the quality of life desired. We all need to live within our means to make sure our future is secure. I believe that you won't be blessed with more unless you wisely use what you have now. People who acquire wealth learn to control small amounts before they acquire large amounts. Use Figure 20.1 to identify the specific profit and loss categories that will work for your business.

21

Coaching Yourself to the Champion Level

One of the reasons we selected real estate sales is due to the opportunities and flexibility our independent career offers us. We are truly an independent contractor: a self-employed individual and business. One of the best things about being an independent contractor is that nobody can tell us what to do, how to do it, or when to do it. We control our success and also our failure. At the same time, one of the worst things about real estate sales is that we are independent contractors. No one tells us what to do, how to do it, or when to do it. It's the yin and yang of the business.

We are self-employed. We are our own employers and our own employees. This creates a unique relationship with the potential of a me/me conflict. There is a personal, internal conflict between diligence and laziness, perseverance and quitting, success and failure. We have the same responsibilities to manage ourselves as we would if we were managing salespeople in a sales manager role. We must manage ourselves as though we are paying someone else an equal amount to do what we do.

We are in a competitive business. We are not an exclusive source of real estate services. We are in competition, because there are more agents than business. Generally speaking, there are a set number of transactions in any given year in any marketplace. If we want to increase our business, we will need to take transactions from someone else.

We are our greatest asset. We have to create income and expand the business. We must be willing to invest in ourselves and in our business. By developing our knowledge, skills, and attitudes, as well as creating systems that are productive, we are guaranteed growth in our business.

Establish Your Own Board of Directors

In any large corporation, the board of directors is a group of high-powered successful business thinkers. They are often people who are outside the company and its structure, thus enabling the board to have greater objectivity than the senior management. They work with the CEO and upper-level management to increase the productivity and profitability of a company. We all need a board of directors that we can trust. We are not looking for a board to rubber-stamp every idea that is brought forward, but rather to objectively look at the business and give sound advice.

This board of directors or advisors doesn't have to be a formal organization. I simply mean you need a person or people in your life to help you with sales, marketing, organization structure, training, financial management, employee issues, evaluating the marketplace, identifying strengths and weaknesses of the business, strategic planning, and providing a little accountability in the core areas.

I often describe a coach's role as fulfilling a number of positions on your board of directors—most important, evaluating objectivity, strategy and tactics creation, and accountability to the implementation. Without a board of directors, advisors, or coach to help in all of these areas, you are at a much higher risk of failure in your business.

> **Champion Rule:** *Call on a person or group of people to help analyze your business.*

In order for you to move your business to the Champion level, change must take place. You can't expect improvement in your results without knowledge, skills, attitude, and activity change. Make a list of the following areas you will need to analyze in order to effect improvement in your current business: sales, marketing, organizational structure, training, financial management, employee issues, evaluating the marketplace, identifying strengths and weaknesses of your business, strategic planning, and providing accountability.

Now please give me permission to be your coach for the next few minutes.

Brainstorm Potential Advisors

Consider your possible options—people you know who could help you in each of those key areas. Who could help you create a better plan and improve your execution in those areas? Is your broker an option? Do you know another agent who is a candidate? At this point, you are not determining whether they *would*—only if you think they are *qualified* to help you.

How about another successful business owner in your community? Is there a consultant, mentor, or coach who could help in one or more of these areas? (It is possible to have more than one option listed for each category; in fact, it is preferable if you do. It gives you more options.)

Once you have completed the list, determine which of these areas will be the most important in raising you (personally) and your business to the Champion Performance level. Prioritize the list from most important to least important. Your mandate is to talk with a person or persons who could help you with your number one problem area. Make a commitment to start that process before the close of business, even if you are just leaving a message for the individual. If you listed no one in the core area, you need to begin your quest to find that person. In the interim, is there a book, CD, or DVD you could buy or a seminar you could attend that would help start you on the path to change and improvement while you find the members needed for your board of directors or advisors?

Power of a Mastermind Group

Another step toward your climb to the Champion level is to become a part of a mastermind group. Napoleon Hill put forth the concept of a mastermind group in his landmark book, *Think and Grow Rich*. Hill defines a *mastermind group* as "a coordination of knowledge and effort, in a spirit of harmony, between two or more people, for the attainment of a definite purpose."

Most people who have had success in their field have done so through the use of a mastermind, either formally or informally. Informally, they look back years later and can see the people or groups that helped them forge their success. Why do it by accident when you can do it by intention? You can be formulating an intended mastermind with anyone you listed on your potential board of directors. Another option is to use an intentional mastermind structure, whereby you create a mastermind group of like-minded and like-goaled individuals into a mutually beneficial team with a definite purpose.

I was in such a group, and it added to my success significantly. It was a group of about 10 agents, and we all had similar production and goals. Our passion to increase and expand our business was at a similar level. I didn't say an equal level, I said similar. We all, over a series of years, added hundreds of thousands of dollars to our gross sales and profits because of this mastermind group. I am still in contact with many from this group, and it has been over 10 years since our last meeting. In forming this type of group, you have a couple of options. You can create a local area group, regionally based group, or nationally based group. There are advantages and disadvantages to each.

Locally Focused Group

With the locally focused group, you can brainstorm specific market-based issues more effectively. You will also gain the advantage of being able to meet more frequently and for shorter periods of time. The challenge with a locally based group is the balance of the competition among agents, since you are all in the same market. There might be less of a tendency to share secrets.

Regionally Focused Group

A regional group expands the potential for differing markets, strategies, and issues. It also increases the sharing between mastermind group participants because the competition is decreased. If you work for a large company, you might be able to secure enough people in the firm to participate regionally. This will help when you are trying to implement new tools or strategies in your business. It can also help when you work with existing tools and strategies created by the company to help you increase your business.

Nationally Focused Group

A nationally focused mastermind group was my preference then—and now. There are certainly disadvantages due to travel proximity and frequency of meetings. I really believe, however, those disadvantages are small when compared to the advantages. With a nationally based mastermind group made up of agents from all parts of the United States and Canada, you create a broader base of knowledge. You benefit from learning about all types of marketplaces. Someone will always be transitioning in or out of a buyer's, neutral, or seller's marketplace. It prepares you for those markets in advance—how to spot them and what to do as your marketplace transitions.

The sharing is unfiltered. Since you are not competing, you will see the true marketing strategy, marketing pieces, checklists, systems, scripts, prelisting packages, and many other tools that will help you build or perfect your tools and systems. If you move the meetings around geographically, you will be able to observe other agents' offices, the internal workings of their systems and staff, and how they operate. This knowledge can be extremely valuable in increasing your ability to leverage through other people.

A nationally based group gives you the opportunity to get out of town and unplug from working *in* your business to working *on* your business. Because the distractions are diminished when you are out of town, you can really focus on a deeper level. It will allow you to see other parts of the country, possibly invest in geographically diverse property, or just have some fun. These trips shouldn't be counted as a vacation, because they're not. However, Joan and I would often take a couple of days on either side to add a little fun and adventure to the business trip.

Change and Grow

My guarantee to you is this: Whatever brought you to the level of success you have today will not be enough to keep you there. You must be willing to change, grow, and learn. To maintain your success, you will need to grow, because your competition is growing and improving. If you want to expand your business and increase your growth, your learning will have to be even greater.

> **Coach's Tip:** *Whatever you play in your car will have influence over your life and success. Make sure the philosophy and personal results the trainers espouse are congruent with what you want to achieve. Take a deep look at the speakers' relationships, family, and character. A lot of people who have achieved wealth and material success have failed in other, more important areas of life. They might have created a lot of income, but lost out in every other account in life. If you follow through and apply their process, you will achieve what they have. However, in some cases, you might not want it.*

One easy way to grow is through CD training. We are in our cars hours a day as we travel to and from appointments, home, work, and so forth. If you live in a large city, you are caught in traffic for a significant chunk of the day, so why not use it toward your growth? Listening to a number of training cassettes during that time dramatically changed my thinking, philosophy of success, skills, knowledge, and attitude. I would not be where I am today without having established the habit of turning off the radio. Even today, the only time music is playing in my car is when Wesley and Annabelle are in it. I've traded the song "Wheel in the Sky" for "Wheels on the Bus," but that is all the music that plays—even today. Don't waste your time; invest it in your future.

Coaching and Objectivity

The real estate industry is inundated with coaches, and many Champion Agents have used the services of a coach or coaches to reach their goals. One of the valuable benefits of a coach is objectivity. It's his or her experience of a personal track record of success. You might now, or in the future, be considering a coach. I would like to share with you a few areas to think about, before you make a large investment, so that you select the right coach or mentor for you.

I founded *Real Estate Champions* as a coaching company in 1998 . . . years before coaching was in vogue. I founded Real Estate Champions to impact people's lives through coaching. The speaking tours, CDs, books, and teleseminars were never part of the original vision. (There is a difference between a coaching company that is built on the framework of coaching and speakers or trainers who see coaching as another revenue opportunity.)

In personal improvement, there are three options for growth: education, training, and coaching. All three of these serve a valuable purpose in one's continuum to achieve the Champion Agent level.

Education

Education is fundamentally the process of acquiring knowledge. It's what you are doing by reading this book. It's what you do when you attend seminars or listen to CDs or DVDs. Education plays a vital role in your success. Most of us spend at least 12 years in school educating ourselves to achieve a high school diploma. The challenge with education is, once you have it, what do you do with it? It's still up to you to use the education.

Training

Training is different from education. You are raising your skill level in a specified area of your business or life. You recognize a deficiency, and you receive training to improve your deficiency. It's more action-oriented and practice-oriented than education. Most training happens live, in real time.

Coaching

Coaching is a personal process of performance improvement. Effective coaching analyzes who you are and where you are going. It also assesses your skills, your business, your goals, your values, and your vision for the future. Coaching then connects with a plan of skill development in a customized format of execution and accountability to raise the odds of your success.

Coaching for peak performers has been around for years. The most successful athletes, for many decades, have been coached to win the big event. Tiger Woods would not be the golfer he is today without his golf coaches. In fact, Tiger did not have a coach during the 24-month period when he didn't win a major championship. Once he started to work with a coach again, he won a major championship within six months. The only difference was the coach. Michael Jordan, John Elway, and Michael Johnson all had coaches. Leaders in the business world, with some of the most successful companies, have coaches. Behind each great milestone or accomplishment stand two people—the one who executes the task or carries out the game plan and the one who helps create the game plan and teaches and coaches the goals and objectives.

Characteristics of a Good Coach

A good coach has five basic traits. When these traits are used to help you move forward in your life, the results are amazing. A coach can help you increase your production and enjoyment in life and can help you craft a life of long-term success.

Clarifying Goals

The first trait of a great coach is the ability to listen, to help you clarify your goals and vision in all areas of your life. Earl Nightingale, the famous speaker, stated, "We are goal-seeking organisms." Your purpose is to set and achieve goals in life. The difficulty for people is not in achieving goals, but in setting them in the first place. You can truly accomplish anything in life provided you first decide to do it.

Establishing Deadlines

The second trait of a successful coach is guiding you to understand that all goals must have deadlines. Deadlines get one's juices and thoughts flowing to create the desired result. Have you ever planned to go away for a vacation, and two days before you are to go, you get a flurry of activity in your business? It is because of the deadline that the activity increases and things begin to happen. How would you like to have that kind of production ongoing?

Creating a Plan for Success

A Champion coach will take the goals and vision you set for yourself and teach you to achieve them. He or she will help you create the step-by-step game plan to achieve the envisioned future.

For example, I had a client in 1998 whose goal was to earn over $250,000 for the year, even though the year before he had earned only $130,000. We worked diligently to break into bite-size pieces what he needed to accomplish in order to achieve his goal. Once the bite-size pieces were defined, we were able to determine the daily disciplines for him to undertake. Because he had to just focus on his daily disciplines, the task was not par-

alyzing. When he fell behind in achieving his goal, it was always caused by his failure to do his daily disciplines. As his coach, I helped him create the game plan and kept him on target to execute it daily. He achieved and broke his goal, earning over $265,000 in 1998, which was more than a 100 percent increase in his business.

Providing Motivation

A Champion coach shows clients the consequences of not following through on their goals and commitments. The coach will provide ongoing motivation and inspiration during the storms of life. It is not the storm that causes the problem, it is how we react to the storm. A Champion coach will help you brace for the storm that otherwise might overwhelm you.

Helping You Evaluate Your Progress

Finally, a successful coach provides accountability and is available for you. A Champion coach will help you evaluate your progress against your goals and vision. He or she will hold you to the standard that you have set for yourself.

Many agents today are working longer hours to keep on the treadmill of life. They often are neglecting time investments in their health, families, and self-development areas of their life. They are spending a tremendous amount of time working in their business. They are truly employees of their real estate businesses rather than owners, CEOs, and visionaries of their multi-million-dollar sales companies. To be an owner means you can walk away for a vacation with your family and the business will continue to turn out your product. Your business continues to earn an income for you while you are lying on the beach. Is the huge price being paid worth the results? Can one grow—with balance?

We live in a time when there is an abundance of information. We can attend seminars, listen to CDs, and read books. We have more resources for growth than at any other time in history. There is one crucial barrier to using the knowledge you have even now. It is action or an implementation strategy. It is someone to hold you accountable for the implementation of the new idea or development of the new skill needed. It is the guidance for creation of the new streamlined system.

A coach has one other important focus. Football coach Tom Landry put it best: "A coach is someone who tells you what you don't want to hear and has you see what you don't want to see, so you can be who you have always known you can be." A Champion coach will shrink the gap between where you are and the true potential that is inside you. If you are not achieving your full potential, you are a prime candidate for coaching. To be successful, a coach must be passionate about your success in life.

Selecting a Coach

I encourage you to select a coach as carefully as you select your doctor or attorney. Coaching has become an industry of generalists. The specialization that occurs in the real estate industry is a rarity in the coaching industry. Most coaches are generalists who work with anyone from any profession.

When you look at the roots of coaching, in athletics and entertainment, you find that people coach only in their field of expertise. An acting coach doesn't coach you to be a better singer; for that you get a vocal coach. A football coach in college or at the professional level doesn't decide to coach baseball instead. (One might coach a Little League team, but nothing at a higher skill level than that.)

My advice is make sure you select a coach who specializes in sales or in real estate sales. Don't select a jack-of-all-trades (master of none). You want to select a coach who has achieved a high level of performance, personally, in real estate sales. You can't teach at a high level what you have never done yourself.

I look forward to the day when I can coach Annabelle's or Wesley's soccer team. If they continue to improve and play for a number of years, my soccer coaching days (at least as the head coach) will come to an end. I didn't play soccer as a child. I can read about it in books that explain how to teach and coach children's soccer, but once they become good and want intermediate or advanced strategy and skills or techniques, I would no longer be qualified as a coach.

Selecting a coach who has played at the highest level of real estate sales success is paramount if you want to be a Champion. You need someone who has been in the trenches and sold real estate. This is true from the founder or CEO of the coaching company on down to each and every coach on the team. Some companies have CEOs or speakers who present the public face of the company but who have never sold real estate as a career. Some companies' coaches have never sold real estate as professionals. How can you coach what you have not done? They will be able to take you only through the basics. Check the credentials of the individual coach as well as those of the company. If the company you are considering doesn't offer a complimentary consultation with the coach you will personally be working with, be wary. Always interview before you commit. Evaluate and interview a few companies and the individual coaches for each company. Don't rush; make the right selection the first time.

Make the Commitment

Successful improvement in your career is based on your commitment. Some of the success of coaching and improvement is squarely on your shoulders. It's in the realization that, coach or no coach, the four probabilities of success—knowledge, skill, attitude and activities, and what you do with them—will determine your success. If you do the activities, you will win. If you don't, you won't. A good coach will hold you accountable to doing them and will help you get your desired result faster and with fewer mistakes. However, you have to commit to execution.

Your commitment to reach the Champion Agent level is about the following four questions. If you can't answer these four questions honestly, then coaching might not be your best option.

1. *Are you really happy with where you are?* Is your career going in the right direction? Are you where you expected or wanted to be? How about your income? Are you making enough money? Are you keeping enough money for yourself? And what about your life balance? Are you taking enough time off for your family and yourself? What about vacations? Most people believe success comes from working harder—24/7 if necessary. Wrong! It comes from having the right attitude, working smart, and effectively managing activities and time.

2. *Do you really want to do better?* Do you really, *really* want to do better? In what specific areas? On a scale of 1 to 10, how committed are you to doing better? You must be totally committed to do better. You will not experience the results that you could through coaching if you are not held accountable to your own goals, plans, implementation, and results.

3. *Are you really willing to change?* Are you really willing to accept and apply advice in all areas of your business, or only in the convenient ones? This is the hardest for most—accepting, applying, and implementing advice to change. Change does not come easily for all people, and old habits are hard to break.

4. *Are you ready to invest in yourself?* Will you really invest in your personal success? First, in personal time and energy. It is a full-time career! Second, financially. The primary reason most do not succeed is simply because they do not invest in their own success, or they invest in the wrong areas. *Investing in high-payoff activities is the key.*

Become a Champion for Life

Becoming a champion is a process that you commit to and work toward each day. It's a decision that is connected to action. It isn't merely an intention. (If we received rewards based on our intentions, we would all be wealthy and thin.) You must be focused on your commitment to excellence. Without it, you will fall far short of the Champion level.

I believe that Champion Performance is attainable for everyone—including you. I am delighted to have had the honor of sharing my personal journey to becoming a Champion with you. I hope your results match and exceed the results of my other clients.

Please feel free to share your journey with us. One of the best parts of my career is the stories I hear from people like yourself. I am here to continue to serve you in your journey. You can reach me through Real Estate Champions at 877-732-4676 or www .RealEstateChampions.com.

My belief is that everyone deserves to be a Champion!

Epilogue

Becoming a Champion isn't the easiest path you could decide to take. It would be easier to decide to be a mediocre agent or even a good agent. The decision to be less than you are capable of being is yours alone. That decision to settle for less is uniquely human. Every other living being, whether a tree, a flower, a squirrel, or a fish, inevitably is trying to do and become the most it possibly can. A tree will grow as tall and large as it can; a flower will bloom and produce as much pollen as it can; a fish will grow as large as it can and produce the largest volume of eggs it can.

As humans, we are the only beings on earth who have the choice to be less than we are capable of. Becoming a Champion requires a passion for reaching your full potential as a real estate agent, business owner, mother, father, husband, wife, friend—whatever roles you are blessed to play in life. Certainly, some of these roles are more significant than others. For me, if writing books, speaking, coaching, and running my company were to ever stand in the way of my becoming a Champion Husband and Champion Dad, the price would be too high and not worth it. I would choose to be less in certain areas and more where it really counts. That's an acceptable trade-off. The challenge is that most of us are still putting in our hours at the office. We are investing 40-plus hours a week at the office. We need to make them Champion hours and minutes! Champions focus on growth and increased revenue in our business or focus on decreasing the time invested in the business.

In the end, your personal knowledge, skills, attitude, and activities will be the pathway to your Championship-level performance. If you have the desire to build a Championship team (as many agents do), you can't do it without first being a Champion yourself. Many agents in the real estate industry are trying to achieve this goal in reverse order. They will never get there and often go broke in the process.

My belief is that a small team (e.g., one administrative assistant and maybe one buyer's agent) enables you to have a better quality of life and more stable revenue. It creates an opportunity to access greater growth and wealth than if you are a sole agent because it enables you to invest in greater amounts of direct income-producing activities. If you are capable, once this small group is controlled, expand it to a larger team. This will give you even more freedom in terms of income, stability, and time off.

I want to caution you as well. Your personal productivity in listing and selling activities is still the most profitable section of your business, and it always will be. Whenever you hire salespeople of any kind, whether it's buyer's agents or listing agents, they will receive a portion of the revenue they produce. What you produce is 100 percent yours. This is where many people miss the curve in the road with large teams. This is the reason I focused 100 percent of this book on what you need to do personally to be a Champion Agent. Until you are a Champion, all the people, staff, buyer's agents, systems, and marketing strategies will have a limited effect on your net profit. When you are a Champion, they will have an explosive effect. The staff will help you expand from where you are today, but they won't help you become a Champion. The first move is yours, not your team's. Once you have mastered becoming a Champion Agent, then you will be ready to build a Champion Team. It all starts with you.

My next book, *The Champion Real Estate Team,* will coach you in the best ways to build a team of Champion Performers. It will teach you the skills to develop the structure and systems to build a Champion-level team. I will also delve deep into leading, monitoring, and coaching your team of people. The book will culminate with developing an ownership mentality in your people, because what gets owned gets done.

We all have the capacity to become Champions. *You* can become a Champion Real Estate Agent. You now have the tools at your fingertips to create leads, convert leads, close prospects, and create vast wealth. You have the knowledge and skills to be able to *decide* what you want, *define* the changes, and *design* the plan. You now have the three Ds of success.

It's time to add the fourth. Just *do* it! I know you can!

There is a pot of gold out there with your name on it. It's time for you to go out and claim it.

You are a Champion!

Dirk Zeller
Real Estate Champions
Bend, OR 97702
541-383-8833
www.RealEstateChampions.com
Info@RealEstateChampions.com

Index

About the Author

Dirk Zeller has been recognized throughout his real estate career as one of the leading agents in North America. He has been described by many industry insiders as the most successful agent in terms of high production with life balance. His ability to sell more than 150 homes annually, while only working Monday through Thursday and taking Friday through Sunday completely off every week, is legendary in the real estate field.

Dirk has turned his success into significance through founding *Real Estate Champions*. *Real Estate Champions* is the premier coaching company in the real estate industry, with clients worldwide. Dirk has created such revolutionary programs as "Protect Your Commission™," "The Champion Listing Agent™," and "Positioning Yourself as the Expert™." These programs, and others like them, have changed the lives of hundreds of thousands of real estate agents worldwide.

Dirk is one of the most widely read authors in the real estate arena. His two books, *Your First Year in Real Estate* and *Success as a Real Estate Agent for Dummies*®, are both highly regarded. His free weekly newsletter, "Coaches Corner," is read by over 200,000 subscribers each week.

Dirk has spoken to agents and managers at the local, regional, national, and international level for most of the large real estate brands. He has shared the stage with such notable speakers as Zig Ziglar, Brian Tracy, and Les Brown.

With all the blessings and success Dirk has attained, his faith and his family are still the primary focus of his life. He and his wife of seventeen years, Joan, are active with their children, four-year-old son Wesley and fourteen-month-old daughter Annabelle. He and his family reside in Bend, Oregon.

You can contact Dirk at:
    Real Estate Champions
    132 Crowell Way, Suite 200
    Bend, OR 97702
    541-383-8833
    Info@RealEstateChampions.com